Advance praise for
Renewing the Promise: A New Vision for Eritrea

Much of the existing discourse analyzes how Eritrea arrived at its current impasse. In this book, Semere Solomon moves beyond diagnosis to chart a way forward, outlining the core principles Eritrea must embrace to achieve prosperity and peaceful coexistence with its neighbors. The book's distinctive strength lies in the author's firsthand involvement during Eritrea's most critical years, combined with his extensive experience in international development. Semere's insight, urgency, and commitment make this work both timely and substantial.

— *Abraham T. Zere, Former Voice of America's Horn Team Lead; Multimedia Journalist, USA*

To overcome Eritrea's deficiencies, the path to prosperity, as Semere demonstrates in this book, prioritizes the respect for human welfare. The vision of Eritrea being reborn as a nation where people live with dignity is a beautiful dream. However, realizing this requires addressing moral decay through a fundamental transformation. Semere shows how the experiences of other nations can liberate us from fear and stagnation. Through physical and intellectual engagement, this transformation can be the key to Eritrea's liberation.

— *Tewolde Stefanos, Entrepreneur, USA*

Having worked alongside Semere for over two decades in international development and education, I can attest to the integrity and insight behind this work. In Renewing the Promise: A New Vision for Eritrea, Semere doesn't just bring analysis, but also a call to action, grounded in lived experience and global best practices. His vision for a people-centered Eritrea, where sovereignty and human welfare are inseparable, is both compelling and achievable. This book is essential reading for policymakers, scholars, and anyone who believes Eritrea can chart a new course.

— *Charito Kruvant, Founder and Chairperson at Creative Associates International, USA*

Semere Solomon's new book aims to diagnose Eritrea's political, social, economic, and geopolitical crises and proposes a comprehensive roadmap for national renewal. It is a timely addition to Eritrean literature on the transition to democracy and is worth reading.

— *Dr. Mohamed Kheir Omer, Writer and Researcher, Norway*

Semere is a skilled development practitioner whose work reflects a commitment to Pan-Africanism and Eritrean freedom, evident in his life history and representation of Eritrea's trajectory. In this book, he advances a key thesis: human welfare forms a fundamental pillar of national growth—a message relevant beyond Eritrea to Africa. Through this work, Semere places himself in the struggle for Eritrean freedom. He details the pre-independence struggle, compares it with present realities, and projects hope for future generations. His narrative encourages youth to engage with African development, liberation history, and self-determination across the continent.

— *Nurudeen Lawal, International Development Practitioner, Team Lead and Founder, Quality Education Development Associates, Nigeria*

Claiming that your esteemed book holds the key to addressing the challenges our country faces now and, in the future, would not be an exaggeration. This book also resonates with those who are struggling to find solutions to our current predicament and are tirelessly debating how to prepare a roadmap for the transition.

— *Semere Fessahaye, Former Professor of Information Technology and Senior Information Technology Engineer, France*

After reading your book with great attention, I was genuinely impressed by its depth and scope. Your ideas, underpinned by solid facts and evidence, set this work apart from others of its genre. The vision of Eritrea we long for after the fall of the Isaias regime is vividly depicted, capturing both its sorrows and its hopes. I thank you for your historic contribution and invite all those who wish Eritrea well and are eager to take action to join this endeavor.

— *Kebreab Yimesghen, Consultant, Social Affairs, USA*

This book arrives at a crucial time, and its significance lies in its ability to spark discussions among Eritreans with diverse viewpoints, all of whom share a vision of a brighter future for their country. Beyond mere analysis, its clear ideas, roadmap, and the hope it instills convince me that it can make an invaluable contribution to establishing a stable, prosperous, and democratic Eritrea.

— *Yusuf Hassen, Senior Civil Engineering Expert, Sweden*

During a time of great uncertainty and crisis, this book serves as a beacon of hope. It dares to put forward the premise that sovereignty alone is not enough if it means sacrificing the Eritrean people's dignity and welfare. His human-centered approach prioritizes self-determination as the path ahead for prosperity, which will allow those of us in exile to one day return and fulfill our beloved nation's unrealized promises.

— *Aida Semere, Senior Program Manager - Health Tech Consulting Team at Leap Orbit, USA*

Renewing the Promise: A New Vision for Eritrea

SEMERE SOLOMON

Copyright © 2026 Semere Solomon
All rights reserved.

Hardcover ISBN: 979-8-218-91486-8

Published in January 2026.

This book is dedicated
to the courageous Eritrean youth
who dared to dream of freedom,
who reject and continue to reject oppression,
who are determined to free their nation from injustice.
Eritrea of the future is yours!

"Development is the process of expanding human freedoms. It is primarily about empowering people to lead lives they have reason to value."

— Amartya Sen, Nobel Laureate, Economist, and Philosopher

Table of Contents

Foreword ·· xiii
Introduction ··· xxi
Acknowledgements ·· xxvii

Chapter 1   Eritrea: Current Situation ·································· 1
Chapter 2   Eritrea: Pre-Change and Post-Change ···················· 19
Chapter 3   A Dual Economic Strategy for Eritrea: Unlocking
            Domestic Potential, Engaging the World ················ 49
Chapter 4   Human Welfare-centered Economic Development ······ 62
Chapter 5   The Development-Governance Nexus: Foundations for
            Sustainable Progress ······································ 71
Chapter 6   Reconceptualizing Sovereignty: Human Welfare
            at its Core ··· 88
Chapter 7   Weaving the Future: How Cultural Threads
            Strengthen the Economic Fabric ························ 99
Chapter 8   Harnessing the Tide: The Eritrean Diaspora's
            Role in National Change ································ 116
Chapter 9   The Case for a Deterrence-Centric Defense in Eritrea ·· 133
Chapter 10 The Pursuit of Smart Diplomacy ························ 150
Chapter 11 Partnership, Not Patronage: Reframing
            International Development ······························ 167
Chapter 12 Diagnosing Our Political Culture ······················· 175

Chapter 13 African Economic Horizons: A Framework for Eritrea · · · 192
Chapter 14 The Next Chapter: Integrating Transitional
             Justice into Eritrea's National Project · · · · · · · · · · · · · · · 204
Chapter 15 The Fate of the Fragmented Landscape of
             Eritrean Opposition · 215

Conclusion Envisioning a New Eritrea · 234
Endnotes · 239
Bibliography · 249

Foreword

Inspired by Eritrea's ongoing political and economic crises, this book by Eritrean veteran and activist Semere Solomon Abbay critically reflects on the country's current state and suggests possible pathways to address its deep-rooted problems and challenges. Like many others familiar with Semere Solomon through his writings, I have always known him as an advocate for freedom. Yet, reading this book stirred a quiet, poignant feeling within me. Growing up in Asmara during the 1960s and 70s, I lived in the same neighborhood as Semere and his esteemed family, in the area known as Collegio La Salle. From friends and playmates, especially his younger brothers Kaleb and Rufael Solomon, I often heard of Semere's academic achievements. At that time, he was a student at Haile Selassie I Secondary School, while I attended Haile Selassie I Elementary & Middle School. Later, Semere moved to Addis Ababa for university, and went on to join the Eritrean People's Liberation Forces—an act that inspired both awe and fear among us adolescents. Additionally, Semere Solomon's mother, Madalena Yosief, and my mother, Wahid Ghebremedhin, were close friends and confidantes. Especially after the Derg military regime came to power in Ethiopia, when their children joined Eritrea's liberation struggle, the two mothers counselled and comforted each other with visits and telephone calls, and our families continue to remember them with fondness and a quiet sense of loss.

These childhood and neighborhood relationships certainly hold a special place for me. However, when asked to read this important book and share my thoughts, the initial ideas that came to my mind were not primarily rooted in childhood memories. Instead, the foundation for the opinions and insights I am about to share lies in the comprehensive, critical analysis and immensely interesting ideas articulated in the book. Especially during this critical and challenging time of transition in the country's history, I consider that there is an urgent need to share one's perspective on such extremely important work by engaging with the questions and solutions it presents. This is, of course, always in the hope that it will help shed light on certain aspects of the book and encourage people to read it, while thinking through and interpreting the questions and answers it offers in their own way.

Renewing the Promise: A New Vision for Eritrea provides a compelling picture and analysis of Eritrea's contemporary political situation, accompanied by the author's nuanced perspectives and thoughtfully proposed solutions to the nation's multifaceted problems. Over the last two decades or so, Eritrea has gone through major historical moments, resulting in a succession of complex problems and challenges. All of these are analyzed in this book within a carefully organized thematic framework designed to promote a clear understanding of the issues and, consequently, the projected remedies. Readers are encouraged to approach this work within this contextual lens.

The issues explored in this volume are vital to Eritrea's sovereignty and illuminate the underlying tensions in the country's political climate. If these challenges remain unaddressed, they could precipitate a profound existential crisis for Eritrea and its population. It is important to note here that the topics addressed are well-known among Eritrean scholars and the general populace alike. Moreover, numerous esteemed Eritrean scholars and others have also conducted extensive studies on these issues across various academic platforms.

This book is a welcome addition to the critical scholarly tradition on Eritrea, as it systematically examines the core issues of Eritrea and, gradually, through evidence and judgment across the chapters, we are made to see a realistic yet compelling image of the country, as I will describe below. The harsh reality of the problems and the resulting crisis—some of which might even be difficult for fair-minded supporters of the Eritrean regime to deny—is as follows. In Eritrea, there is no government that operates under a constitution. There is no freedom of speech or press. People are arrested without legal proceedings, and once detained, they face no formal charges in court. Thousands of political and religious prisoners, along with conscientious objectors of various kinds, are held without trial in many prisons and secret detention centers. Their confinement is not just indefinite detention without trial; until they are fortunate enough to be released, they must also endure extremely harsh prison conditions. Under these circumstances, torture and illness cause their bodies to deteriorate, their minds to break, and their morals to decline, subjecting them to both physical and psychological hardships. Besides the widespread violation of basic human rights in Eritrea, another deeply troubling truth must also be noted: those released from prison often refuse to discuss the reasons for their detention or the conditions they endured. This silence arises from the regime's influence—whether through direct threats or by instilling fear within the community—that serious consequences might follow the victims if they "do not keep their mouths shut," meaning if they speak openly about their experiences. The author has thoroughly documented in this volume the pervasiveness and tragic consequences of state repression and human rights abuses across the areas listed above and beyond.

Concerning Eritrea's economy, the book accurately argues that, despite its wealth of natural resources and the reputedly hardworking, resilient nature of its people, the country remains one of the poorest and least developed in the world. A clear sign of this poverty is the over 600,000 Eritreans who have fled to distant parts of the world to start new lives, sending remittances back home to support their families and relatives left behind. The causes of poverty and migration are complex, meeting at the intersection of multiple factors. However, notably, the main reasons young people migrate are the country's indefinite military conscription and regional conflicts involving the Eritrean government, both justified and unjustified. These factors, in a reciprocal cause-and-effect cycle, have significantly contributed to Eritrea's poverty and underdevelopment.

The main strength of this book lies in its broad coverage and in-depth analysis of the topics it addresses. Consisting of 15 chapters, each is dedicated to a specific subject. Through detailed examinations in each chapter, the book cumulatively explores the root causes of the country's ongoing issues. This step-by-step analytical approach provides ample critical focus, resulting in insights that help clarify and suggest solutions to the problems and challenges faced. Carefully reading and reflecting on all the chapters not only offers a complete view of the core issues confronting Eritrean society regarding freedom and development but also presents a range of ideas and proposals for what Eritreans need to do to transition from oppression and poverty toward building a nation based on democratic principles and accountability.

In the "Introduction" of this book, the author explains the purpose of his work, stating that "Renewing the Promise: A New Vision for Eritrea" serves as a sequel to his first book, "Eritrea's Hard-Won Independence and Unmet Expectations" (published in 2024 in Tigrinya and English). This second book builds on the first, aiming to provide more updated information, delve deeper into the topics and questions raised earlier, and offer concrete solutions. The promise is largely maintained: the new book consistently follows this core structure—critique followed by solution.

Chapter 7 stands out as a particularly strong critical reflection and timely reminder for Eritreans seeking the rule of law and justice. In my view, the author in this chapter describes—with skill and beauty that has rare precedent in the Tigrinya language—the civilization and culture of tolerance within Eritrean society, emphasizing the importance of honoring and preserving it. He writes:

> The Eritrean people embraced Christianity and Islam early in their history. The translation of the Holy Bible into Ge'ez, supported by its nine saints, is a legacy spanning several centuries. Above all, the Eritrean people have lived—and continue to live—in coexistence and mutual acceptance, regardless of their religious differences. Eritrea is dotted with churches, monasteries, and mosques that reflect its deep-rooted religious faith. Another defining feature of the Eritrean people is their value system, characterized by integrity and reverence for God. They have maintained customs and laws that emphasize community solidarity, cultivated over a long period. Their respect for the rule of law is one of their admirable characteristics, marked by mutual cooperation and respect for the law.

It is also helpful to consider the significance of the book's title, as it is crucial for understanding both its structure and the urgency conveyed by its tone, as originally conceived and published in its Tigrinya title. The Tigrinya title, "Eritrea: Qelesti Hasabat NiHwyet Hager" (literally translated as "Eritrea: Guiding Thoughts for National Healing or Salvation"), presents a distinctive combination: the first part refers to "Guiding Thoughts," while the second emphasizes "Healing." The first half refers to the ideas, perspectives, and practical solutions outlined in the book, whereas the word "healing" in the second part metaphorically suggests that these ideas aim to "cure" the nation from a specific kind of affliction or crisis—precisely aligning with the book's claimed goal. In the English edition, this semantic nuance is maintained—where possible—by highlighting the urgency and directness of the book's narrative tone. While preserving the core meaning, the English title, "Renewing the Promise: A New Vision for Eritrea," explicitly emphasizes the urgency and time-sensitivity of the book's message. In scholarly terms, this genre of writing is often called a "Manifesto." Classic examples include Karl Marx and Friedrich Engels' "The Communist Manifesto" (1848), France's "Declaration of the Rights of Man and of the Citizen" (1789), the United States' "Declaration of Independence" (1776), and within Eritrea, "Where is Your Brother?" (Pastoral Letter of the Catholic Bishops, 2014). Manifestos serve as advocacy tools—using clear, precise, specific, urgent, and insistent language—to present ideas, address societal issues, and propose solutions. They are distinguished not only by their clarity of analysis and problem description but also by their capacity to outline key issues, guide readers toward a course of action, foster decision-making, and motivate mobilization. This work aligns with the "Manifesto" genre. It appears, indeed, that, without explicitly stating so, the author follows this model, balancing his critical analysis of the situation with persuasive arguments to promote the outlined pathways as a call to action. It must be further underlined that this call stems from a genuine concern and the desire to inspire collective effort toward national salvation.

There is another important matter I believe readers should be aware, especially those English readers who follow Eritrean politics but may not be familiar with Eritrean languages. In the past, we have seen various writings—similar in form and tone, if not in content—from different authors and groups that aim to help heal the country from its problems. However, we have also noticed that some of the solutions these agents suggest as cures seem to be worse than the "illness." Particularly, those writers or groups that promote harmful politics disguised as "national salvation" are the ones that have contributed to deepening mistrust and divisions among Eritreans along religious, ethnic, and regional lines.

Before concluding my remarks, I want to briefly return to the memory I previously shared at the outset of this foreword—my remembrance of Asmara and the family of the late Solomon Abbay. In the neighborhood where we grew up, the Solomon family is still honored by both past and present residents as a family of patriots. This reputation comes from their long-time involvement and enormous sacrifice in the liberation efforts and struggle of the Eritrean people, especially those led by the Eritrean People's Liberation Front (EPLF). I want to emphasize that my use of the word "enormous" in the preceding line is not meant to diminish, in any way, the sacrifices of other Eritrean families, many of whom also endured great hardship and loss. Instead, it is to highlight that this family had five siblings who fought in the Independence War, and several family members who dedicated their lives to service within the organization's civilian institutions, both inside and outside Eritrea. Tragically, two of the sons, Rufael and Bihon Solomon, died in the war. Such a family background—marked by service and sacrifice—uniquely positions the book and its author, giving them a special onto-epistemic and moral authority. As the Eritrean saying goes, "Only the wounded can truly speak." Recognizing that the author's insights and ideas are deeply rooted in Eritrean history, sacrifice, and personal experience indeed increases the credibility and weight of this testimony.

Professor Ghirmai Negash
January 2026
Ohio University, USA

Introduction

IN 2024, I published a book in Tigrigna and English titled 'Eritrea's Hard-won Independence and Unmet Expectations.' The book is divided into three parts. The first part offers a concise analytical history of the Eritrean people's armed struggle, along with the pre- and post-colonial periods. The second part examines Eritrea's current and future trajectory, while the third part delves into my background and personal memories. After the book's release, I engaged in discussions with readers in various public forums. Many interested readers and listeners generously dedicated their time to thoughtfully review the book and provide written feedback on the topics addressed in the second part of the book.

The second part of the book comprises nine chapters, aiming to analyze the political, economic, social, and geopolitical realities of post-independence Eritrea. It also seeks to offer evidence-based recommendations to address pertinent questions. Additionally, it presents studies conducted and conclusions drawn by scholars and experts who have thoroughly researched specific topics to describe the system in power in Eritrea since 1991 and to explain its behavior. The research focuses on answering questions that concern all Eritreans: How did we arrive at our current situation? What are the reasons? Where did we go wrong? If we were to look back, what could have been done better? There is a wise saying: 'Rulers come and go, but the people remain the constant bedrock of the nation.' If this saying holds true, it can serve as a theme for discussion to prevent the repetition of past mistakes and to ensure that the next generation, learning from the previous one, can build its country and determine a better path forward.

The analysis provided by 'Eritrea's Hard-won Independence and Unmet Expectations' was fundamentally designed to draw valuable lessons, serving as a cautionary tale to avert similar mistakes in the future.

The book I am currently presenting to readers, titled 'Renewing the Promise: A New Vision for Eritrea,' serves as a sequel to my first book. It seeks to thoroughly explore the broader issue of how the unfulfilled goals of social justice, which were integral to the overall struggle for national sovereignty and territorial integrity of Eritrea, continue to be deferred. Comprising 15 chapters, the book is structured to provide an in-depth examination of the aforementioned questions. Each chapter complements and connects with the others to offer a comprehensive approach. The chapters aim to shed light on the developments in political, economic, social, cultural, and growth trajectories, as well as geopolitical spheres, since independence. Additionally, to define and understand the nature of the system, the book references studies and analyses conducted by scholars and experts on this subject.

These chapters delve deeply into their respective themes, offering comprehensive analyses. They address the following questions: What are the critical objectives, roadmaps, and priorities for systemic change in Eritrea, both before and after the change? What does the goal of a transitional government entail, and what pathways does it outline? What priorities should Eritrea consider to secure progress and become a prosperous nation? Where can these solutions be found? What are the prerequisites for economic growth? What should Eritrea's economic growth and development roadmap look like? How can human welfare be prioritized? What is the meaning of sovereignty, and for whom should it be prioritized? What role does culture play in nation-building? How are good governance and economic development related? How is the prevailing repressive political culture in Eritrea characterized, and how can it be corrected? On what foundations should Eritrea's philosophy of national security be based? What type of foreign policy should Eritrea pursue, given its strategic location along the Red Sea and Horn of Africa? What steps should Eritrea take to become an economically developed and globally competitive nation?

As Eritrea's growth and development hinge on internal stability, what role should transitional justice play during a transitional government to ensure social cohesion? In other words, how should it be managed? What lessons can be learned from the experiences of other countries? Specifically, based on Africa's experience, what pathways can lead Eritrea to prosperity? How does external support align with developmental cooperation? How is the Eritrean opposition characterized? How can it transform itself into a viable political alternative? These questions deserve proper answers.

This book also explores the significant role of the Eritrean Diaspora in nation-building, posing questions and providing analyses about this crucial segment of Eritrean society—its status, characteristics, and potential.

Undoubtedly, the questions mentioned above present a considerable challenge to address comprehensively within a single book due to their extensive scope, depth, and complexity. The significance of these topics also necessitates thorough studies to adequately explore them. In my efforts, I have strived to ensure that the approach remains not overly academic, while also ensuring that the analysis appropriately reflects the importance and gravity of the questions.

Moreover, I do not believe this work has fully explored all the topics that have been discussed. It is an endeavor driven by the desire to ensure these objectives are effectively realized, allowing other professionals to develop them through their research undertakings further. My hope and aspiration is that additional initiatives will be pursued by other researchers and writers.

In writing this second book, I have endeavored to ensure that my analyses are as objective and balanced as possible. Throughout this process, I found it particularly helpful to compare global experiences, especially those of countries with socio-economic conditions similar to those of Eritrea.

Drawing from a variety of books, essays, and other informational sources, the insights and the experience I acquired as a member of the civil service of the Provisional Government of Eritrea, along with my active participation at a higher level during the first seven years following independence, proved invaluable in my analyses.

For twenty-four years, encompassing 17 years in the field and seven years post-independence, I dedicated myself to the national liberation and reconstruction of my country. After Eritrea gained independence, and until my departure in 1998, I served as the Director General of the Planning and Development Department within the Ministry of Education. With the extensive experiences I have accumulated and the relationships I have built with various individuals, I am confident that my perspectives are both grounded in reality and genuine. Furthermore, my twenty-five years of experience in international development were utilized in the analysis of this book.

With an academic background in Educational Planning and Management, complemented by a diploma and a Master's degree in Sustainable Development and International Diplomacy, I have had the privilege of serving various international institutions, notably the United Nations (UN) and the United States Agency for International Development (USAID), in diverse roles. This extensive experience, spanning over twenty-five years, began after I left my beloved country in 1998.

My career in international development has taken me to various parts of the world, including Africa, the Middle East, Southeast Asia, and several countries in Central Asia, allowing me to observe their circumstances firsthand. I believe this experience has significantly shaped and enriched my international perspective on the political and developmental issues I had the privilege of being part of.

Unreservedly, the careful observation and monitoring of the events and decisions that have led to the current turmoil in Eritrea, which I have conducted over the years, are reflected in my analysis.

This book essentially serves as a collection of my thoughts aimed at systematically exploring various thematic issues in depth. I hope you, the reader, will perceive these themes as gifts or harbingers of good news. I kindly request and appeal to you to recognize that, although the chapters may appear to be standalone, they are indeed interconnected and related, as previously indicated.

In conclusion, I am filled with immense joy as I present this second book to you, the reader. I sincerely hope it fulfills the expectations of my companions from the armed struggle and my cherished readers.

Acknowledgments

WRITING THIS BOOK was a journey I did not undertake alone. I am deeply grateful to the many individuals who supported, challenged, and encouraged me along the way.

I am deeply grateful to Ghirmay Negash, Professor of Post-colonial Studies and Director, African Studies Program, Ohio University, for dedicating his valuable time to reviewing the Tigrigna version of the manuscript and for offering insights that significantly enhanced the quality of the book. His contributions were indispensable in finalizing the work you now hold. I would like to express that the joy I feel at the prospect of this book's publication is immeasurable. His scholarly advice and encouragement were immensely helpful.

I am deeply grateful to Michael Woldemariam, Jerrold Keilson, Eduardo Velez, Semere Fessaheye, Mohammed Kheir, Tewolde Stifanos, and Kebreab Yimesghen for reading the manuscript, providing feedback, and sharing invaluable suggestions. Their suggestions have greatly refined the arguments presented in various sections of the book.

I also extend my thanks to my daughter, Seble Semere, for the time she dedicated to understanding the essence of this book and designing the book's stunning cover by collaborating with her sister, Aida Semere, and her cousin, Dr. Shiden Mehari. In this endeavor, she stood by me as a companion.

I am grateful to the members of 'Ilal Mezanu' (Peer Dialogue) for offering me opportunities to engage in discussions on various pertinent issues at different times and for generously sharing their knowledge with me.

I am deeply indebted to the readers of my previously published books, whose encouragement has inspired me to continue writing, express my views on various topics, and share my experiences. Without their support, this book would not have been completed.

Finally, I would like to extend my heartfelt thanks to my wife, Faiza Adem, and all my family members. Bringing this book to its current stage required time away from you, and I am grateful for your patience and understanding. I could not have achieved this without your enduring love and encouragement.

Chapter 1

Eritrea: Current Situation

THIRTY-FOUR YEARS AFTER achieving independence, Eritrea is marked by a lack of freedom, widespread poverty, a struggling economy, unstable political conditions, and a fragile social fabric. It is almost unimaginable that Eritrea would find itself in such a predicament after a decades-long liberation struggle. Therefore, it is crucial to present ideas for exploring this situation rather than ignoring the facts.

Eritrea remains under the rule of a one-person dictatorship, with President Isaias Afwerki in power since its independence. A constitution ratified in 1997 has never been implemented, and the legislative body has been inactive for over twenty-four years. The People's Front for Democracy and Justice (PFDJ) is the sole political party.

The system seems structurally designed for political repression and continues to operate systematically in this manner. The disappearance of the G-15[i], comprising senior government and party officials, the Forto group (a movement staged in 2013 to topple the government), political opponents, journalists, and other dissenting citizens, remains unresolved. The number of citizens taken from their homes, disappeared, and held without trial in the system's prisons, often indefinitely, continues to grow.

Transnational violence persists, and exiled Eritreans consistently face intimidation from the regime.

The authoritarian regime in Eritrea has not spared religious institutions or their leaders. Abune Antonios, the Patriarch of the Eritrean Orthodox Church, was deposed and died under house arrest on February 9, 2022, at the age of 94. On October 15, 2022, Abune Fikremariam Hagos, the head of the Catholic Church of Segheneiti, was arrested at Asmara's International Airport upon returning from a European trip. Various sources confirm that he was held without charges at Adi Abeito prison. Abune Fikremariam and another Catholic priest, Abba Mehreteab, were released on January 4, 2023. On October 20, 2017, Hajji Musa Mohammed Nur, a respected nonagenarian who served as the Honorary President and board chairman of the Al Diaa Islamic School, was detained along with others for opposing government interference in the school's operations. This led to peaceful protests. In March 2018, Hajji Musa Mohammed Nur died in a hospital shortly after being admitted. The government continues to imprison members of unrecognized faiths, such as Jehovah's Witnesses and non-Lutheran Evangelical churches[ii], and conducts oppressive campaigns to force them to renounce their beliefs.

All citizens have an obligation to participate in an indefinite and ongoing national service. The harsh treatment and widespread torture within this service have driven hundreds of thousands of young and middle-aged Eritreans to flee their homes and seek refuge abroad. According to United Nations documents, by 2024, an estimated 663,085 Eritreans were living in exile (UNHCR, 2023). The primary host countries include Sudan, South Sudan, Ethiopia, Kenya, Angola, Germany, Sweden, Switzerland, Norway, the United States, various Middle Eastern countries, Canada, Israel, Australia, and Uganda.

On October 4, 2024, the UN Human Rights Council issued a statement revealing that the Eritrean government was attempting to evade scrutiny over its human rights record. According to a report by the Special

Rapporteur, Eritrea is plagued by illegal and systematic arbitrary arrests and enforced disappearances, with no guarantee of the right to freedom of belief. The report also highlights the detrimental impact of indefinite national service in Eritrea, which consumes much of the citizens' lives in service to the government (UNHRC, 2025).[iii]

In summary, the political situation has deteriorated alarmingly, with signs of instability becoming increasingly evident. Owing to a severe lack of accountability and transparency, political opposition and concerns have become commonplace. Citizens, unable to hold their leaders and government accountable, are increasingly succumbing to a sense of hopelessness. Despite internal and external pressures, Eritrea remains a country with no inclination towards political reform.

Eritrea's economy is primarily based on small-scale subsistence agriculture, with modern agriculture still in its infancy. Manufacturing, the second-largest sector, is underperforming, while service sectors like tourism and finance are also in their early stages. Overall, Eritrea's economy can be described as subsistence-based. The only significant export-oriented manufacturing sectors are gold, copper, and zinc mining, with potash exports expected to begin soon. The Economic Intelligence Unit magazine reports that this is expected to boost the Gross Domestic Product (GDP), forecasting a 1.4% growth in Eritrea's economy by 2025, compared to the global GDP growth projection of 2.5% for that year. Several sources indicate that a significant portion of Eritrea's GDP comes from mining.

Another crucial economic source is revenue from Eritreans in the diaspora, estimated to be hundreds of millions of dollars from a 2% income tax and remittances sent to Eritrea. Although it is challenging to measure the exact contribution of remittances to the national GDP due to a severe lack of transparency and data, it undoubtedly amounts to a big percentage of the GDP. Another challenge in measuring GDP per capita in Eritrea, is that we don't have an accurate sense of the actual size of the population, since there is no publicly available census.

Apart from the well-known Colluli Potash Project, a Chinese investment, there are no other promising investment prospects. The outcome of the recent investment agreement initiated by the governments of Eritrea and Italy is currently under discussion.

In its annual (2024) report on the Human Development Index, the UNDP ranks Eritrea 175th out of 195 countries, a dismal indicator by any measure. It also states Eritrea's population as 3,684,032.[iv]

Human capital, once a source of strength, has become a cause of concern. The mass exodus of professionals, academics, and youth has created significant voids and intellectual stagnation in the country. This exodus is evident not only in the internal labor market but also in the educational sector, which struggles to find qualified teachers and is in a state of continuous decline.

The infrastructure in Eritrea remains underdeveloped. The government often acknowledges that the infrastructure is not developed to the required level. There is no functional railway line, except for a small section. The two ports, Massawa and Assab, have potential but are underutilized; the facilities there are outdated.

Electricity is a perpetual problem, with unreliable supplies and frequent power outages common. The supply of clean water and health services is similarly problematic. Internet service coverage in Eritrea is among the lowest in Africa and is extremely slow. One of the major problems is that the government does not encourage private-sector development. Given its strategic location and the potential for human capital absorption, Eritrea's economy has the potential to grow. However, underdeveloped infrastructure remains a major obstacle.

While regional conflicts, ongoing instability, and the economic siege imposed on the country are often cited as reasons, the primary impediment to Eritrea's progress lies in the government's outdated ideologies and misunderstanding of development, coupled with a profound lack of political will and poor external relations. The main challenges include:

- Inability to foster an environment conducive to both foreign and domestic investment;
- Policies that make domestic capital owners feel besieged, driving them to seek opportunities abroad;
- The presence of barriers rather than support for the private sector;
- Insufficient utilization of the nation's human potential;
- Lack of recognition and encouragement for intellectual capacity;
- The ruling political party's dominance over most of the economy, lacking accountability and transparency;
- Failure to integrate into the global economy;
- Absence of partnership-based collaboration and integration with neighboring countries, the region, and the world; and
- The massive exodus of the most vibrant segment of society—youth—making it clear how tragic the situation has become.

The situation in Eritrea has been appalling and concerning for some time. The constantly shifting regional political dynamics and alignments have exacerbated this situation. A military confrontation with Ethiopia is increasingly likely.

Eritrean youth have begun to express their stifled voices. Known as the "Blue Wave" or "Brigade Nhamedu," their movement has been spreading like wildfire across Europe, the Middle East, North America, and within Africa. This movement is led by Eritrean youth who have endured various hardships. Some were shot and killed while trying to flee to Sudan and Ethiopia to escape national service; others were subjected to forced labor; some faced torture and abuse while trekking across the Sahara Desert seeking refuge, and some risked their lives crossing the Mediterranean Sea. These young men and women bitterly curse the system that has ruined their lives. They feel anger and hatred and feel deeply wronged by the system. They express their opposition and desire for change with a high level of political dedication and activism.

The Blue Wave still needs to state its long-term objectives in clearer terms, expand its base and alliances, refine its strategy, and intensify its efforts to achieve its goals. This strategy requires organizational refinement to effectively counter the deceitful attempts by the Eritrean regime to dismantle it. A more systematic approach is necessary to thwart the regime's schemes and rally the diaspora's youth around noble national goals, ultimately freeing the nation from repression and establishing a constitutionally governed government.

Currently, the Eritrean political opposition is fragmented and disorganized, operating inconsistently. Although efforts are underway to unite on a common platform, the prolonged persistence of this situation without change is concerning. The number of opposition movements is high, and they spend significant time and energy smearing each other. Their social media outlets sow discord and hatred. The absence of a common platform to confront the Asmara regime remains a significant obstacle to the effectiveness of these groups. Some seem to focus more on carving out their opposition niche than on promoting the broader goal of change. It is also a well-known fact that the PFDJ's espionage networks infiltrate opposition camps and attempt to weaken them by creating ethnic, religious, and even regional divisions. The potential harm this could cause to the cohesion and unity of Eritrea's political opposition, both now and in the future, is evident.

Regional Situation

Eritrea, a small nation in the Horn of Africa, is situated on the western shore of the Red Sea. It shares borders with Sudan to the west, Ethiopia to the south, and Djibouti to the southeast. Additionally, Eritrea boasts a coastline that extends over a thousand kilometers along the Red Sea. Its strategic position renders it a crucial factor in the geopolitics of this volatile region, encompassing both the Horn of Africa and the Middle East.

Ethiopia

Ethiopia is currently facing a profound crisis, largely due to its leaders' political failures. The political reform process initiated within the EPRDF was derailed, resulting in a political landscape dominated by the vested interests of competing factions. The power struggle, and consequently the struggle for resources, between the Prosperity Party and the Tigrai People's Liberation Front (TPLF) escalated into open conflict during the 2020 war. Although a temporary solution was brokered by the Pretoria Agreement, a political resolution remains elusive. The constitutionally recognized land rights of the Tigray region have not been restored to their pre-war status, and displaced Tigrayans have yet to return to their villages. Services in the Tigray region remain adequately unrestored, and representatives of the Tigray region have not returned to the Ethiopian Federal Council.

Consequently, both parties are more inclined to advance their agendas by forming alliances with other political organizations. The "political engagement" that has emerged between the PFDJ and TPLF exemplifies this trend. However, because it lacks a shared strategic goal and does not prioritize the interests of both peoples, its outcome is likely to be perilous for both. Moreover, it has been perceived as interference in Ethiopia's internal affairs. The temporary alliance between the PFDJ and the Amhara Fano has produced similar sentiment in the corridors of power in Addis Abeba.

Forces known as the Fano and the Oromo Liberation Army continue to express grievances against the federal government, posing a significant threat to the country's security. Given the political nature of the forces involved in this conflict, a political solution seems distant.

Following the initial political honeymoon between the Prosperity Party and the PFDJ, their relationship has increasingly deteriorated. This political alignment was characterized by a profound lack of transparency and accountability and a relationship based on temporary interests on the other. A significant development in this context is Ethiopia's ruling party, the Prosperity Party, pursuing maritime ownership along the Red Sea, raising considerable concerns in the region. Despite its failed attempts in Somaliland, the Prosperity Party continues to engage in diplomatic, political, and military maneuvers to achieve its maritime ambitions.

The tension between the PFDJ and the Prosperity Party has escalated beyond maritime ownership to encompass control over the politics of the Horn of Africa. Both parties are forming various political alliances to counter each other. It is an open secret that the Prosperity Party has started collaborating with Eritrean opposition forces operating in exile to challenge the PFDJ.

The ever-shifting regional political dynamics and reconfiguration of alliances have further complicated the situation. Military confrontations seem increasingly imminent, with war drums echoing these developments. Predicting outcomes is challenging, primarily because the political forces involved in this contest are numerous, each with their own vested interests they are unwilling to relinquish, compounded by the volatile nature of these alliances themselves.

The primary actors are the Prosperity Party, the PFDJ, and the TPLF. The secondary actors include Fano (or Amhara opposition) and the Oromo Liberation Front (OLF). Other potential groups that could emerge as players are not yet significant. These actors share similar characteristics, regardless of their stated goals and interests, which can be summarized as follows.

It is misleading to assert that these groups or the majority of them prioritize public interest over their political agendas. They relentlessly pursue political goals and actions marked by short-sightedness. Some habitually employ coercion against their people within their areas of influence. These forces reject political pluralism, do not engage in inclusive politics, and believe that violence is the solution to political disagreements.

Sporadic violent conflicts and clashes among these various groups over the past 30 years affirm the general assessment indicated above. Moreover, the political alliances they formed aimed to achieve short-term benefits. Examples include the PFDJ-EPRDF, PFDJ-TPLF, PFDJ-Prosperity Party, EPRDF-Eritrean Opposition Groups, Prosperity Party-Fano, Prosperity Party-OLF, and PFDJ-Anti-EPRDF/TPLF Forces. Political entities with such characteristics and the alliances they forge at different times are incapable of acting as peacemakers or contributing to regional stability; instead, their inherent nature perpetuates instability in the region. Their history clearly supports this. Regrettably, they continue to pose a threat to the region's security. The political volatility we are witnessing is a natural outcome of unresolved political grievances and entrenched political cultures of elimination that have accumulated over the past decades.

Furthermore, Ethiopia's quest for access and maritime ownership along the Red Sea has compounded the already existing problem. It should be noted that Eritrea, as a sovereign nation, has every right to defend itself from this threat using all means at its disposal. These include political and military. The best way to challenge this threat, though, is by forming a government of national reconciliation, keeping in mind the following considerations: -

National reconciliation as the bulwark against war: At this moment of existential threat, it is imperative to address the Eritrean government's actions directly. The paths of isolation, internal repression, and reactive saber-rattling have not only failed to ensure national security but have also actively contributed to the precariousness of the current situation. There is no better time or pressing need for a profound and strategic shift. To navigate this crisis and secure the future of the nation, the government must immediately set aside its differences with the opposition and call upon all Eritreans to form an inclusive government for national reconciliation and unity.

The failure of exclusion and the imperative of unity: For decades, the Eritrean government operated under a model of absolute control and exclusion. It has refused to implement the ratified constitution, rejected political pluralism, declined to release prisoners of conscience, and systematically silenced dissent. This has created a façade of stability, masking profound internal discontent and a crippling lack of national cohesion. A state in war with its people cannot effectively address external threats.

The Government must understand this reality on the ground. The strength of a nation facing an imminent threat lies not only in its military arsenal but also in the unified will of its people. By continuing to treat a significant portion of its citizenry as adversaries, the PFDJ is fighting on two fronts, internal and external, and weakens its position on both. The "politics of exclusion" is a fatal luxury in this volatile hour. The imminent threat from Ethiopia's reckless maritime ambitions demands a response that is strategic rather than merely militaristic.

A government of national reconciliation: the only viable path: This is not a plea for weakness, but a call for supreme strength—the strength that comes from unity and solidarity. The government must demonstrate maturity and genuine care for its people. It should take the following actions:

- Initiating an unconditional national dialogue: This immediately calls upon all Eritrean opposition forces, civic societies, and religious and intellectual leaders, both inside the country and in the diaspora, to form a transitional council for national salvation with a genuine intent to form a government of national reconciliation.
- Establishing a government of national unity: This inclusive body must be tasked with overseeing the crisis, representing a unified Eritrea in diplomatic efforts, and beginning the process of implementing the constitution and the rule of law.

- Releasing Prisoners of Conscience: Emptying the Prisons of All Political Detainees. This is a fundamental act of good faith that would unleash the nation's intellectual and moral capacity and rally the population behind a common cause.

Mobilizing for diplomacy, not just for war: A national unity government can wield tools that an isolated regime cannot. The focus must be on robust diplomatic mobilization to stop wars before they start.

Therefore, a unified diplomatic front is required to address these issues. An inclusive government can legitimately knock on the doors of global powers—the US, the EU, China, Russia, and the UN—and present a coherent appeal for peace and assistance. It can be argued from the position of moral authority that represents all Eritreans.

Immediate actions are required to leverage regional and international efforts to address these issues. With a unified voice, Eritrea can more effectively pressure the IGAD and the African Union to move beyond statements and exert real diplomatic pressure on Ethiopia to abandon its quest for maritime ownership and return to international law.

There is also a pressing need to neutralize proxy dynamics in the Middle East. A reconciled Eritrea committed to the rule of law is less fertile for external interference. It can deny Ethiopia and other countries the pretext to meddle in its internal affairs by presenting a stable and united front.

A final chance for legacy and survival: The Government of Eritrea stands at a historic crossroads, forced to confront the hard truth that its past policies precipitated the crisis. Decades of failure to build a constitutional state that tolerates dissent, creates an economically viable nation, develops a deterrence-centered defense doctrine, and establishes a reputation as a reliable partner for peace have left the nation profoundly vulnerable.

Now is the time for wisdom, not arrogance, exclusion, and isolation. It is time for statecraft, not just warfare. The proverb, "The wise man builds fences before the wolf appears," has never been more relevant. The strongest fence Eritrea can build is national unity and reconciliation.

By opening up the political space and calling all Eritreans to the decision-making table on issues that concern their survival, the government can transform this moment of peril into an opportunity for national rebirth. This is the only way to secure peace for the people of Eritrea, protect the sovereignty of the nation, and ensure that future generations inherit a country defined not by perpetual war and autocracy but by stability, the rule of law, and mutual respect. The time to act is now.

Whether the government has the political will to listen to this call—that is, in view of galvanizing the support that the current situation demands—remains to be seen. I hope we will have a government that heeds the hearts and minds of its citizens.

Sudan

The people of Sudan have endured decades of oppressive leadership, paying a heavy price. The legitimate concerns raised by the Sudanese about their dire situation and their calls for change were co-opted by senior officers of the Sudanese Armed Forces and the Rapid Support Forces (RSF). Consequently, Sudan is currently grappling with political and economic crises. This political conflict has reversed the economic growth and social progress that Sudan has achieved in recent decades. The civil war has caused immense human suffering and economic devastation. By becoming a battleground for regional powers, Sudan has invited significant external interference into its affairs. It has become a country where proxy wars are waged, with Saudi Arabia, the UAE, Egypt, Ethiopia, and Eritrea each contributing to the ongoing conflict in their own way. Major world powers are, in one way or another, stakeholders in this conflict.

Somalia

The collapse of the Somali state in the early 1990s marked a new chapter in its history. Since then, the militant group "Al-Shabaab" has emerged as a significant force, extending its influence beyond present-day Somalia and contributing to the instability of the Horn of Africa. Al-Shabaab's primary goal is to establish an Islamic government governed by Sharia law, further exacerbating the already volatile conditions in a region characterized by countries embroiled in war and devastated by civil strife. These militant groups also have the potential to spread their influence to neighboring countries such as Eritrea, Ethiopia, Kenya, and Djibouti. Addressing the persistent threat of expanding militancy in this critical region requires ongoing regional and international efforts.

The government led by President Hassan Sheikh Mohamud is weak, with the Federal Government lacking effective control over the sub-administrative units (statelets) that make up the federal state. In March 2024, the Federal Government passed a law amending the country's Constitution, which strengthened the executive branch's power and introduced indirect rather than direct elections. This decision was opposed by the established administrative units that formed the federal state, leading to a deterioration in relations. Currently, the United States appears more inclined to engage with administrative units, such as Somaliland and Puntland, rather than the Federal Government.

An unresolved political issue remains between the Federal Government and Somaliland, which seeks to declare independence. The recent port access agreement between Ethiopia and Somaliland has caused significant concern for the Federal Government. Analyses and information suggest that the situation could have worsened without Turkey's mediation. The tripartite pact between Somalia, Egypt, and Eritrea is a consequence of this tension. This pact, which targets Ethiopia, aims to address the recurring question and ambition of Ethiopia's guaranteed sea access, which it continues to pursue.

Djibouti

Djibouti's strategic position at the intersection of Africa, the Middle East, and Asia plays a crucial role in global trade, with over 12% of the world's trade passing through this strait.[v] Additionally, its unique strategic importance has led several world powers to establish military bases there. Currently, the USA, China, France, Japan, Italy, Germany, and Saudi Arabia have set up and maintained military installations.[vi] Moreover, 95% of Ethiopia's trade transitions occur through Djibouti.[vii] The country has adeptly maintained a policy of neutrality, carefully managing its relationships with various international and regional forces through a cautious and balanced approach.

The phenomenon of proxy wars

In this region, political forces and groups consistently strive to engage in regional politics in various capacities to exert their influence over the region. Moreover, they are all involved in proxy wars and readily serve regional interests. Here are a few examples:

1. Eritrea participated as a military partner in a campaign led by the United Arab Emirates and Saudi Arabia to combat the Houthis in Yemen, simultaneously serving the interests of the United States and the West. Additionally, during the civil war that erupted in Ethiopia in 2020 between the Prosperity Party and the TPLF, Eritrea sided with the Prosperity Party and its allies and attacked the TPLF. PFDJ officials openly refer to this participation or alliance as "the war they were invited to participate in."
2. Ethiopia has maintained its presence in Somalia for decades as part of a UN-mandated peacekeeping force aimed at stabilizing the region, with the United States as the main financier of this project.

3. Ethiopia and Eritrea have taken sides in the ongoing civil war in Sudan, participating either directly or indirectly.
4. Various sources have confirmed that Eritrea provided political and logistical support to the militant extremist group Al-Shabaab, which operates in Somalia. The Eritrean government has also acknowledged that Al-Shabaab had an office in Eritrea. More recently, it has become publicly known that the Eritrean government is supporting the current Somali government by training Somali soldiers in Eritrea.
5. Turkey and the United Arab Emirates played a significant role in curtailing the TPLF's counter-offensive in the Ethiopian civil war of 2020 by siding with the Prosperity Party and its allies.
6. Conversely, the tripartite pact between Eritrea, Somalia, and Egypt aims to address Ethiopia's recurring quest for guaranteed sea access. Egypt is also using this pact to negotiate with Ethiopia regarding the contentious Grand Ethiopian Renaissance Dam (GERD).

The possibility of change in Eritrea - Scenarios

There is a growing belief that the current personal dictatorship in Eritrea is nearing its end. Increasingly, statements suggesting that "its days are numbered" are being made by people closely associated with the regime. This is not primarily due to the efforts of opposition forces but rather because the politics the government has pursued have led to a dead end. The internal networks that were once tightly held and controlled have transitioned to a state of extreme brittleness and vulnerability. According to all indicators, the system is in a precarious state. The question on the minds of many Eritreans is: how will change come? Based on an analysis of the current information, several plausible scenarios can be proposed.

First, like other dictatorial systems worldwide, coercion is the main instrument of the Eritrean system of governance. Therefore, it does not hesitate to use coercive tools against government officials (whether from the military and security apparatus or civil service) suspected of dissent. For example, imprisonment (such as that of Colonel Le'ake, the Naval Force Commander), threats, and even assassination attempts (such as the attempted assassination of Minister Sebhat Ephrem at his residence).

Given its repressive conduct, the regime can target prominent and mid-level cadres (elites) under its command—senior and mid-level military officers, security and police officials, civil servants (especially educated middle-aged youth), and PFDJ members—at any time. This has happened before. To cite some examples: the G-15, the Forto uprising by senior government and party officials, and the movement led by the alumni of the Revolution School. It is important to remember that most members of these movements are imprisoned.

Therefore, change will come through a division created within the ruling clique (involving competing interests) or through revolt by competing factions. As the political scientist Milan Svolik states: "In such systems, the main political transaction is not between the ruler and the people, but between the different 'cubs of the litter.' Ultimately, one transition scenario may be internal rupture and rebellion."[viii]

Second, a promising path for change lies in a collaboration between pro-justice forces in the diaspora and those advocating for change within the country. The Eritrean diaspora's potential contribution to the struggle for change, in alignment with the internal movement sharing similar goals, is crucial. To achieve this, it is essential to work towards an agreement on a minimum program. This involves forming a broader united front that brings together the majority of political organizations abroad, civic society, and activists in the diaspora, reaching a consensus on three fundamental objectives: (1) regime change; (2) the establishment of an inclusive transitional government that includes all Eritrean stakeholders, grounded in the rule of law, accountability, and transparency; and (3) the creation of a constitutional government, paving the way for national reconstruction and sustainable development. A pro-justice force that embraces these core objectives internally and collaborates with the growing movement in Eritrea is a viable prospect.

This joint endeavor must develop and implement an outreach strategy to promote these non-negotiable objectives and expose the regime's destructive nature. The primary aim is to win the hearts and minds of the Eritrean people and establish credibility as a reliable ally for change to the internal pro-justice forces in Eritrea. Achieving this goal may require diplomatic efforts, forming partnerships and alliances based on cooperation and engagement, and building and strengthening ties with various regional and international bodies with an interest in the region. Engagement should not only explain the country's situation but also highlight the benefits of such changes. Additionally, mobilizing the diaspora community according to their professions and interests is crucial, as is developing the capacity for continuous policy research and development on various topics that will serve the post-change period.

Regardless of the diaspora's extensive efforts for change, it must be understood that change will ultimately be confirmed from within the country and by insiders or the inner circle of the regime. Therefore, the diaspora must consistently recognize and strive to ensure that Eritreans inside Eritrea—within the military, civil service, and other sectors—who are fighting for justice, become reliable allies and partners in the cause of change. Consequently, the diaspora's strategy must focus on building a bridge between themselves and the forces of change inside Eritrea.

Third, the potential for a significant and widespread event originating in Ethiopia cannot be overlooked in the short term. As we have all observed, the alliance between Prime Minister Abiy and President Isaias, along with the relationship between their countries, has been deteriorating for some time now. It has become apparent even to the average person that they are entangled in political intrigue, each seeking to undermine the other's power. The voices we hear are merely precursors to wars. The ever-shifting alignment of forces in the region—PFDJ, Prosperity Party, TPLF, Fano, and the Oromo Liberation Army—could lead to conflict at any time. There is ample reason to believe that regional stakeholders have the capacity to intervene in an impending conflict. Recent events in the region have made this clear. Although predicting the outcome of such a bloody conflict is extremely challenging, one reality is certain: if this conflict erupts, it could fundamentally alter the region's political landscape.

Fourth, Natasha Ezrow, a scholar of history and political science, observes that when a dictator seizes power, he often experiences overwhelming insecurity or intense fear for his survival, which leads to severe paranoia. This feeling is intensified by the lack of succession mechanisms (Ezrow, 2011). Considering the dictator's age and health, a scenario in which he naturally departs from this world through death could also occur. In Eritrea, the issue of power succession has been stalled for decades, and raising it is still considered taboo. In a country like Eritrea, where there are no viable institutions—be it a political party, legislative body, judicial body, or executive branch—the likelihood of chaos erupting at the sign of change is very high.

Furthermore, it is suggested that if Isaias and his clique were to disappear from the political scene for various reasons, the only alternative would be a civil war among senior military officers over the question of "who takes power?" and the ensuing chaos, with a high probability of clashes among them. Some political analysts also believe that ensuring a smooth transfer of power could be challenging, indicating that turbulent experiments may occur. To prevent chaos, robust institutions, political competence, and the involvement of political stakeholders, including the people, are necessary.

Chapter 2

Eritrea: Pre and Post-Change

IN THE POST-INDEPENDENCE era, Eritrea was marked by poverty, limited economic capacity, a small population, and low standards of living. Despite these challenges, Eritrea had the potential for reconstruction, thanks to its invaluable assets: relentless, dedicated, perseverant, and innovative human capital. The Eritrean people not only endured thirty years of war but were also the primary architects of their independence. This remarkable victory laid the groundwork for a promising developmental journey, leading many observers to call Eritrea the "Beacon of Hope" for the Horn of Africa.

However, the experience of the past thirty-four years has shattered this dream. Thirty-four years after gaining independence, Eritrea is facing significant challenges.

The potential of two generations has been eroded; deliberate efforts have dismantled the country's social fabric; the rich culture of diversity nurtured over many years has been distorted or destroyed; improper interference in and manipulation of religion and religious institutions has become entrenched; the rule of law has been undermined, and lawlessness has been institutionalized. Any opposing voice or view has been suppressed by force or coercion.

The youth have been subjected to endless national service and transformed into instruments of forced labor. As a result, hundreds of thousands of young men and women have been driven into exile.

The violation of fundamental human rights has become commonplace, veteran fighters have been marginalized, and society's thinking has been systematically steered to align solely with the narrative desired by the regime. Consequently, Eritrea has become isolated from its neighbors and the rest of the world.

The political situation has deteriorated to alarming levels, with no signs of stability on the horizon. Widespread political resistance and dissent have emerged due to a lack of transparency and accountability in the government. Citizens, unable to hold their leaders and government accountable, are increasingly engulfed by a sense of hopelessness. The PFDJ regime relies on four fundamental pillars to maintain its grip on power.

The first pillar involves strengthening the national security apparatus, which includes security forces, military structures, police, and a reserve army. The regime consistently employs terror as a tool to maintain its authority over the people. Although these security and military structures have different names, they often operate under mutual suspicion and distrust. Ultimately, the regime is controlled by a clique focused solely on maintaining its power and dominance.

The second pillar focuses on controlling and managing financial resources, primarily through the illicit trade of valuable national assets, such as gold and other minerals, and leveraging contributions from various commercial entities controlled by the PFDJ. These entities operate covertly and often within the commercial and financial systems to sustain the regime's financial base. They not only engage in these activities but also accumulate financial assets through illicit activities.

Moreover, the regime benefits from the financial proceeds of the 2% tax policy traditionally imposed on the diaspora, a practice known as "milking of the diaspora." This mechanism enables the regime to collect hundreds of millions of dollars annually, which it uses to fund its coercive apparatus. Eritrean embassies, by prioritizing the collection of money from the diaspora and monitoring their citizens, often neglect the usual functions of an embassy and engage in transnational repression.

Compounding this issue is the regime's arbitrary control of foreign currency exchange rates, which deviates from international financial norms. Despite the diaspora's goodwill to support their families, what ultimately ends up in the regime's coffers is substantial or outrightly plundered.

The third pillar focuses on the regime's policy of strictly controlling life opportunities. The PFDJ regime has made support and assistance for various life milestones—such as international travel, education or training, healthcare, and property ownership—conditional. In this system, citizens' ability to build their lives or advance their careers depends on the regime's goodwill. If dissent is detected, these benefits are indefinitely suspended, subjecting entire families to severe repercussions.

All employment opportunities in Eritrea are exclusively offered and managed by the government or the ruling party (PFDJ). In such a tightly controlled environment, it is easy to imagine the consequences for anyone who dares to express dissenting views. From the "freezing"[ix] that has affected many mid- and high-level civil servants, consequences can escalate to imprisonment.

Under this regime, traveling abroad is extremely difficult. The process of obtaining permission for citizens needing to travel for medical reasons is very strict and granted only to those with special connections. The opportunity to own a house is also entirely under the regime's control. An individual's chance of owning a home is determined by their loyalty and closeness to the ruling party (PFDJ). Consequently, even those who wish to keep their homes have no choice but to align themselves with the regime, as their entire lives are under the complete control of this overarching system.

The fourth pillar involves maintaining absolute control over narratives while effectively silencing alternative perspectives. These narratives primarily emphasize internal and external conspiracies against the country, centering on the idea that 'the existence of Eritrea is under threat.' According to the PFDJ's doctrine, the nation has consistently faced threats of expansion and aggression because of its strategic location along the Red Sea. This narrative claims that the country has paid a significant price, prompting its citizens to view it as a valuable national asset. However, this does not justify the promotion of nationalism rooted in suspicion towards others and hatred. Yet, the PFDJ argues that even when reconciling with adversaries, there must always be others to confront, or imaginary foes to be fabricated to sustain the system's narrative of fear.

The PFDJ's narrative was built around strong anti-Woyane [TPLF] rhetoric, particularly targeting the West, especially America, by accusing it of conspiring with the TPLF to undermine Eritrea. This accusation is used to attack, oppose, and condemn such actors. Slogans like "America and the West are the main enemies of the Eritrean people," "They are the major obstacles to Eritrea's reconstruction and development process," and "They oppose the developmental strides Eritrea is making based on its own resources and capacities," are common refrains frequently echoed by official news outlets.

This narrative is both continuous and all-encompassing in nature. Under the PFDJ regime, there is no distinction between the government, PFDJ, and the state. In some cases, this lack of separation even includes President Isaias Afwerki himself. The PFDJ is synonymous with the government, the government with the state, and the state with the PFDJ. The PFDJ is equated with President Isaias. Consequently, anyone who does not support the PFDJ, the Eritrean government, or President Isaias is considered to be unpatriotic. For this reason, they are categorized as enemies of the nation. Those associated with the nation's enemies are subsequently labeled as traitors, Woyane [TPLF], mercenaries, collaborators, or CIA agents.

To instill or indoctrinate these narratives into the populace, the regime operates a sophisticated propaganda machine. It excels in censorship and information control by keeping the internet and telecoms infrastructure in Eritrea substandard to ensure that people do not have access to external sources of information. It also allocates endless resources for this purpose. After the Ministry of Defense, propaganda receives the second-largest budget allocation.

Pre-transition: observations and reflections

When examining the categorization of the system in Eritrea, it is crucial to recognize that it operates as a personalistic dictatorship. To thoroughly grasp the characteristics and comparisons of such regimes, we may need to consult a series of studies by political science experts and historians on the nature and traits of dictatorships.

In a lecture titled "The End of Personalistic Dictatorships - How Personalistic Rulers Lose Their Power," Dr. Ezrow,[x] a professor at Essex University, defines dictatorship as "a type of government that lacks an executive turnover or change." She further explains that there are five types of systems based on dictatorship, and according to her indicators, the system in Eritrea aligns with a personalistic dictatorship (Ezrow, 2011).

Another scholar, Milan (W) Svolik, in his book "The Politics of Authoritarian Rule," analyzes 303 rulers who were in power between 1946 and 2008 and how they ended up relinquishing power. He reveals that thirty-two (10.6%) were removed by popular uprising, thirty (9.9%) were forced out by their own will due to public pressure, twenty (6.6%) were killed or assassinated, and sixteen (5.3%) were ousted by foreign military intervention. He notes that the remaining 205 rulers (67.7% or two-thirds) were removed by their own inner circles, often actors from the regime's coercive apparatus, typically through a coup d'état within the government (Svolik, 2012).

"In conclusion," Svolik states, "in such systems, the main political conflict is not between the ruler and the people, but rather among the different factions of the inner circle. Ultimately, the solution is a coup or rebellion." (Svolik, 2012).

Ezrow also highlights that the gravest threats to a personalistic ruler stem from those within the inner circle, as they possess the greatest potential to execute a coup d'état. She elaborates by noting that a personal ruler's survival in power hinges on the political dynamics within the ruling elite (Ezrow, 2011).

The series of coups d'état in West Africa from 2020 to 2023, including those in Gabon, Mali, Guinea, Chad, Burkina Faso, and Niger, supports this argument. The attempted efforts to challenge the President in Eritrea in 2000 and 2013 (that can be categorized as a coup) were not exceptions to these patterns. Another example is the 1990 coup attempt by Major General Mer'id Negusse against his superior, the former President of Ethiopia, Colonel Meghistu Hailemariam.

Based on the evidence presented, the challenges of a system rooted in personalistic dictatorship can be summarized in the scenarios outlined in Chapter 1, titled "Eritrea: Current Situation." Briefly, the first scenario might involve a change initiated by the inner circle, potentially involving military and civil service personnel in the leadership. The second scenario could be a change driven by these internal forces in collaboration with Eritreans abroad seeking justice and reform. The third scenario involves changes through foreign intervention. The fourth scenario could result from the natural death of the personalist ruler, potentially sparking a power struggle among senior army and security officers within the ruling elite.

The importance of a post-transition roadmap, the establishment of a transitional and constitutional government

Eritrea's current system is on the brink of internal collapse, with widespread discussions regarding Eritrea's future. The once tightly controlled and disciplined internal coercive apparatus now exhibits significant dysfunctions. Numerous events underscore a serious decline in its grip of power. In Eritrea, institutions and institutional processes have long shown signs of deterioration, giving way to a firmly entrenched, one-man dictatorship. This fragile structure, characterized by a lack of accountability, weak institutions, corruption, and totalitarianism, undermines national stability. Consequently, a spirit of despair and distrust has taken hold among citizens.

This institutional degradation and erosion extend to the legislative and judicial branches of the government. The National Assembly, the highest legislative body, has not convened for more than 20 years. The centralized power structure stifles and nullifies institutions, particularly government bodies with distinct mandates and policies, often bypassed by PFDJ party cadres. The cabinet of ministers rarely meets, and when it does, it operates in secrecy, leaving the public uninformed about its activities.

The Eritrean people, increasingly frustrated by the deteriorating conditions in their country, have called and are calling for change or reform. Even regime supporters are now advocating ideas such as establishing a transitional government and opening up alternative political spaces. Many are convinced that change is inevitable and view it as a matter of time. However, some argue that the government's instillation of fear and a culture of submission have prevented people from mobilizing for change or reform. Others believe that the ruling party's coercive apparatus instills fear of consequences, causing hesitation in efforts to bring about change. Nevertheless, there is a desire and need for change.

However, the main issue is how the changes desired by the Eritrean people can be expressed or achieved. In this regard, both within Eritrea and among the diaspora, citizens—whether they support or oppose the

PFDJ regime—are frequently seen engaging in discussions among themselves through various means and on different occasions.

As explored in Chapter 1, there are speculations about what Eritrea might look like after the change. A major concern is the transition of power. Since the topic of succession has been treated as a taboo for decades, it is believed that if President Isaias were to leave the political scene for any reason, the most likely outcome would be a power struggle among different interest groups within the regime, each vying for control. Additionally, given the existing divisions and fragmentation among the Eritrean opposition, this lack of unity could present a significant challenge in ensuring a smooth power transition. This concern suggests a potential reality in which the aftermath may be unclear or unpredictable.

In one way or another, everything in life, without exception, has a beginning and an end. This fundamental truth is affirmed by the laws of both natural and social sciences. Many administrations have risen, only to eventually decline and disappear thereafter. Similarly, while the people and their land endure and will continue to exist, the governments that rule them and the political organizations and personalities that lead them share the same fate. From birth to adulthood, and finally, having withstood the test of time, they move towards their demise or conclusion.

The fate of the current Eritrean government is no different from what is discussed above. In light of this, it is crucial to consider possible developments, identify potential opportunities, anticipate potential threats/dangers, propose ideas to avert them, and pave the way for a smooth transition to constitutional Eritrea. The significance and purpose of the proposed roadmap stem from this fact.

Models of transitional governments

Transitional governments are temporary administrations set up after political upheavals such as revolutions, civil wars, government collapses, and voluntary regime dissolutions. Although their characteristics may differ based on their unique situations, they share certain commonalities. Here are some examples:

Post-Revolutionary Transitional Government - Tunisia's National Constituent Assembly (2011 – 2014): Following the ousting of President Zine El Abidine Ben Ali during the Arab Spring uprising, a transitional government was established to draft a constitution and prepare for democratic elections. Led by Prime Minister Beji Caid Essebsi, this government implemented fundamental constitutional reforms and facilitated a democratic transition.

Post-Conflict Transitional Government - South Africa's Government of National Unity (1994): After the end of the apartheid system of racial segregation, a transitional power-sharing government led by Nelson Mandela was established. Its goal was to negotiate the establishment of a majority-rule government. The power-sharing arrangement between the African National Congress (ANC) and the National Party focused on reconciliation and the conduct of democratic elections.

Military-Led Transitional Government - Egypt's Supreme Council of the Armed Forces (2011 – 2012): After President Hosni Mubarak was ousted, the Egyptian military assumed control of the country until elections were held. However, owing to its inherently undemocratic structure, the promise of a smooth transition to democracy ultimately failed to materialize.

United Nations-Supported Transitional Government - United Nations Transitional Authority in Cambodia (UNTAC) (1992 – 1993): Following years of civil war, the United Nations was tasked with temporarily administering Cambodia to conduct free elections. Its mandate included international supervision, demobilization of former combatants, and organizing elections.

Interim Administration Established by Force - Afghanistan's Interim Administration (2001 – 2004): After the U.S.-led war and the fall of the Taliban, a transitional government led by Hamid Karzai was established to prepare for elections. Although it was inclusive, incorporating various ethnic and political groups, it was fragile and heavily reliant on foreign support.

Mali's Transitional Government (2020 - Present): Following a military coup, an interim civilian-military transitional government was established with the stated goal of holding elections in the country. This framework, composed of military and civilian members, faced challenges to its legitimacy and created complications in returning to democracy.

Syria (2024-25): The Syrian Transitional Government was established on March 29, 2025. Ahmed al-Sharaa was appointed interim president and formed a twenty-three-member cabinet of ministers. This transitional government, formed by Hayat Tahrir al-Sham (HTS), the Salvation Army, technocrats, civil society, and former ministers from Bashar al-Assad's government, includes representatives from groups such as Alawites, Christians, Kurds, and Druze. This transition is expected to take five years.

The characteristics of transitional governments can be summarized as follows.

Temporary:

- These types of arrangements are necessary to ensure a smooth transition to a constitutional government.

- These interim governments are established to function only until a permanent structure is established.
- They may be led by a diverse array of entities, including civilians, military officers, technocrats, international organizations, or a combination of all or some of the indicated entities.
- Their objectives may encompass bringing about constitutional reform, conducting elections, demobilizing combatants, and fostering reconciliation.
- They often grapple with legitimacy issues, even with support from internal or external forces. Earning the population's trust remains a formidable challenge.

Post-change challenges

The severity of the challenges encountered after regime change is closely tied to the thoroughness and sophistication of the preparations made during the pre-change phase. Essentially, the more comprehensive the preparations are, the better equipped people are to avoid potential challenges. Neglecting this could lead to an increase in problems in the future.

The main challenges can be summarized as follows: -

Institutional deterioration: The current system in Eritrea has led to weakened institutions to the point where it would not be an exaggeration to say that they are non-functional. This situation breeds a lack of trust in these institutions. Additionally, it has hindered the ability of government ministries to operate effectively because of insufficient capacity. Building the capacity of ministries and other government institutions will be a significant undertaking.

Political polarization: Following the fall of the dictatorship, society can become deeply politically polarized over issues of power, ideology, and the nation's future. Therefore, it is crucial to replace the current government with a legitimate and stable one. This necessitates efforts to reconcile seemingly conflicting viewpoints, manage visible tensions or power struggles, and foster institutional trust within the community.

Economic collapse: Dictatorial regimes often leave a country's economy in disarray, marked by total control and marginalization of key economic actors. This is common in Eritrea. In this context, developing infrastructure and ensuring economic stability will be major challenges. Issues such as unemployment, poverty alleviation, the revival of paralyzed institutions, and the equitable distribution of resources must be addressed, which can be a lengthy process.

Deep-seated mistrust: The mistrust that has been sown during the dictatorship era is likely to persist even after regime change, posing a challenge that can undermine social cohesion and the building of national identity.

The conduct of transitional justice: Addressing human rights violations and other unjust acts committed in the past is delicate and requires careful handling as resistance to it will be inevitable.

Rebuilding diplomatic relations: Reestablishing diplomatic relations and enhancing international cooperation will be challenging since relationships with other nations were damaged due to the erroneous foreign policy of the dictatorial system.

Regional instability: The potential instability in our region and its potential impact necessitate planning how to manage it. We also need to determine how we will interact with our neighbors, regions, and the world.

Restoring security: Restoring security and reforming the security apparatus are important challenges the new government might need to address.

What needs to be done?

To address these challenges, the establishment of an interim administration rooted in good governance is crucial. This requires mechanisms for transitional justice, economic reform, and cultivating societal trust. It must be specifically tailored to Eritrea's unique history, multicultural composition, and the pervasive nature of the dictatorial system that has ruled the country for decades. The following steps are essential:

A bridge must be built between pro-democracy and justice forces operating abroad and groups inside Eritrea working towards similar goals. Creating conditions for collaboration and building trust is crucial. This can only be achieved through opening active channels of communication and establishing synergy.

Pro-change and justice forces, both within the country and in the diaspora, must unite under a single program to achieve this. Their leadership should be identified and established, their strategy (roadmap) clarified, their priorities articulated, and a platform capable of delivering practical results should be prepared. These elements should align with the following overarching objectives:

- Regime change;
- Establishing an inclusive transitional government that encompasses all Eritreans based on the rule of law, accountability, and transparency; and
- Transitioning towards nation-building and sustainable development through the establishment of a constitutional government.

To effectively mobilize pro-change and justice forces both within and outside the country, it is essential to develop and implement outreach strategies centered on the aforementioned non-negotiable objectives while exposing the regime's destructive nature. This approach is crucial for winning the hearts and minds of the Eritrean people and establishing credibility as genuine advocates of social justice. A credible demand for justice will require an appeal to the army and security forces, veteran freedom fighters, war-disabled, civil service members, activists, fathers, mothers, religious leaders, and traditional leaders.

To support efforts aimed at achieving these objectives, forging alliances and partnerships and engaging in dialogue and cooperation with regional and international bodies based on shared interests is indispensable. Proactive diplomatic efforts are crucial to this endeavor. The narrative should not only be geared towards defining or analysing the country's situation but also emphasize the mutual benefits that both parties can gain from the change.

Furthermore, as previously mentioned, the diaspora community can be organized according to their professions and interests, enabling them to engage in discussions on key topics and develop important draft policy documents that could be used as references by the interim government. These may include, but are not limited to, a draft National Charter, Refugee Resettlement Policy, Transitional Justice Policy, Macroeconomic Policy, Professional Army Building Policy, Foreign Policy, and Demobilization Policy for combatants.

Achieving these goals will require persistent and uninterrupted efforts.

A Roadmap for a Transitional Government in Eritrea

The roadmap for the transitional government encompasses the following attributes:

a. This roadmap is crafted to serve as a guiding framework for the post-change phase, delineating a vision for structuring a transitional government and facilitating the shift to a constitutional one.
b. The proposed vision for Eritrea's transitional government is: "The establishment of a democratic and prosperous nation, founded on a national covenant that ensures the rule of law, where the rights of all citizens are guaranteed, popular participation is anchored in all spheres of life, social justice and peace are established, and relations with neighbors and the world are based on mutual respect and cooperation."
c. Political transitions are inherently fraught with complex challenges. The thirty-four years of the post-independence period that Eritrea underwent make its situation particularly unique. The regime left no stone unturned in its efforts to cling to power. By creating conditions that prevent dialogue, the opportunity to address the nation's problems through peaceful and democratic means has become very slim. Under such conditions, there are no other options but to consider alternative approaches. Achieving this requires significant and sophisticated political and diplomatic capacity and skills, as well as visionary, transitional leadership.

To accomplish the above, it is essential to have a roadmap that prioritizes the critical tasks mentioned above and that guides the activities of the transitional government. Such a roadmap can also serve as a consensus-building mechanism.

Foundational principles of a transitional government

The foundational principles of a transitional government encompass the following:

- Acknowledging the significant sacrifices made by the Eritrean people in their pursuit of independence;
- Cherishing the love and resilience the Eritrean people have for their nation;
- Placing the interests of the Eritrean people above all else, while ensuring this does not come at the expense of other peoples or groups;
- Embracing and celebrating Eritrea's ethnic, religious, cultural, and political diversity, rather than merely tolerating it;
- Ensuring and safeguarding freedom of expression;
- Resolving internal political differences through democratic dialogue;
- Developing a comprehensive roadmap to enhance the human capital;
- Committing to a process of reconciliation, recovery, and integration to build a healthy society; and
- Promoting mutual respect, cooperation, and peaceful coexistence with neighboring countries and the world.

Goals and priorities

In response to the significant and existential national challenges previously mentioned, ensuring Eritrea's survival as a nation is urgent and crucial. To achieve this, concentrated efforts on the following priorities are essential:

- Establishment of a Transitional Government: Convening an inclusive National Conference with all relevant Eritrean stakeholders to form a provisional transitional government that will guide the country towards a democratic transition.

♦ Formation of a Constitutional Government: Drafting and implementing a democratic constitution, followed by conducting free, fair, and just elections.

The need for a deliberate facilitation of the process

To achieve such a transformation, the facilitation role of a widely accepted and credible political force is crucial to prevent a political vacuum. This body comprises justice-seeking Eritreans from within the country and the diaspora. In Eritrea, there appears to be growing momentum for change, although its internal dynamics largely remain hidden from public view. This movement encompasses Eritreans from diverse backgrounds—military and security personnel, police, civil servants, youth, women, and others—who share a profound frustration and anger over their country's current state and a strong desire for freedom and justice. They are ready to make the necessary sacrifices to rescue Eritrea from the brink of collapse, with their sole agenda being the salvation of their nation and the fulfillment of their people's aspirations.

Despite its limitations, the Eritrean diaspora can play a pivotal role in supporting and co-leading such change. Therefore, it is essential to focus on developing shared goals, dismantling divisive thinking, establishing responsible mass media, and cultivating a collective will, all of which are vital for establishing a constitutional government in Eritrea. Although the diaspora has the potential to seek change, there is a prevailing belief that change will ultimately originate from within the country and its inner circles, as discussed previously.

The diaspora must consistently remember that Eritreans advocating for change and justice within Eritrea, whether in the army and security apparatus or outside it, can be strong and reliable allies in this quest. Consequently, <u>the diaspora's strategy should aim to build a bridge between themselves and the forces for change and justice within Eritrea</u>, thereby creating a collective momentum to bring about positive change, establish a transitional government, and lay the foundation for a constitutional one. For this political initiative to be meaningful, a clear vision of Eritrea's future is required.

This leadership, which is facilitating the transitional process, will form a viable coalition with the forces that have long been struggling for change and should conduct its activities in consultation with them. It is essential for this internal force to mobilize all the nation's resources, especially political support from citizens within Eritrea. This should not be seen as an option but rather as a strategic imperative for the future. Therefore, formulating a roadmap for political transition is the first step toward building momentum and creating a situation in which normal life is reinstated.

This roadmap should follow a clear path to building a constitutional Eritrea, based on fundamental democratic principles.

It serves as a critical document, delineating the objectives and aspirations of the transition. It specifies the scope, depth, and methodology of political transition, foresees potential risks, taps on potential opportunities, and underlines the ultimate goals that require attention.

This roadmap outlines the timeline for political transition (or transitional government), the roles and responsibilities of various stakeholders, and other critical issues that must be addressed. Moreover, it plays a crucial role in ensuring that the desired outcome is achieved during the transition by managing change peacefully and in an inclusive manner.

To define the transition process, it enumerates the key milestones and timelines that the coalition movement for change, both domestically and internationally, must accomplish to transition Eritrea to a system focused on good governance. This ensures that the transition is completed within a reasonable time frame.

The legitimate body, a coalition of forces seeking change and justice both domestically and internationally, that represents the transitional government, must clearly communicate the government's program to the people, outline its limitations, and affirm its commitment to prioritizing the welfare of the populace. The transitional government is tasked with overseeing and facilitating the transition process from its inception until a constitutional government is established.

This legal body, entrusted with guiding and facilitating the change process, is responsible for setting the stage for the National Dialogue Conference. Following a successful dialogue, the transitional government will spearhead an inclusive effort to draft a new constitution, building on a review of the previously drafted constitution/s. This new constitution will embody universal principles of freedom and justice, take into account Eritrea's socio-economic structure, and reflect the perspectives, culture, and values the Eritrean people cherish.

To transition to a constitutional government, it is crucial to foster an environment conducive to civil discourse, ensuring inclusivity, transparency, and participation by all citizens in the political process. Above all, this body promotes a culture of resolving differences through dialogue, encouraging unity and reconciliation, while firmly opposing the use of force to settle conflicts. It will establish independent institutions, such as an Electoral Commission, a judicial system, and various regulatory bodies, to strengthen the rule of law and democratic processes. Additionally, it will ensure the credibility and transparency of free and fair elections within a defined timeframe.

The transitional government should leverage the potential of the Eritrean diaspora to mobilize resources and secure financial, logistical, technical, and material support. It should also engage with various international partners to obtain technical and financial assistance, fostering a spirit of trust, public engagement, and participation by creating conditions for timely connections with Eritreans living abroad.

During the transition process, the transitional government must prioritize the rule of law and ensure that justice is served. It should also focus on maintaining the stability and security of the population, taking all necessary measures to prevent acts of revenge or retribution. Additionally, it must ensure that all government institutions operate with clear mandates, accountability, and transparency.

The transitional government should embark on a process of national healing, peace, and reconciliation to address the country's internal divisions. To achieve this, a well-defined strategy and profound vision are essential. The success of such efforts often depends on the inclusive participation and goodwill of all citizens, along with the support of the broader international community. To put this into action, a framework for justice and reconciliation should be established to implement transitional justice mechanisms, which help address past wrongdoings and foster national reconciliation. Civic education should be crafted and disseminated to promote democratic values and enhance civic participation, thereby making education and public awareness more effective and widespread.

It facilitates the release of all prisoners of conscience, practically demonstrating a commitment to upholding human rights, and prepares the ground for these individuals to receive the necessary support they need for their rehabilitation and to start their new lives.

The interim government should prioritize the delivery of essential social services such as education and healthcare to meet the needs of the Eritrean people. It must also extend support to disabled war veterans. Collaboration with host countries and international organizations is crucial for effectively addressing the issue of Eritrean refugees displaced from their places of origin.

It should forge strong relationships with neighboring countries and the international community based on international norms, mutual respect, and cooperation. It should re-establish diplomatic ties with all neighboring and global nations, particularly Ethiopia and the Sudan, in accordance with the principles that govern international relations.

To improve Eritrea's image, which has been marred by the previous regime's controversial actions, it should undertake robust public relations and diplomatic campaigns to improve its image. Reviewing existing bilateral and multilateral agreements or treaties and formulating and implementing new ones will be essential.

The transitional government must ensure internal stability and human security while safeguarding national sovereignty. To enhance citizen security, professional military and security forces should be established, and new opportunities should be provided to members of the national service who wish to pursue new roles in their lives.

Timely public engagements and discourses should be initiated and conducted, emphasizing transparency and accountability. During these occasions, both the challenges and opportunities the nation faces should be presented to the people. Developing a robust communications strategy and initiating public engagement are vital to building trust among Eritrean citizens and uniting them around a common platform.

The transitional government will formulate a comprehensive policy to advance Eritrea's economy and infrastructure. It will manage the national economy and ensure the availability of essential goods and services for the population. To promote transparency, the national budget will be made public. The government will also ensure the payment of civil service salaries and guarantee access to water, electricity, and other essential services. Additionally, it will review and renew all existing contracts, with particular emphasis on those related to mining. An environment conducive to the growth of all economic sectors—agriculture, industry, and services—will be nurtured to enhance their contributions to the national economy.

Sustainable development relies on strong economic foundations across all sectors, necessitating a framework that fosters prosperity in all areas. Achieving this requires a national development strategy crafted through dialogue and discourse aimed at eradicating poverty in the country. A macroeconomic policy will be developed to promote entrepreneurship, encourage capital accumulation and investment, boost exports, foster balanced trade relations with neighboring and developed countries, and prioritize regional integration, all of which will be supported by sound fiscal and monetary policies.

Shortly after the transitional government is established, a conference of domestic and international investors will be convened to create conditions for economic prosperity in the country. These relationships are grounded in principles of partnership, providing a platform for the national economy to benefit from international support in the short, medium, and long term.

In summary, the transitional government will make a concerted effort to build an Eritrea rooted in social justice, freedom, and liberty, thereby ensuring sustainable development and success.

Transitional period

The transitional period refers to the time following the change, which culminates in the establishment of a constitutional government. This transitional government may remain in place for up to thirty-six months, given the complexity of the transition and tasks needed to be accomplished before setting up a constitutional government.

Structure of the transitional government

The political entity representing the transitional period is responsible for forming a caretaker government. This government will have full executive authority to manage state affairs during the transition period. The cabinet, led by a caretaker president, will consist of competent professionals and citizens from across society.

Conference for national dialogue: Aims and responsibilities

Convening the Conference for National Dialogue is a sacred objective, characterized by openness, transparency, inclusivity, and a conducive environment for deliberation. The responsibilities of the Conference for National Dialogue include the following: -

- It is essential to invite Eritreans from all social strata—particularly political organizations, civic societies, religious and traditional leaders, prominent individuals, and representatives of the diaspora—to participate in the National Conference to finalize the roadmap for a political transition. These participants will represent the diverse socioeconomic, political, and cultural structures of society. Equitable representation of women is not merely an option; it is a priority. To accomplish this, a preparatory committee will be appointed to facilitate the process.
- The Conference for National Dialogue shall prioritize the establishment of a transitional government. It will approve the Charter of the Transitional Government and deliberate on norms and principles for establishing a transitional national assembly, the constitution-drafting process, national reconciliation and healing, restructuring institutional systems, establishing the rule of law, reforming the justice system, Eritrea's relations with its neighbors and the world, security and stability issues, economic recovery, the expansion of social services, and other related matters. Recommendations relevant to these matters will be presented to the Transitional Government of Eritrea.
- The Conference for National Dialogue shall be convened within a short period (three to four months) following the change.

Transitional Government of Eritrea (TGE)

The Transitional National Assembly will function as a legislative body until a constitutional government is established. The elected members of this assembly are tasked with implementing the decisions, policies, and directives recommended by the National Dialogue. Additionally, it ensures representation across most Eritrean social strata. Its functions include adopting and implementing the National Charter[xi] as its guiding framework. This dynamic National Charter is designed to uphold the values, dignity, and institutional frameworks of a transitioning nation. The TGE will fulfill several key functions, including:

- Promulgating and enacting provisional laws;
- Ratifying the draft constitution and affirming its legitimacy through a referendum;
- Approving the budget and overseeing its implementation;
- Promulgating and implementing laws concerning political parties; and
- Approving and implementing electoral laws proposed by the Electoral Commission in line with the given mandate and the nation's priorities.

Additionally, it establishes the following commissions to execute their missions and oversee their operations: the National Commission for Reconciliation and Stability, Electoral Commission, Constitutional Review Commission, Commission for the Resettlement of Displaced Citizens and Refugees, Commission for the Rehabilitation and Integration of Former National Service Members, and Commission for the Investigation of Human Rights Violations.

Transitional Justice

In the absence of justice, citizens continue to endure relentless instances of detention, killings, torture, and disappearances. The suffering inflicted on victims and their families is significant and long-lasting. To halt the perpetuation of such a horrific culture and create conditions for victims of the defunct system to receive justice, it is essential to adopt and implement a highly credible, systematic, and process and outcome-oriented approach. This approach must provide victims with various opportunities to obtain justice.

Transitional Justice serves as a tool for societies transitioning from conflict, collapse, and authoritarian rule to peace and democracy, addressing widespread human rights violations and injustices. Its application necessitates a thorough analysis, broad public participation, and a balance between justice, reconciliation, and stability.

When implemented with consideration of local specific realities and in accordance with international norms and standards, Transitional Justice can yield sustainable outcomes. It includes elements such as truth-seeking and reconciliation, accountability and justice, reparations for victims, institutional reform, memorialization, and education.

The process of Transitional Justice involves ensuring that it is conducted under a legitimate mandate, assessing the specific situation, consulting with stakeholders, adopting a comprehensive framework, mobilizing resources, building the capacities needed for its implementation, promoting public dialogue and reconciliation, and planning and implementation that adapt to time and circumstances.

It is also important to acknowledge that in any transition scenario, segments of the former regime might display resistance, which may make it difficult to co-opt them in support of the broader transition. Accountability often sounds great in principle, but political realities may make it hard.

All these functions require expertise or highly qualified and dignified professionals and people with conscience to manage, oversee, and implement them.

Challenges of the new constitutional Eritrea

Understanding the factors that will persist and influence Eritrea's development is crucial. These include: The Red Sea's strategic importance to the global community, which will subject Eritrea to scrutiny from both regional and international powers, Ethiopia's maritime ambitions, particularly its desire for sea access, which will remain a significant concern for Eritrea, the ongoing political instability in the Horn of Africa, rooted in historical context and unresolved political grievances, which may eventually lead to a reconfiguration of political alliances, and the potential for proxy wars, driven by the aforementioned factors.

How can Eritrea address these challenges?

Eritrea's stability hinges on its ability to avert and manage threats to its security and well-being. The initial step in alleviating this tension is to fully acknowledge their existence and comprehend them. Moreover, it is crucial to identify and rectify Eritrea's misguided and confrontational domestic and foreign policies, which could potentially lead to instability.

Equally important is Eritrea's ability to understand to shifts in the global political landscape. Moreover, decisions that clash with the interests of the international community could jeopardize Eritrea's national security, leading to political and diplomatic attacks and sanctions by powerful nations. To avert such potential threats, Eritrea can adopt several strategies.

First, Eritrea must endeavor to establish itself as a stabilizing and peaceful partner in the global community. It should launch a robust diplomatic initiative to counter the persistent narrative that it has always been and is part of Ethiopia, while demonstrating its commitment to peace and regional stability and proving itself as a security guarantor in the region.

Second, Eritrea should impress upon the international community that Ethiopia's stability aligns with its own and the region's strategic interests and that fostering improved relations with its neighbors, grounded in mutual respect, should be a priority. Additionally, Eritrea should exhibit goodwill in addressing Ethiopia's security concerns and propose solutions that resonate with international norms and benefit both parties. The only viable resolution lies in peaceful and diplomatic efforts.

Third, Eritrea can fortify itself by building a resilient economy that can withstand political shocks. This involves crafting sound economic policies, enhancing domestic production capacity, creating favorable conditions for foreign investment, and expanding and developing its human capital. To bolster its economic strength, Eritrea must leverage appropriate technology.

Fourth, developing a modern and professional army is essential to ensure national security. Such an army can underpin the region's security framework—established through alliances—and serve as a deterrent or leverage against potential external threats. Establishing military cooperation with major global powers is another avenue worth exploring, as it can serve as a shield against external pressures and threats of aggression.

Fifth, Eritrea must address the issue of population growth seriously. At times, a larger population can help deflect external threats from neighboring countries. According to records from the National Statistics and Evaluation Office, in 2001, the Ministry of Local Government of Eritrea estimated the country's total population to be approximately 3.2 million people. Due to mass migration, Eritrea's population has not grown as expected. Given the rapidly increasing populations of neighboring countries, Eritrea should closely monitor these issues. It is important to recognize that, in our world, having a small population can sometimes be a vulnerability.

Sixth, addressing extremist tendencies is inherently linked to a country's political, social, and economic dynamics. Containing or eliminating religious, ethnic, or political extremism requires sustained effort. A constitutional government can ensure political, religious, and ethnic freedom, establish fundamental human and political rights, end illegal detentions and exile, adopt a resilient economy to provide a decent life for its people, and collaborate with neighboring countries to jointly address these deficiencies.

Ultimately, Eritrea must strive to learn, master, and utilize the art of diplomatic engagement. The political situation in the Red Sea region demands diverse, far-sighted, and adaptive approaches. In a world where national, regional, and global interests intersect, Eritrea cannot exist in isolation. It must abandon its "I am the victim" stance. In its diplomatic efforts, pursuing a win-win solution for all should be the central element of its strategy. A former Chancellor of Germany, Otto von Bismarck, once said, "Politics is the art of the possible, the attainable — the art of the next best." From this, we can draw invaluable lessons.

The vision
Eritrea aspires to be a nation admired by its neighbors and the international community. This admiration stems not only from the considerable sacrifices made during the struggle for independence but also from a nation-building initiative driven by well-defined strategies and goals. This initiative entails robust institutions, a resilient and modern economy, highly skilled and competent human capital, balanced diplomacy in foreign affairs, and a sincere desire to improve the quality of life for the Eritrean people.

At the heart of this vision is the creation of conditions for the rule of law, which serves as the foundation of a society that values a fair and orderly system of governance. Upholding the principles of freedom and social justice, along with pursuing economic development that meets the needs of various regions in the country, is essential. Good governance and institutional frameworks emphasize building a collective consensus and prioritizing fair representation.

Traditional customs and laws that once supported the systems and stability will be refined through dialogue and consensus. Discriminatory practices against women and other historical disadvantages are re-evaluated.

The journey toward change may be gradual, but the change itself will be significant and sustainable. Instead of sudden transformations, steady and managed changes are preferred. Change is viewed positively only when it is sustainable and profound. A slow process of change may seem lengthy in a single human life, but it is not so in the lifetime of a nation.

The preservation, respect, transmission, and inheritance of Eritrea's value systems, traditions, history, and faith are crucial. Even when faced with challenges, trusting that history, with all its dark chapters, has proven to be a wise teacher that offers invaluable lessons that are essential for maintaining national identity and pride. Reviving Eritrea's rich, ancient, and modern history, supported by archaeological and historical research, and preserving its historical civilizations and sites are of utmost importance. In particular, the preservation of heritage sites such as Adulis, Zula, and Belew Kelew reinforces the continuity of cultural identity. This vision honors history and tradition and instills pride in those who contribute to the nation's progress.

We are dedicated to ensuring that Eritrea coexists peacefully with its neighboring countries, engaging with them respectfully, encouraging regional collaboration for shared objectives, and resolving conflicts through peaceful means.

Religious freedom is an essential pillar of society that is often unrecognized. Faith acts as a stabilizing force within communities and is closely tied to social values and norms such as respecting elders, fostering collective trust, and cultivating virtuous character traits. Embracing change should be viewed as a natural progression. While it may sometimes seem slow or exhausting, it should never be perceived as a barrier to progress.

To address current challenges, it is vital to learn from past institutions, whether governmental or otherwise. The goal is to create an environment that promotes "normalcy[xii] as a way of life," where individuals can live their lives without fear, express their ideas freely, and participate as equal citizens or human beings in building the nation.

In this vision, parents instill their values and culture in their children, showing love and care, and raising independent thinkers.

The justice system functions transparently, ensuring that the law's supremacy is applied equally to everyone. In a nation governed by laws, policies, and systems, outcomes are predictable. Dialogue is practiced as a standard to accommodate diverse perspectives.

Eritrea's advancement fundamentally relies on identifying, mobilizing, and utilizing domestic resources, community-based development initiatives, and promoting fundamental individual responsibilities. A responsible approach that includes everyone and pays attention to vulnerable segments of the population is crucial.

Educational institutions, research centers, and centers of excellence must be empowered to promote knowledge and innovation.

This vision envisions a future for Eritrea characterized by prosperity, stability, and cultural diversity, affirming not only its history but also the dignity of the nation in which so much hope has been invested.

This vision promotes social justice and equitable sharing of national resources among the people. This vision will prevent a wide gap between the rich and the poor. Social justice prioritizes essential services, such as education and healthcare.

This vision ensures the full participation of women, who make up half of society, and fulfills their needs and aspirations. It regards all Eritrean nationalities equally and strives for a better future for all.

Chapter 3

A Dual Economic Strategy for Eritrea: Unlocking Domestic Potential, Engaging the World

BEFORE EXPLORING SPECIFIC concepts that illuminate the economic development roadmap, it is crucial to discuss development as a concept. This involves examining the conditions under which development efforts take place, recognizing that domestic development is intertwined with regional and international economic systems, and briefly reviewing and summarizing the experiences and lessons from various global development initiatives, which are vital for embarking on this path.

Development as a concept

Human beings inherently strive to bring about positive change and improvement in their lives, actively engaging in shaping their vision to achieve it. Each society, with its unique characteristics, chooses its own path or strategy to achieve the desired change. These strategies align with and reflect the specific goals and conditions of the country or society, thereby defining and limiting the complexity of the development processes.

However, development is a dynamic concept that embodies fundamental aspirations and offers opportunities for a decent life. It enhances the capacity for creativity and innovation, paving the way for a better future for all. At its core, development should be rooted in domestic values and interests, driven by local initiatives, and owned by the people and their chosen leaders. Because the development drive is a managed process, there is no universal formula or one-size-fits-all solution applicable globally. Solutions must be relevant to unique circumstances and acceptable to the specific needs and conditions of each society.

For economic growth to be sustainable, it must be inclusive, benefit everyone equitably, generate lasting national benefits, and responsibly utilize environmental resources without depleting them. As some economists assert, development is a comprehensive process encompassing social structures, popular perceptions, national institutions, the pattern of economic growth, and activities aimed at eradicating poverty and backwardness at their roots. It is essentially a journey of change that can transform people's living conditions from an unacceptable situation to a better one.

International and regional actors, along with development partners, can significantly contribute by providing technological, technical, and financial support. However, it is essential to acknowledge that this support should never supplant the leadership, resources, aspirations, or ownership of the local community. A country prospers when an environment is fostered that enables people's talents, aspirations, and resilience to flourish and expand. Good governance boosts productivity at higher levels, and development efforts rely on human creativity and the private sector's contributions as vital components.

The Human Development Report 2011, presented by the UNDP, underscores the importance of equity and sustainability in the development process, highlighting the interconnectedness of these two elements. This approach emphasizes achieving a high quality of life and ensuring social justice for all. The report concludes that sustainability requires us to carefully consider our lifestyle choices and recognize that our actions have consequences for the seven billion people alive today and the billions more who will follow in future generations.

Efforts to better understand and address societal needs and priorities often yield significant and valuable results, thereby making the process worthwhile. By doing so, development partners can align their sustainable initiatives and achieve their goals more effectively. Ultimately, development initiatives aim to empower a country's citizens, within their specific contexts, to realize the future they envision and enjoy its benefits.

Culture can be a powerful driver of societal progress, as it defines a society's identity and fosters a sense of belonging and pride that supports local advancement. Culture strengthens social cohesion and the spirit of integration in society. For a society that takes pride in its culture, heritage, and history, the outcome of its efforts is likely to be sustainable, even if the progress is slow. This is because culture is a crucial element underpinning historical continuity, enabling societies to utilize their traditional and modern institutions, beliefs, and value systems to navigate the development process and ensure that their aspirations remain sustainable.

From international assistance to development cooperation

Development cooperation fosters genuine partnerships and integration between countries, whether developed or developing. This concept emphasizes inclusivity and prioritizes the needs, values, and priorities of local communities, thereby creating opportunities for sustainable development and addressing local challenges. Prioritizing local priorities in setting the development agenda is an essential principle that must not be compromised.

Development cooperation should establish systems that generate long-term, visionary solutions rather than short-term ones. It should focus on strategies that build human capital and promote infrastructure-focused initiatives, aiming for comprehensive social progress. It also encourages the creation of solutions that value creativity and local realities, inevitably creating dynamics that can address and resolve complex developmental challenges.

For development efforts to be effective and reach a commendable level, development cooperation must foster relationships that are centered on entrepreneurship. This should not solely be about job creation and good intentions, but must also involve generating shared economic benefits. This, in turn, lays the foundation for building relationships among partners based on transparency, mutual responsibility, and obligations. Development cooperation helps establish a sustainable framework by ensuring that endeavors are aligned with business logic.

Foreign direct investment (FDI) plays a vital role in this cooperation. By attracting such investments, local development initiatives can boost economic activities and productivity. Foreign direct investment not only injects capital into the local economy but also facilitates technology transfer, skill development, and improved market access, all of which can stimulate economic growth.

Foreign direct investment is crucial for fostering cooperation. By attracting such investments, development initiatives can enhance economic activities and productivity. It not only injects capital into the local economy but also facilitates technology transfer, skills development, and improved market access, all of which can stimulate economic growth.

Development cooperation should promote trade exchanges between developed nations and those on the path to development, creating opportunities for developing countries to integrate into global supply chains and markets. Additionally, it aids in diversifying the economy, enhancing living standards, and forging strong global partnerships.

Moving beyond the traditional donor-recipient dynamic, development cooperation should foster equality and mutual benefit among stakeholders.

This transformation creates dynamics in which all stakeholders can generate shared value through interaction.

The concept of "travel companions" describes this type of partnership. Therefore, development cooperation should emphasize collaboration. Viewed broadly, it should also cultivate a spirit of trust and strengthen long-term relationships, which are fundamental prerequisites for sustainable growth and innovation.

An additional advantage of developmental cooperation is the conducive environment it creates for all stakeholders to collaborate. In such a framework, there is a significant opportunity for every voice to be heard. This, of course, provides small or developing countries with the opportunity to compete fairly in the global market and contribute to the unbalanced global economy.

Another solution is to attract domestic investment. When local stakeholders lead the financing and implementation of development projects, the initiatives often align with their needs and priorities. Local leadership fosters ownership and sustainable growth and significantly increases the likelihood that development projects will be effective. However, ensuring this requires the formulation and implementation of a sound macroeconomic policy that is aligned with reality. This macroeconomic policy must encourage entrepreneurship, investment, and competition. Furthermore, it should promote the expansion of strong international trade relations and partnerships with neighboring countries and regional cooperation.

Mobilizing domestic resources is a cornerstone of the development processes. When domestic capacities and resources are effectively identified and utilized, there is no reason why development efforts cannot succeed, with citizens becoming the primary agents of their development. This approach not only fosters a dynamic conducive to sustainable growth but also establishes a foundation for successful and meaningful developmental initiatives in the future.

Equally important for development is ensuring a fair and equitable distribution of national wealth among the populace. It is essential to prevent a significant gap from being created between the rich and the poor. For instance, Nigeria, with a daily oil production capacity of 1.8 million barrels, has 40.1% of its population living below the poverty line. A person or household living on less than $2.15 per day is considered to be below this line. Similarly, Gabon, despite its wealth in natural resources and having one of the highest GDP per capita in Africa ($8,017), still sees 33.4% of its population living in poverty, with an unemployment rate of 28.8%. These examples highlight a common issue: in countries where transparency, good governance, and sound economic policies are lacking, people may continue to live in abject poverty despite having abundant resources.

Eritrea's development roadmap: Some lessons

As discussed in Chapter 1, Eritrea's economy primarily depends on subsistence agriculture, with limited adoption of modern agricultural practices. Manufacturing remains underdeveloped, while service sectors such as tourism and the financial sector have minimal impact. The economy's main exports include gold, copper, and zinc, with potash exports anticipated in the future. Additional support comes from diaspora taxes and remittances from Eritreans living overseas.

Over the past thirty-four years, Eritrea has experienced no significant economic growth or improvement in its citizens' living standards. Suffice it to mention the President's repeated official statements that there is no economy in Eritrea, and if there is any, it is subsistence-based. While wars with neighboring countries, a no-war-no-peace situation, and economic sanctions are often cited as reasons, I believe the root cause lies in the government's outdated political will and understanding of development, as reflected in its practices. This can be summarized as follows: the failure to create a conducive environment for foreign or local investment; treating domestic investors with suspicion, prompting them to move their capital abroad; viewing the private sector as an obstacle to economic grwoth and development rather than promoting it; not fully utilizing the country's human resource potential; neglecting the development and use of intellectual capacity; the ruling political party's control over the majority of the economy and its lack of transparency; insufficient efforts to integrate into the global economy; failing to establish partnership-based relations with developed countries, the region, and the world; and the absence of meaningful regional cooperation. Adding to these issues is the massive exodus of the productive segment of society, particularly the youth, which further illustrates the dismal situation in the country.

Eritrea, or any country with a similar economy, should not be expected to passively receive assistance, whether in the form of loans, aid, or otherwise, that does not align with its priorities or needs. Therefore, I believe it is crucial for Eritrea or any host country on a development path to assume ownership and leadership of programs funded by external aid. Sustainable cooperation must always be centered on society's needs and values.

Like any other developing nation, Eritrea must acknowledge that in today's interconnected world, no country can thrive in isolation. Engaging with other sovereign states and devising mutually beneficial collaborative solutions is crucial. This collaborative approach, rather than a zero-sum game, underscores the importance of cooperation and interdependence, necessitating concerted efforts to achieve shared goals. Often, there are no viable alternatives to this method when tackling complex global challenges.

Eritrea's inability to leverage the benefits of domestic capacity and international cooperation is largely due to its self-imposed isolation. The post-independence period, spanning approximately six to seven years, demonstrates the significant efforts made to develop domestic capacities and resources and promote national priorities in collaboration with international institutions, which had a substantial impact.

Moreover, the steadily waning and cautious international support for developing nations should serve as a wake-up call for the global community to take action. Recent funding cuts at the United States Agency for International Development (USAID) and reductions in aid budgets, along with impending cuts by some Western European countries—Great Britain by 40%, France by 35%, and Germany by a similar figure—illustrate this trend.

In light of these funding cuts, developing countries should regard international aid as a supplement, rather than the primary driver or catalyst for change. As these countries advance on their development trajectory, it is crucial for them to strengthen their engagement with regional and international partners. However, this engagement must be rooted in partnerships that offer mutual benefits and integration. For effective development planning, the following perspectives should be considered:

Efforts to improve good governance

Effective governance is essential for promoting economic development and preventing policy errors and market imbalances. The World Bank defines governance as the manner in which power is exercised within a nation, which is shaped by its established customs and institutions. This definition encompasses the government's ability to formulate and implement sound policies, adhere to them, and be held accountable, while upholding institutions that regulate economic and social interactions between citizens and the government. According to World Bank experts, this concept includes a) accountability, meaning those in authority must answer for their actions, whether successful or not; b) inclusiveness, ensuring all stakeholders have the opportunity to participate in decision-making; and c) predictability, achieved through the proper establishment of robust policies, laws, and systems.

Additionally, a governance framework must ensure transparency by holding the government accountable to keep its citizens informed of all decisions and policies. A vital aspect of this principle is the development and reinforcement of good governance, which involves the separation of powers, accountability, transparency, adherence to the rule of law, and the creation of strong institutions.

Formulation and implementation of context-appropriate policies
Emerging nations possess untapped resources that can lead to economic prosperity. To harness this potential, it is crucial to align domestic policies with strategies that attract foreign investment and technology transfers. This approach can unlock the full capabilities of the private sector, fostering mutually beneficial trade and business partnerships through bilateral agreements that benefit all the parties involved. It is vital to develop and implement policies grounded in local values and tailored to the specific conditions and developmental stages of each country. Achieving this requires the complete eradication of corruption, which has been a significant barrier to progress in this regard. This not only enhances the benefits of effective governance but also aids in combating it. African political leaders must explore new methods to align with their citizens' values.

From uni-partnership to diversified partnerships
Relying heavily on international aid makes nations vulnerable to unpredictable global economies. Therefore, for developing countries, diversifying partnerships and forming broad alliances with various stakeholders, such as regional blocs, the private sector, and civil society, should be seen as a strategic necessity rather than just an option. This involves initiatives such as enhancing domestic capacities, revamping the education system to meet 21st-century demands, and investing in human capital development.

These efforts lay the groundwork for cultivating a skilled workforce essential for sustainable development.

Laying the foundations of a private sector economy

A nation's progress is intricately linked to the entrepreneurial spirit of its citizens and the strength, competence, and aspirations of its private sector. In developing countries, a vibrant and robust private sector is a driving force behind economic growth and vitality. By strengthening their private sectors and collaborating with local and international investors, these countries can shift from relying on aid to becoming active participants in the global economy. Economically advanced nations can initiate agreements upon projects (by all stakeholders) to create lucrative investment opportunities in developing areas, while host governments, such as Eritrea's, can foster an investment-friendly environment through partnerships.

This approach can lead to mutually beneficial outcomes for all parties involved. Nations must engage in trade partnerships that are advantageous to both sides to reduce their reliance on international aid and become significant players in the global market. This requires fostering collaboration between the public and private sectors and promoting investment in key areas. Ultimately, this results in sustainable development, the spread of prosperity, and an improved quality of life for the population.

Encouraging public-private partnership

The public and private sectors should not view each other as adversaries. In development projects, they function as strategic partners or allies, complementing each other. The government creates a supportive and favorable environment for the private sector to thrive. The private sector plays a vital role in a nation's economy by investing, generating employment, and fostering entrepreneurial activities. Public-private partnerships and investments in key sectors promote sustainable economic growth in developing nations, leading to prosperity and improved living standards for the population. This cooperative strategy, which aligns with the interests of various stakeholders, has the potential to unlock the extensive transformative power inherent in local capabilities.

Leapfrogging certain phases

Developing countries must harness the potential of technology and artificial intelligence to achieve and accelerate economic growth, a process known as "leapfrogging." The entire world has witnessed what can be accomplished using modern technologies. To tap into this potential, it is essential to build digital infrastructure and invest in education. Engaging with global technology companies and governments helps secure and enhance the resources and capabilities required in this sector. It is also crucial to invest in mobile connectivity and education (human capacity development). Digital electronic commerce (e-commerce) enables local businesses to reach wider markets, thereby promoting entrepreneurship and economic diversification. Mobile payment systems and microfinance provide access to citizens excluded or marginalized from the traditional financial systems, allowing them to participate in building the national economy. Such initiatives can have a multiplier effect on a country's development journey.

Expanding regional cooperation

In today's complex world, developing nations must recognize that pursuing development in isolation is unsustainable, even if they manage to ensure their own safety or economic security. Engaging with others to devise mutually beneficial solutions is essential. This collaborative approach fosters cooperation and interdependence, which are crucial for addressing complex global challenges. Moreover, regional collaboration opens access to larger markets and enhances the region's investment climate. Investors are drawn to stable, predictable, and cohesive markets with minimal barriers and low tariffs. To achieve this, a robust infrastructure and consistent regulatory framework must be established.

From a single-product economy to a diversified economy

Transitioning from an economy reliant on a single product to a diversified economy offers significant advantages for developing countries. This shift reduces dependence on a single commodity for income and helps to mitigate potential economic shocks. Countries such as Mauritius in Africa and several countries in Southeast Asia have collectively addressed this challenge, serving as role models for others. Therefore, countries must focus on utilizing their raw mineral resources and developing industries based on processed natural resources to ensure sustainable development in the future. Economically, this concept is often referred to as "value-added."

Taxation is also another viable source of revenue, and improving the tax system is essential. Countries with underdeveloped tax systems often struggle to adequately fund social services. For instance, in developed nations, tax revenue constitutes 30% to 50% of GDP, whereas in developing countries, it accounts for only 10% to 25%.

Job creation

To effectively establish a viable economy, macro policies must prioritize job creation by stimulating the dynamic private sector. This approach is vital for developing human capital and accommodating the demands of an expanding workforce. By addressing the underlying causes of state fragility and mass migration, it promises to strengthen global stability.

Selective government involvement in the economy

Similar to other countries, governments can collaborate with the private sector to invest in strategic economic sectors associated with national security. However, this collaboration should not undermine the role of the private sector. These sectors may include infrastructure (such as roads, railways, air and sea transport, energy, and water supply), services (such as education and health), and critical mineral extraction. Funding for these investments can come from state assets and loans from international financial institutions, provided that appropriate guarantees are available. All public investment projects must undergo feasibility studies. When the government invests in the national economy, it must do so in a transparent and accountable way. In essence, the public should have the right to be clearly informed about these investments, including their objectives, timelines from start to finish, sources of funding, and the return on investment.

All governments engage with their economies, differing in terms of the extent, methods, and openness of their involvement. Singapore and Norway demonstrate collaborative and transparent approaches by using state capital to support private-sector activities. Singapore's Temasek Holdings and GIC hold substantial equity in key companies in the telecommunications, aviation, finance, and technology sectors. France maintains stakes in vital national security companies in the energy (EDF), aerospace (Airbus), and rail (SNCF) sectors. China steers its economy through five-year plans and state-owned banks and enterprises in the infrastructure and energy sectors. The South Korean government has worked with family-owned conglomerates (Chaebols), such as Samsung and Hyundai. Norway's Government Pension Fund Global (GPFG) manages public investment from oil revenue without directing the domestic industry. Although market-driven, the United States provides significant public funding for strategic research in defense and health, leading to innovations such as the Internet and mRNA vaccines.

Chapter 4

Reorienting Economic Development Toward Human Welfare

Like all nations worldwide, those on the path to development are tasked with meeting the basic and increasingly complex needs of their citizens. These needs or rights, to some extent, reflect a nation's level of advancement and encompass its social, economic, and political rights. To achieve this goal, leading economists have consistently focused their research, theories, and reflections on the subject. As a result, the world has gained more knowledge and experience through these discussions. However, since a definitive conclusion has not yet been reached, research and studies continue to be conducted with greater depth and sophistication.

One group of researchers contends that ensuring continuous or infinite growth is essential for the fundamental functioning of the economy and for addressing the basic or progressively increasing needs of citizens.

Another group of researchers in this field, while agreeing with the aforementioned perspective, believes that infinite growth should not be the ultimate goal of the economy. They must also be able to answer the following questions: Under what conditions does economic growth occur? What are the determinants of economic growth? How should growth be sustainably managed? How are resources allocated and distributed? What is the role of growth in changing people's livelihoods? Does resource use consider environmental costs or lead to environmental degradation? What policies or strategies should guide this development? This fundamental inquiry aims to provide preliminary answers to these questions.

Growth and development: Their differences

Herman Daly, a well-known economist, describes growth as an increase in productivity, whereas he defines development as an enhancement in the quality and variety of goods and services produced (Daly, 2009). Additionally, Daly and Farley (2009) characterized development as the creation of goods and services that aim to improve human well-being. This perspective suggests that, according to economists Michael Todaro and Stephen Smith, development involves going beyond the conventional distribution of resources to meet the demands of sustainable development. Moreover, they assert that by addressing economic, social, and political issues, development brings significant changes in the lives of the impoverished.

The aforementioned scholars and researchers describe development as follows: "Development is a comprehensive process that involves reorganizing social structures, popular attitudes, national institutions, accelerating economic growth, reducing inequality, and eradicating absolute poverty. Essentially, it is a process of change that can enable a transition from an unsatisfactory state of living to a better one" (Todaro, 2003). In essence, while growth pertains to the quantitative expansion of the economy, development focuses on transforming the standard of living or life of a society to enhance human well-being. In other words, people-centered economic development seeks to achieve economic growth and a decent and sustainable standard of living for the population.

Our understanding of growth and development

Although growth and development are distinct concepts, they are evaluated using different frameworks. Growth is typically measured by an increase in Gross Domestic Product (GDP) or GDP per capita, whereas development is assessed through various dimensions or aspects of that growth. This includes indicators used by organizations like UNDP, such as reducing illiteracy, expanding health services, and increasing home ownership rates (Todaro, 2003). Moreover, Daly argues that development can reveal whether poor developing nations are capable of advancing to the next stage of economic progress. Unlike growth, development is a more comprehensive concept that addresses current needs without compromising the ability of future generations to meet their needs (Daly, 1996). This suggests that while people have the right to utilize the resources available in their environment, it should not lead to environmental degradation. This highlights the importance of considering future generations.

Guiding principles

As previously discussed, the people-centered development approach employs indicators that extend beyond GDP, emphasizing sustainable access to opportunities, inclusive decision-making that encourages public participation, and enhancing sustainable livelihoods. These principles are embodied in the following guidelines:

- Development should prioritize fulfilling human needs rather than treating people as mere ' instruments.
- Engagement of communities in the development process should be authentic, and participants should have a voice in shaping the policies.
- The impetus for development must originate from and be owned by the people rather than being imposed through a top-down, command-based approach.

- Development strategy should aim to enhance human capacity through education, health services, and social security, thereby elevating individuals to a more advanced level.
- It must be an approach that actively combats inequality rather than perpetuating it.
- The safety, needs, rights, and potential of future generations must be considered, not just those of the current generation.
- Development should never serve as a justification or pretext for environmental destruction. Environmental management should balance conservation and rehabilitation efforts with resource utilization.
- It must be inclusive and ensure access to educational opportunities, health services, and other resources for women in particular and other marginalized groups.
- Both inclusive development and sovereignty are grounded in human welfare.

The journey of growth towards enhanced human well-being

As previously discussed, policymakers are responsible for fostering ongoing growth to enhance human well-being. Knowledge and technology are pivotal in this endeavor and require special attention. Modern society cannot sustain growth without the industrial revolution, information technology, artificial intelligence, or advanced management systems. However, growth involves more than these elements. Key components of sustainable growth include implementing market-driven strategies, ensuring food security, crafting and executing effective fiscal, monetary, and trade policies, generating employment opportunities, and building human capital. By transforming raw materials into finished goods and services, these efforts enhance societal well-being and meet the needs of society. This raises questions about how the factors influencing ever-changing human needs are addressed. Is resource allocation effective? Is it fair? These questions highlight the importance of human welfare.

There was a time when human security was linked to growth in Gross Domestic Product (GDP), based on the belief that as GDP increased, people's lives would improve correspondingly. However, this perspective overlooks the resource distribution methods. This type of growth model often leads to a concentration of a nation's resources in the hands of a few, leaving the majority of society lagging behind in terms of development. Consequently, an increase in GDP does not automatically lead to better societal well-being (Daly, 2009). Human welfare is closely tied to the fair and equitable allocation of a country's resources.

Understanding human welfare

Human security encompasses the overall welfare of a community and its living conditions. It includes various aspects, such as essential needs, such as food, clean water, basic healthcare, education, stable and adequate housing, job opportunities, shelter, financial stability, personal safety, social unity, human rights, freedom from discrimination, clean air, sustainable living conditions, political rights, and mental well-being. Beyond these elements, human welfare involves personal safety, political stability, adherence to the rule of law, and social security. In our modern, technologically advanced society, affordable and widespread Internet access should be considered a right rather than a luxury.

The objective of the Eritrean struggle for independence

Reflecting on the past, the Eritrean people's war for independence had a primary goal, while not neglecting its other objectives, of a broadly defined political mission aimed at achieving social justice. Fundamentally, the movement sought to secure basic human rights, the right to an improved quality of life, the right to express opinions freely and without fear, the right to education and political involvement, the right to access fair and efficient public services, the right to economic advancement, the right to religious freedom, the right to preserve cultural heritage, the right to live according to one's own choices, and the protection of the rule of law. It was also committed to peacefully resolving conflicts and coexisting harmoniously. Additionally, it aimed to establish relationships and a shared existence with neighboring countries based on respect for sovereignty, mutual respect, and cooperation, just as it expected others to respect and engage with it to do the same.

The goals mentioned above align with and support the fundamental concepts of human welfare.

Eritrea, in which Eritrean citizens reside, should be committed to the people-centered principles mentioned above. However, it is not necessary for all these principles to be realized immediately, nor do they need to be perfect. As long as the path enhances human welfare, it should be supported. This process is dynamic and often involves unforeseen changes. The key is to demonstrate political will and establish frameworks that facilitate the realization of the goal by setting milestones with specific timelines. It should be acknowledged that some might view this aspiration as living in a dream world. Nevertheless, it is within our reach to achieve this.

A people-focused Eritrea, where Eritrean citizens live without fear, can offer the opportunity for a fulfilling life that meets the basic needs of its people. This approach unlocks the potential for creativity and innovation, paving the way for a brighter future while fundamentally ensuring that development is centered on local rights and needs and delivered through local initiatives.

Eritrea should be a nation in which its people and elected leaders hold each other accountable. The country must ensure the rights of its citizens, be governed by the rule of law, and be guided by accountability and transparency. It should encourage public participation, promote dialogue, and view consultation as a vital tool for making policy decisions. Eritrea should be built on institutional processes and institutions, establishing and enforcing laws and regulations that ensure the welfare of its citizens. To ensure the well-being of its people, Eritrea must aim to elevate human resources and their potential to a higher level.

Knowledge, skills, and abilities empower citizens to achieve economic growth, creating opportunities for them to become more productive and contribute more to the growth of the national economy. Eritrea's investment in education can yield significant returns compared to individual costs. Writing, reading, arithmetic, and other basic life skills enhance workforce quality. Education is a crucial pillar for raising living standards, lifting people out of poverty, and promoting economic growth. Both economic growth and productive human capital are required for the standard of living to improve. This is possible when changes are evident in the type of knowledge within society, which is achievable only through education and training (Cipher, 2004).

An Eritrea that prioritizes its youth focuses on educating them to become productive citizens rather than preparing them for emigration to other countries. This approach equips them with the knowledge to engage with global advancements in fields such as science, technology, arts, and sports, allowing them to become acquainted with and leverage these assets. It instills strong moral and social values that they practice daily, nurturing a deep love for their country and fellow citizens. It fosters a sense of devotion to their nation and a tireless pursuit of their ambitions, helping them develop critical thinking skills and become skilled and competent professionals.

In Eritrea, which values the welfare and dignity of its people, educational institutions, research centers, and centers of excellence should aim to become hubs of scholarship and innovation.

An Eritrea dedicated to fulfilling the universal needs of its people must focus on integrating, mobilizing, and utilizing domestic resources and community-based development initiatives to achieve this. It should also support individual initiatives. Essentially, it must adopt an inclusive strategy that provides opportunities for disadvantaged groups.

In an Eritrea that prioritizes the welfare of its people, the nation must rally its people for the common good while cherishing their diversity. While some may argue that achieving this is a utopian dream, it is attainable with the help of a political will that helps its realization.

To focus on the welfare of its citizens, Eritrea must ensure fair and equitable distribution of national resources. It is also crucial to prevent the widening of the gap between the rich and the poor.

For Eritrea to truly prioritize its citizens, it must cultivate a culture of conflict resolution that is deeply embedded in its cultural and societal norms, value systems, adherence to the rule of law, accountability, consultation, predictability, certainty, checks and balances, representation, inclusivity, transparency, and competence, all implemented through a well-defined and robust institutional framework. Weakened institutions require restoration. These elements foster an environment that enhances public trust in the government. They aim to eradicate suspicion, corruption, injustice, social malaise, fear, oppression, hopelessness (where fleeing the country seems the only option), anxiety, various illnesses, and premature death. Addressing societal differences requires a culture of conflict resolution through peaceful means and processes, rather than confrontation. Popular protests, civil disobedience, and uprisings are outcomes of oppressive rule.

For Eritrea to truly enhance the quality of life of its people, it must eliminate corruption, ensure that citizens live with dignity, improve living standards, foster a dynamic private sector, and encourage both domestic and foreign investment. Establishing a foundation for personal initiatives, managing public debt responsibly, maintaining a stable currency, practicing fiscal discipline within a high-investment framework, and nurturing partnerships between the public and private sectors are also essential.

An Eritrea that prioritizes the welfare of its citizens will preserve its social fabric and prevent the fragmentation of families and exile (especially the youth). The core value of the Eritrean people lies in a nation that guarantees social justice and expands social services to all citizens.

It is also crucial to reinstate the role of religious institutions and the traditions and systems of honor that help them fulfil their missions.

Eritrea is not a country that merely stumbles upon growth or pays attention to progress only incidentally. This is a fundamental and foundational issue. This beautiful nation, which some of us inhabit and others view from afar, is, in reality, characterized by poverty rather than a fair distribution of national resources.

At its core, an Eritrea focused on the welfare of its people must ensure the meaningful participation of women, who make up half of society, guarantee their economic freedom, and uphold their rights and their dignity.

Chapter 5

The Development-Governance Nexus: Foundations for Sustainable Progress

NATION-BUILDING IS A complex and multifaceted endeavor. In countries such as Eritrea, which has endured an authoritarian regime for over three decades, the challenge is even more daunting.

Over the past thirty-four years, Eritrea has neither achieved economic growth nor improved the living conditions of its people. While the 'no war, no peace' situation and the economic blockade stemming from conflicts with neighboring countries could be cited as contributing factors, I believe the primary issue lies in the government's flawed political will and misguided understanding of governance. This does not imply that the first two factors are insignificant.

As discussed in earlier chapters, flawed political will and ineffective policies manifest in several ways: the failure to create an environment conducive to economic growth; policies that drive local entrepreneurs to leave the country (it is widely known that their assets worth tens of millions have been relocated to neighboring countries); hindering rather than supporting private enterprises; failing to fully harness the country's human potential; and neglecting the development and utilization of academic potential.

Additional factors contributing to this stifled economic situation include the ruling political party's opaque and unaccountable control over most of the economy, lack of efforts to integrate into the global economy, failure to establish mutually beneficial partnerships with neighboring countries, the region, and the world, inability to participate in regional integration, and dysfunctional institutional operations. When we consider the massive exodus of youth, the severity of the situation becomes evident.

What factors contribute to equitable and inclusive growth? Sustainable and inclusive growth are essential elements of economic progress, evaluated not only by productivity levels and quality but also by changes in societies' living standards. Essentially, it addresses the question: "What was the previous standard of living, and how has it improved?"

Development is a key concept that is centered on human well-being. To achieve this, nations on the development path, including Eritrea, must meet and interlink certain prerequisites. These include:

- **Ensuring effective governance;**
- Directing development efforts towards underserved or marginalized groups to enhance their livelihoods;
- Promoting environmental conservation;
- Creating and executing comprehensive or sector-specific economic policies that respect and address the traditions of the general populace;
- Crafting development strategies that empower women;
- Leveraging a society's cultural and value systems as significant tools in the development process;
- Boosting national security and political stability,
- Emphasizing an agricultural development strategy to secure food supply;
- Developing and implementing robust human resource policies;
- Enhancing the equitable distribution of national resources; and

♦ Strengthening cooperative economic, trade, security, diplomatic, and cultural partnerships at the regional and global levels.

Each of these prerequisites poses significant questions, as they all have a considerable impact on a nation's economic growth and are interdependent on each other. However, the focus here is to underscore the importance of good governance in a country's economic advancement and elucidate the mutually beneficial relationship between these two aspects.

Effective governance and economic progress

Nations aspiring to develop must establish stability to achieve their objectives. This stability is fundamentally anchored in good governance. Essentially, people can lead peaceful lives only in a supportive environment. Effective governance comprises several key elements: adherence to the rule of law, separation of powers, accountability, transparency, institutional functionality, constitutional governance that protects the rights of all citizens, safeguarding of fundamental human rights, predictability, inclusiveness, consultation, development and promotion of institutional capacity, and a political culture that resolves domestic political differences peacefully and orderly. It also includes providing space for responsible press and facilitating interactions between the population and the government.

These elements contribute to building public trust in the government. They encourage creativity and innovation across various fields, create opportunities for long-term development planning, and lay the foundation for sustainable economic growth. Economic growth generates employment opportunities, helps reduce income inequality, and creates pathways for eradicating poverty and improving living standards. Since effective governance promotes policy predictability, it fosters an environment conducive to both domestic and foreign investment, thereby incentivizing individual initiatives. It also establishes a healthy relationship between the government and the private sector.

Effective governance enhances the delivery of quality social services by fostering societal contributions. It strengthens stability by uniting society around both modern and traditional value systems. By nature, effective governance provides citizens with the opportunity to live fulfilling lives within their communities. It creates avenues for citizens to contribute to their country's growth by investing their resources and encourages them to seize the available opportunities to be part of the nation-building process. Additionally, it discourages migration to other countries. Even when migration occurs, it ensures that individuals maintain a connection with their homeland, encouraging them to invest and engage more actively in their country's development. The economic contributions of the Chinese, Egyptian, Filipino, and Turkish diasporas to their home countries are evident.

Effective governance promotes the representative participation of various societal segments in matters that concern them, creating opportunities for national dialogue and fostering harmony. It serves as a solid foundation and cornerstone of family well-being and strengthens social cohesion.

However, the lack of effective governance leads to instability, which can result in resistance or popular uprisings. It also creates a breeding ground for dissatisfaction and an unsustainable future.

The separation of powers among the legislative, executive, and judicial branches, the establishment of the rule of law, and the definition of the state's role and institutional functions are vital for economic progress. These components are crucial for addressing policy shortcomings and rectifying market imbalances. According to Webster's Dictionary, governance is described as 'the method or system of authority that tends to continue in the administration and management of the economic and social resources of a country for development.'

The World Bank defines governance as 'the manner in which power is exercised in the management of a country's economic and social resources for development.' This includes the capacity of governments to formulate and implement effective policies and maintain institutions that govern economic and social interactions among citizens and between citizens and the state. The World Bank has identified six key dimensions for evaluating governance: Voice and Accountability, Political Stability and Absence of Violence/Terrorism, Government Effectiveness, Regulatory Quality, Rule of Law, and Control of Corruption (World Bank, 2023).

In their book, "An Introduction to Sustainable Development," Rogers et al. explore how weak governance impedes development, complicates the process, and leads to uneven negative impacts that disproportionately affect the poor. They argue that effective governance requires accountability, public participation, administrative equity, transparency, and predictability (Rogers, 2009).

Accountability means that those in power are answerable for their actions. Equity ensures that all citizens can participate in decision-making, and the proper implementation of sound policies, laws, and systems fosters policy predictability. Furthermore, they highlight that a governance system must be transparent, enabling citizens to remain informed about governmental decisions and policies.

Calderisi suggests that to stimulate economic growth and attract significant foreign investment, governments must align their actions, prioritize and sequence them effectively, implement coherent policies, and establish essential institutions. He contends that this strategy, rather than relying on aid from foreign donors, should have its own logical foundation (Calderisi, 2006). In their article "Explaining African Economic Performance," Collier and Gunning argue that in many African countries, there is a negative correlation between economic growth and the amount of foreign development aid (Overseas Development Aid – ODA) due to weak policies (Collier, 1999). In his renowned lecture, "New Rules for Rebuilding a Broken Nation" (delivered at the US Foreign Service Association), Paul Collier emphasized the importance of a clean government that creates jobs for the youth and supports the provision of social services. "This," he asserts, "can help countries transition from a politics of plunder to a politics of hope" (Collier, 2009).

The mandates of the state

The primary role of the state is to formulate development policies and strategies and ensure their implementation. Governments are tasked with clearly defining their mission, establishing core values and objectives, and steering the future of the nation. This mission encompasses providing services to citizens, upholding the rule of law, promoting economic growth, providing security against internal and external threats, constructing the necessary infrastructure for economic development, and ensuring equitable access to quality education, basic healthcare, and various social services. It also involves fostering positive relationships and partnerships with neighboring countries and the global community for their mutual benefit. All these elements must be considered within the current socio-economic context and articulated in clear and comprehensive policy documents. In all these roles, equity should be prioritized.

Another critical government responsibility is to develop a strategic plan. The government must clearly outline how it will implement these objectives and policies. What strategy will it adopt? How will it mobilize domestic and external resources, and what role will the private sector play in this endeavor? What responsibilities do citizens have in achieving these objectives? What kind of partnership is necessary between the private and public sectors? What will be the role of foreign direct investment? How will this be channeled into the country? Through which means will it be utilized? These questions require further exploration.

The third essential task of the state is to establish laws and regulatory mechanisms that are characterized by transparency. This includes property rights, anti-corruption measures, and other factors. According to the United Nations Economic and Social Commission for Asia and the Pacific (UN ESCAP), this regulatory framework encompasses legal instruments, rules, norms, procedures, and institutions. These norms serve various purposes, such as ensuring public benefits, protecting technical, safety, and quality standards, and ensuring compliance with established operational procedures.

The fourth role of the state is to develop a human resource development (HRD) policy aimed at building the skilled human capacity required for national reconstruction and development. Essential questions that need to be addressed can include the following: What kind of capacity is required for national reconstruction? What kind of skills? What kind of ethics? Does the education provided produce the skilled labor required in the 21st century? Does the education and training provided encourage research, innovation, and critical thinking, and is this aligned with the national reconstruction policies? The foundation is an educated populace and a trained workforce.

Eritrea's education system is marked by limited access and unequal distribution at all levels, low academic standards, and a shortage of qualified teachers. Furthermore, vocational training institutions suffer from poor quality and limited access, inadequate infrastructure, and a lack of teaching and learning materials. The general population contends with high illiteracy rates and a weak reading culture, compounded by limited access to non-formal education and inadequate assessment methods.

An Eritrean education professional, who prefers to remain anonymous, observes that higher education in Eritrea caters to only a small segment of youth. There is a dearth of qualified teachers and educational resources, a lack of research infrastructure and funding, and the quality of education is very low, prompting capable Eritrean scholars to seek opportunities abroad.

To enhance national economic development, the following measures are proposed: a) Given the widespread illiteracy in Eritrea, it is crucial for all Eritreans to complete basic and middle-level education, ensuring they become literate citizens with essential writing, reading, and arithmetic skills, civic education, and basic life skills. b) Secondary education should prepare citizens to either pursue higher education or acquire the skills, knowledge, and abilities necessary to enter the workforce. c) Youth who have the opportunity to pursue higher education should become citizens specializing in research and critical thinking, equipped with technology and progress, and possess a vision aligned with the 21st century. Ultimately, the goal is to cultivate an educated population and skilled workforce.

The fifth responsibility of the state is to establish a skilled, impartial, and competitive governmental body (bureaucracy) capable of effectively implementing and regulating policies related to quality and standards. The primary duty of this bureaucracy is to provide public services. Efficient tax collection can significantly boost a nation's Gross Domestic Product (GDP). Developing a transparent and efficient tax system to collect government revenue and provide services effectively is a crucial function of the government structure.

The sixth responsibility of the state is to create reliable and modern infrastructure. This involves mobilizing both domestic and international resources (through loans or other agreements), constructing transportation networks (land, sea, and air), setting up airports and ports, ensuring a reliable and extensive energy supply with equitable distribution, enhancing water supply, developing a sewage system, establishing solid waste management systems, and advancing modern communication systems (such as broadband Internet and mobile networks) that meet global standards. Additionally, it includes building residential housing that is financially affordable to citizens and creating modern financial institutions (banks, stock markets, digital payment platforms) and other service-providing entities. These efforts enable the private sector to thrive and invest, thereby significantly contributing to the country's economic growth.

The governance system under the PFDJ

The governance framework under the PFDJ deviates from conventional norms, failing to adhere to standard practices, ignoring essential governance principles, and lacking transparency. This is attributed to several factors:

Separation of Power: Authority is centralized in a single individual, with no separation among the three branches of government—Legislative, Executive, and Judiciary. The National Assembly has been ineffective, as it has neither passed legislation nor met for more than twenty-five years, and the judiciary lacks autonomy. Another tier of courts, akin to the Special Court and answerable to the President's Office, intervenes in and adjudicates matters outside their jurisdiction. The executive branch is largely inactive and has not addressed national issues for decades. This has resulted in a scenario where no branch can hold the others accountable.

Accountability: Authority is concentrated in one person who is not accountable to any other entity. He is not answerable to the National Assembly or the press. Government activities are not audited, and the utilization of state resources is opaque to say the least and often characterized by favoritism. Nobody is responsible for the failure of the economy or whether social services have been adequately provided and satisfactory. The following questions also remain unanswered. Are people living comfortably? Are children receiving quality education? Have the country's relations with neighbors, regions, and the world improved or deteriorated? To what extent has the nation's wealth increased?

Human rights: The government's conduct is marked by violations of fundamental freedoms—belief, worship, thought, speech, assembly, writing, free movement, dignity, and expression—as well as arbitrary arrests, denial of the right to be brought before a court (habeas corpus), prisons unaccountable to the judiciary, and the injustice and abuse inflicted upon citizens.

Institutions and institutional procedures: In Eritrea, the institutional framework and procedures are frail, compounded by a one-person rule. The Eritrean system is characterized by arbitrary processes that lack transparency. Essentially, the country is being driven towards danger by a weak governance structure characterized by a lack of accountability, ineffective institutions, and corruption. This has inevitably fostered a sense of hopelessness and mistrust among the population. The erosion and weakening of institutions have also affected the legislative and judicial branches. Centralized governance has sidelined institutions, especially those with independent mandates and policies. The cabinet seldom meets, and when it does, it operates in secrecy, leaving the public uninformed. The Eritrean system has dismantled many institutions, rendering them ineffective and unable to function. This has inevitably resulted in a lack of public confidence in these institutions. Additionally, government ministries have shockingly contributed to their own dysfunction and lack of capacity.

Transparency: Topics such as the budget (revenue and expenditure, recuurent and capital), war mobilization, the implementation of development programs, national security issues, mining contracts, the 2% tax collected from the diaspora, and other funds, annual economic growth rates across sectors (agriculture, mining, services - GDP), state revenues from taxes, transparency in issuing licenses, assets controlled by PFDJ-owned companies (and government-owned companies), foreign exchange, etc., are absent from the Eritrean system's discourse.

Consultation: To claim there is no culture of consultation is an understatement. National matters are neither discussed with the public nor deliberated within the National Assembly. A secretive modus operandi is deeply ingrained in the political system. People remain uninformed about issues and are only left to speculate. Decisions on war and peace are made by a single individual, and the same applies to diplomatic relations in the region.

Consequences of poor governance

As detailed in Chapter 2, thirty-four years after the declaration of independence, Eritrea's situation is precarious and deeply troubling.

Weakening of the social fabric

The militarization of society is a defining characteristic of Eritrea's current state. The repressive system established in Asmara employs this mechanism for societal control, intensifying tensions by fostering intergenerational resentment and stifling the country's ability to harness its citizens' motivation and creativity.

Another crucial social aspect is the weakening of the strong social fabric that once united diverse communities. Trust in institutions has eroded, and divisions have emerged among the citizens. As social stratification deepens, the nation's diversity, rather than serving as a source of national strength, has been co-opted for the PFDJ's political agenda.

Economic stagnation: The aforementioned factors clearly indicate that while economic institutions expected to generate employment are shrinking, the existing ones are becoming increasingly fragile. The PFDJ controls the nation's assets, which are primarily derived from mining, contraband, and other enterprises. Typically, these assets are allocated to strengthen the military (weapons, training, logistics, etc.), maintain security and intelligence systems, and operate propaganda mechanisms (notably festivals and holidays). Overall, they are used to sustaining an authoritarian regime.

Living conditions and distrust: Conditions conducive to improving people's living standards are absent, and opportunities for better livelihoods are uncertain. Food security, defined as access to a balanced diet, is not guaranteed. This economy is characterized by a weak private sector and a lack of both domestic and foreign investment. Investment in infrastructure is virtually nonexistent, except for the small and large dams built across the country with no economic purpose. There is no fertile ground for fostering individual initiatives. Furthermore, the relationship between the public and private sectors is entangled in mutual distrust.

The Eritrean economy

As previously discussed, Eritrea's economy is predominantly weak, with industries such as tourism and financial services still in their infancy. Essentially, the economy is based on subsistence. The only manufacturing sectors oriented towards exports are mining operations for gold, copper, and zinc, with potash exports anticipated in the future.

Despite a coastline that extends for a thousand kilometers, the marine resource sector remains underdeveloped. Eritrea has resources such as fish, precious corals, and petroleum that could be harnessed for economic growth. Additionally, there is potential for a tourism industry that could generate significant foreign currency and opportunities to develop untapped financial services.

Eritrea could have capitalized on the services provided by its ports to boost its economy. For instance, in 1994/95, the port of Assab handled 73% of Ethiopia's imports and 51.7% of its exports, whereas Djibouti managed only 0.8% of Ethiopia's imports and 3.2% of its exports. Currently, the Port of Djibouti handles 95% of Ethiopia's exports and imports, with Ethiopia paying Djibouti approximately one billion dollars annually for these services. It is easy to envision the financial benefits Eritrea could have gained from this revenue if it were accessible.

Another crucial component of the country's economy is the 2% tax levied on Eritreans residing abroad, along with the remittances they send back to Eritrea. The Eritrean economy not only heavily relies on these remittances but also exemplifies a system that exploits its citizens, primarily due to the government-instituted unfair exchange rates. Unlike other nations, Eritrea has not effectively harnessed the potential of its diaspora. For instance, the Vietnamese diaspora, numbering approximately five million worldwide, contributes approximately $16 billion annually in remittances to Vietnam, significantly impacting its economy. These individuals not only send money but also return with skills and education acquired abroad. Given that the Eritrean diaspora exceeds one million, it is conceivable that potential remittances could reach as much as three billion dollars annually. However, the real question is whether the Eritrean government will seize the opportunity to tap into the diaspora's potential or not. The answer is clear.

These facts do not lay the foundation for sustainable growth and development; instead, they are detrimental to it. It can be argued that Eritrea is characterized by pervasive, deep-rooted poverty.

Obtaining accurate international data on Eritrea's GDP per capita is challenging because the state keeps this information confidential. The World Bank's 2011 report estimated Eritrea's GDP per capita at $643.8.

The International Monetary Fund (IMF) lacks data on Eritrea's economy. According to the CIA's "The World Factbook," Eritrea's GDP per capita was $1,600 in 2017. In contrast, the GDP per capita for other African nations in 2022 was as follows: Ethiopia at $2,440, Sudan at $3,600, Djibouti at $5,000, and Botswana at $15,000.

The research institute "Trade Economics" reported that Eritrea's GDP growth rate in 2023 was 2.9%. In the same year, Ethiopia and Djibouti experienced growth rates of 7.9% and 5.7%, respectively. According to the African Development Bank, Eritrea's real GDP growth declined to 2.3% in 2022.

Over the past thirty-four years, the Eritrean government has not only failed to build basic infrastructure but has also struggled to maintain the infrastructure inherited from the colonial period due to a lack of both capability and political will. The government's persistent inability to provide consistent electricity and water, maintain existing factories, construct new ones, fully develop its two ports, and expand Internet access are all additional issues of concern. According to the International Telecommunication Union, mobile cellular subscriptions per 100 inhabitants in 2021 were 50, and the percentage of Eritrean households using the Internet at home was 1.92%, compared to Ethiopia (18%), Djibouti (52.6%), Kenya (24.1%), Sudan (16.2%), and Rwanda (18.5%) (ITU, n.d.). Furthermore, the failure to build residential housing and develop financial institutions that serve the population is a significant concern.

For a country that has not achieved progress on the path to development after thirty-four years, the focus should be on governance. This entails:

- Development of a comprehensive development strategy;
- Crafting homegrown policies tailored to specific conditions;
- Building robust and transparent institutions;
- Adoption of standards of practice that facilitate policy implementation; and
- Eliminating the characteristics of lawlessness.

The government's responsibilities must be clearly defined, and the conditions under which its efforts to enhance living standards reach the populace should be transparent. The Eritrean government is tasked with governing through appropriate channels, necessitating a special commitment, as the success or failure of its mission hinges on the organization, governance, and management of its mandates.

It is essential to ensure that young people are educated to meet global standards in knowledge, technology, arts, and sports. This education should not only enable them to access and excel in these fields but also instill high ethical standards and social values in their daily lives. It should foster a love for the country and its people, instill national pride, encourage the relentless pursuit of goals, and promote innovative and critical thinking, talent cultivation, and skill development.

The potential for human capital development in Eritrea has been tested, with numerous professionals sent abroad for education and training and many students pursuing higher education in countries such as South Africa. However, the results were unsatisfactory. This is because if trained individuals return to find an environment that is not conducive to working or serving in their profession, lacks institutional procedures, or does not provide respect and incentives commensurate with their professional status, their skills are inevitably wasted.

In light of the current ineffective and lawless governance, society risks falling into deep political divisions over power, ideology, and national resources, even in post-change Eritrea. However, establishing a legitimate and sound system of governance is possible. This requires efforts to promote the inclusion of diverse and competing ideas, ensure the smooth and stable exercise of power, and build public trust in institutions.

Authoritarian governments often disrupt a country's economy by exerting complete control and sidelining crucial economic sectors, a situation that is particularly evident in Eritrea. The lack of infrastructure development and economic stability can create a significant poverty trap, necessitating the resolution of lawlessness and impunity, careful fiscal expansion, reform of party-owned enterprises, and fair resource distribution. This process can be gradual and time-consuming.

The distrust fostered during the dictatorship persists, inevitably weakening social cohesion and complicating the formation of a national identity.

Addressing human rights violations and other injustices with appropriate attention and caution is critical. Promoting a culture of tolerance to enhance security and eliminate coercion should also be an important objective.

Due to foreign policies pursued by the government and strained diplomatic relations resulting from conflicts, the government faces the challenge of repairing and strengthening international cooperation. It is crucial to consider the potential instability in our region, the costs we might incur, and plan how to prevent and manage it. Additionally, it is necessary to determine how to engage with neighbors, regions, and the world.

Conclusion

As previously discussed, the link between effective governance and economic advancement is undeniable. Transparent, accountable, and robust institutional governance creates an environment that supports sustainable economic growth. Similarly, strong economic progress can provide the resources needed to strengthen the structures that are essential for governance. Together, they form a cycle of mutual reinforcement, promoting development, social equity, and resilience, which can readily restore normalcy in the community.

Enhancing this synergy requires intentional policies, visionary leadership, and genuine public engagement. Nations that prioritize governance reforms alongside economic strategies gain the advantage of more effectively mobilizing internal capacity, reducing poverty, and promoting shared prosperity. In an era where global challenges are escalating and becoming more interconnected, the relationship between governance and economic prosperity will continue to deepen. This naturally promises a stable and promising future for their mutual relationships.

Chapter 6

Reconceptualizing Sovereignty: Human Welfare at its Core

What does sovereignty mean? What advantages does it offer? How can it be centered on human welfare?

Sovereignty empowers a nation and its people to advance confidently in their identity, ensuring their welfare and preserving their dignity. Through insightful leadership and strategic policies aligned with national goals and ambitions, a country can build resilience, withstand various challenges, and influence its surroundings, provided it remains focused on the welfare of the people. The fundamental concern is achieving self-determination—the power and capability to shape one's future. This necessitates the enactment of decisions and policies that prioritize enduring national interests over short-term ones.

After enduring fifty years of political and armed struggle marked by immense sacrifice, the people of Eritrea achieved national sovereignty through a referendum, joining the global community. Yet, the primary objective has always been, and remains, to leverage this achievement as a foundation or tool to transition into a stable, law-abiding government, and from there, to embark on a path of reconstruction and sustainable development. How far have we progressed on this journey? What have we accomplished thus far? What hardships have we faced? Were they avoidable? If not, what are the reasons? What price have we paid, and what lessons must we learn from our past? What actions are necessary? Answering these questions is essential.

Sovereignty plays a crucial role in nurturing a nation's development and facilitating its transition from one state to another. It lays the foundation for self-determination, instills confidence, and empowers countries to formulate and execute policies that benefit their citizens. As a nation, sovereignty allows one to fulfill one's obligations to one's people in an organized and dignified manner across various domains while also meeting one's responsibilities to the global community. The following points summarize this:

Governance system
A sovereign nation independently establishes its legal framework, develops policies and strategies, and chooses its form of government. It also charts the political course based on its unique culture, history, and values. In Eritrea's case, the current system should have considered and should continue to consider the diverse socioeconomic makeup of its population, the history of its political and armed struggle for independence, and the goals it has set for itself. Moreover, it should consider the country's strategic location with its associated risks and opportunities, geopolitical dynamics, the extent and use of its natural resources and assets, and the spectrum of political opinions.

Thus, sovereignty provides a strong foundation for creating a governance system that incorporates these elements. When a governance system embraces inclusiveness and the rule of law and fosters an environment of forgiveness, reconciliation, and coexistence, it enables citizens to hold their heads high, trust the system they live under, engage optimistically with their country's progress, and elevate the nation to greater heights. The neighborhood, region, and world will regard them with respect and honor. This governance system is resilient to potential crises. Conversely, a governance system lacking institutional confidence, transparency, and accountability breeds corruption and erodes citizens' trust in the government.

Management of the economy

A sovereign nation independently manages its economy by formulating and implementing trade and taxation policies and laws that it oversees to foster growth. Additionally, it negotiates its trade agreements and manages its resources sustainably. A country whose economic policies prioritize sovereignty and create an environment in which its natural resources benefit its people fairly and equitably has a strong chance of success.

Eritrea, with its small population and limited resources, has an economy plagued by extreme poverty. As a small nation with limited resources, where will the means for its reconstruction come from? How can the weak institutions inherited from the Ethiopian system and those of the PFDJ system, entrenched in outdated and inefficient bureaucratic practices, adapt or transform to effectively meet the new realities? How can human capital be developed to align with the needs of national reconstruction? Furthermore, how can the country's underdeveloped, rudimentary infrastructure be revitalized? These challenges necessitate a comprehensive national reconstruction roadmap that addresses these issues. Sovereignty, as a principle, was intended to be a tool to solve these problems. However, the results have not materialized, and citizens have not prospered.

National defense and security

Sovereignty empowers a nation to safeguard its borders, regulate the movement of citizens and foreigners, and maintain internal order. It also enables a country to resist external forces that seek to exert military or political pressure to destabilize it. For Eritrea, sovereignty has been and remains an opportunity to build resilience to external aggression.

A national defense strategy rooted in the philosophy of deterrence fosters peaceful coexistence among sovereign nations and minimizes unnecessary conflicts. The harsh realities of war are well known, and diplomacy offers a more effective means of resolving disputes. Alternatively, deterrent strategies, such as establishing a modern and professional army, can be employed. However, the aim of creating such an army is not to provoke or prepare for conflict with neighboring countries but to serve as a deterrent and bolster national security. It also ensures that neighboring countries regard the nation with respect.

Preserving sovereignty does not necessitate resolving every dispute with neighboring countries through military force. War should be the last resort, employed only when all avenues for peace are exhausted. Over the past thirty-four years, Eritrea's approach to resolving conflicts with its neighbors has not been beneficial for its sovereignty. There is also ample reason to believe that regional stakeholders possess the capacity to intervene in an impending conflict.

It should be noted that, regardless of its justification, the PFDJ has routinely meddled in the politics of neighboring countries-- often without careful consideration of the costs and potential blowback. As a result, Eritrea's human capital has suffered, its economy has plummeted, its development trajectory has been curtailed, its potential for human development and economic growth has been squandered, and its reputation as a "beacon of hope" in the world has been tarnished. Rather than serving as a stabilizing force in the region, it has become a source of instability. Have citizens benefited from this? The answer is clear.

The ruling party in Eritrea, the PFDJ, consistently employs a fear narrative to justify its prolonged grip on power and governance through coercion. It has fostered a sense of victimhood among the populace through extensive propaganda efforts. For instance, the PFDJ has persistently claimed that as long as the Woyane (TPLF) remained in power in neighboring Ethiopia, there could be no opportunity to restore normalcy in Eritrea. Under this pretext, crucial national priorities, such as ratifying a constitution, legally implementing national service, initiating development programs, and addressing human rights issues, have been indefinitely postponed.

Conducting smart diplomacy

Sovereignty empowers nations to participate in diplomatic forums as equals, enabling them to negotiate, prioritize their interests, and independently form alliances. The modern world presents unprecedented opportunities for interaction and interdependence among countries. In this interconnected environment, survival, let alone thriving, is impossible without understanding the universal rules of engagement. A nation's survival depends on its grasp of these rules; failing to do so increases the risk of marginalization and isolation. It is an undeniable truth that acquiring comprehensive knowledge of the world's rules of engagement and the skills to navigate the international system is essential. The common global practice, though not universally followed, is to pursue policies that prioritize national interests without harming others or infringing on their rights. In international diplomacy, this involves creating conditions under which all parties involved can achieve a win-win solution.

By adhering to international norms and sharing common spaces, countries can alleviate regional tensions and instability, foster growth and prosperity, and pave the way for mutual learning among nations. Sovereignty also enables a nation to determine its political direction without being confined to a single political bloc. While a country cannot choose its geography, it can select a path that influences its future.

The destinies of neighboring countries are interconnected, and a crisis in one area can affect all surrounding nations. Moreover, neighboring countries often face similar challenges. Issues such as climate change, refugee crises, various forms of terrorism, and the fight against illegal human and drug trafficking and other illicit trade activities exemplify these shared challenges.

Building partnerships and fostering mutual cooperation through genuine and warm relationships with neighboring countries, grounded in respect for sovereignty and territorial integrity, is vital to a nation's stability. Beyond enhancing national security, such relationships can pave the way for a stable and prosperous future for countries in a region. In areas marked by instability, additional efforts are needed to regulate, manage, improve, and stabilize the situation. Sovereignty is a key principle that opens opportunities for building strategic partnerships with other sovereign nations.

Therefore, Eritrea should prioritize refining its understanding of global and regional politics to establish regional stability and develop and implement a foreign policy that helps avert potential conflicts. The ancient Chinese military strategist Sun Tzu famously said, "The supreme art of war is to subdue the enemy without fighting." Although the context of this quote differs, it underscores that diplomacy and conflict resolution through dialogue offer greater advantages over direct military confrontation, which is inherently brutal.

The military conflicts involving Eritrea and its neighboring countries—Yemen, Djibouti, Ethiopia, and, to some extent, Sudan—were entirely unnecessary. While each of these conflicts had its own specific triggers, there was no reason they could not have been resolved through dialogue.

Eritrea had the opportunity to benefit from adhering to the principles of engagement and leveraging its sovereignty to its advantage. However, owing to its misguided foreign policy, which is out of sync with international norms, Eritrea has become a pariah state, an outcast, and a spoiler. This misalignment has significantly contributed to the erosion of sovereignty. The other issue that needs to be mentioned here is that foreign policy has been the exclusive purview of President Isaias. In a system without constraints, misunderstandings on the international scene often reflect his personality and erratic nature.

Establishing the rule of law

Sovereignty enables the creation of an independent legal system that protects it from arbitrary external influences. It also allows for the enactment of laws that reflect the will of the people. According to the United Nations, the rule of law embodies fundamental governance principles in which individuals, institutions, and other legal entities, whether governmental or private, are subject to the law. These laws are enacted legitimately, applied impartially and fairly, and adjudicated by independent bodies, all in alignment with international human rights norms and standards.

In Eritrea, while decrees and proclamations are occasionally enacted, do they truly align with international human rights norms and standards? Are citizens genuinely regarded as equal under the law? It is challenging to assert that they are adjudicated freely, as reality suggests otherwise. This inevitably undermines citizens' confidence in the governance system, leading to dissatisfaction and unease.

Establishing good governance

Although sovereignty is important, the core element of a flourishing nation is effective governance. Prioritizing good governance is essential for emerging economies. This entails several critical actions: crafting policies tailored to specific circumstances, establishing institutions that uphold accountability and transparency, adopting standards of practice for policy implementation, addressing or eradicating lawlessness, and ensuring that the development strategy is inclusive for all.

Good governance is characterized by several elements: adherence to the rule of law, separation of the three branches of government, accountability, transparency, institutional integrity, a constitutional framework that includes every citizen, establishment of fundamental human rights, reliability and predictability, inclusivity, consultation, fostering a political culture to resolve differences through peaceful dialogue, creating space for a responsible press, and encouraging consultation between the people and the government.

The current governance system in Eritrea lacks these elements, resulting in minimal citizen security. When citizen security is compromised, it indicates that the governance system is not centered on human welfare.

Shaping the nation's destiny

Sovereignty serves as the foundation for a nation to shape its destiny, safeguard its interests, and secure sustainable growth. History teaches us that countries that have not preserved their sovereignty have not succeeded in reducing instability, while those that were capable of defending it cleared their path to growth. The social and political instability witnessed in Eritrea today contributes to distracting the country's future. Solutions are needed to avert such catastrophes.

Thirty-four years after independence, Eritrea is in a precarious condition. Two generations have been squandered, the social fabric has frayed, and the culture of tolerance has been dismantled. Governmental control over religion has become deeply rooted, laws have been weakened, and dissent has been stifled. The youth are trapped in perpetual national service, driving many into exile, while human rights abuses have become commonplace. Veteran fighters are sidelined, and societal thinking is manipulated to conform to the system. Consequently, Eritrea remains isolated from its neighbors and the global community.

The political climate has reached a critical point, with no stability in sight. The lack of transparency has led to widespread political dissatisfaction and frustration. As citizens find themselves unable to hold their leaders and government accountable, a sense of despair is increasingly taking hold of the populace.

Enhancing human capital

Sovereignty plays a crucial role in elevating a country's human capital. The enhancement of knowledge, skills, and abilities drives the economic progress of both individuals and communities. Educated individuals are more productive and contribute significantly more to economic growth than those without education. Education yields a greater return than personal investments, a shift that necessitates substantial reforms in the educational system. Such progress is realized through education and training (Cipher, 2004).

Equally crucial is the promotion of innovation and seizing the opportunities it offers. Although innovation is frequently associated with modern technology, its influence extends far beyond mere technological progress. Fundamentally, innovation generates and broadens opportunities for human potential, fostering growth and enabling the exploitation of opportunities at advanced levels. The goal is to ensure the development of human capital, particularly by integrating the younger generation into the education system and providing them with quality education. The ultimate aim is to cultivate valuable human capital.

In light of these advancements, Eritrea finds itself at a unique crossroads, empowering its youth by harnessing advanced education and technology to achieve its developmental goals. Furthermore, Eritrea can seamlessly incorporate digital technology into its education system, potentially facilitating the dissemination and sharing of technological advancements. This strategy could nurture a new generation that is well-versed in digital education and equipped to address the economic and diplomatic challenges of the twenty-first century. Thus, Eritrea can position itself as a significant global player. However, this opportunity was not fully capitalized on, which also significantly impacted Eritrean sovereignty.

Nurturing patriotism
Sovereignty plays a crucial role in fostering patriotism, a concept encompassing political, social, cultural, and ideological dimensions that prioritize a nation's interests, culture, identity, or unity. When we refer to people, we mean a group defined by a shared heritage, language, history, or beliefs. Patriotism manifests in various forms (Gellner, 1983) and cultivates a shared identity and unity among its members. This underscores the significance of national sovereignty and the right to self-determination and self-governance, which are often linked to strong national sentiments. It also emphasizes the preservation and development of national culture, history, and experience. Moreover, it can serve as a unifying narrative for political movements aimed at establishing a new nation (Anderson 1983). In the twentieth century, patriotism was pivotal in movements for liberation and self-determination against European colonial powers (Smith, 1991) and played a vital role in Eritrea's struggle for independence.

Patriotism strengthens social cohesion, national solidarity, and a sense of belonging. However, it can also have negative effects. These arise when ethnic groups or political movements (or parties) that perceive themselves as superior exploit them for narrow political objectives. When taken to such extremes, it can result in intense hatred, exclusion, chauvinism, and intolerance, all of which are harmful.

Considering the conceptual framework mentioned above, effective strategies can be employed to promote patriotism by leveraging Eritrea's sovereignty as a tool. However, this should not come at the expense of other countries and people. It must embody the most noble elements of society's identity.

Chapter 7

Weaving the Future: How Cultural Threads Strengthen the Economic Fabric

CULTURE IS A dynamic force that defines our identity and is constantly evolving. It shapes our understanding of both our immediate environment and the broader world, influencing our interactions within and beyond our community. Culture encompasses language, ideas, beliefs, value systems, experiences, norms, institutions, tools, artistic expression, rituals, and customs. Moreover, experts in this field often assert that distinguishing between culture and religion can be challenging.

Culture nurtures human creativity and has a symbiotic relationship with economic development. Throughout history, it has played a pivotal role in the construction of empires and the subjugation of others. Military conquests have frequently been achieved through the imposition of cultural dominance, leading to subjugation. The European domination of Africa and the rise of Nazi Germany serve as notable examples.

Contrary to this narrative, culture can act as a catalyst for freedom and social transformation. Its role in dismantling monarchies and forming republics underscores this potential aspect.

Culture celebrates the uniqueness of individual identity and shared experiences. Therefore, when contemplating social transformation, it is crucial to incorporate our understanding of culture into developmental initiatives. As our cultural awareness increases, we can expect significant social and economic progress. However, achieving balanced social, economic, or political interactions among people is unlikely until they begin to see each other as equals. Cultural values rooted in class, gender, ethnicity, and religious discrimination, as seen in some countries, can impede progress. Therefore, these issues should be critically examined.

In our interconnected world, while diversity is ostensibly respected, we cannot ignore the pervasive influence of the dominant Western culture in global media. This highlights the importance of consistently passing down cultural values and heritage across generations to counter this cultural dominance.

Societies grounded in their culture, identity, history, values, and customs achieve sustainable development, albeit gradually, rather than experiencing temporary growth. On a national level, values and customs based on unity, mutual understanding, and respect for identity and diversity foster a sense of belonging and solidarity, thereby strengthening the society.

Culture can be a powerful tool for establishing governance structures that mirror the social values and customs of diverse communities within a nation. In developing nations, particularly in Africa, societies with traditional systems, such as councils of elders, play a crucial role in facilitating communication with the central government. This interaction is essential for achieving sustainable development.

Culture nurtures a sense of communal unity, and embracing and tolerating diversity are vital for sustainable development and progress. Recognizing the transformative power of culture is key to driving comprehensive and sustainable development. To achieve this, our approach must be culturally sensitive and should respect and preserve the unique values and experiences of each society. When societies integrate their traditional and modern institutions, beliefs, and value systems into the development process, it contributes to making their realities more sustainable.

For our intervention to be effective, several factors must be considered. These include:

a. The pursuit of change is intrinsic to all societies, and the desire for transformation is fundamental. The energy required to drive this change is generated when individuals actively participate and collectively invest their intellect and resources to achieve their goals. This consultation process significantly influences the success rate.
b. Each society is unique. Every society has distinct characteristics. The chosen path of development or strategy must align with these features and their pace. Moreover, these changes can often span generations.
c. Social change is a complex and interconnected process, which makes one-size-fits-all solutions challenging. Instead, solutions must consider the specific needs and contexts of each society.
d. Societies' existing structures are foundational. When societies utilize their existing organizational structures, especially traditional ones, along with their value systems and beliefs as a blueprint, the outcomes reinforce their educational endeavors.

Practical implications

The pace of economic development and progress is shaped by various social and political factors. Countries can achieve significant advancements when the appropriate conditions are in place. These conditions may include sound economic policies grounded in good governance and inclusiveness, the creation of an investment-friendly environment, the development of human capital through education and training, the expansion of job opportunities, and the enhancement of cultural values embedded in the social structure that define a society's identity. As societies focus on their needs and priorities, their chances of success increase, regardless of the challenges they face. Recognizing culture as a crucial element in shaping a shared vision enhances our perspective on sustainable development, making it complete and more comprehensive.

Relevant and appropriate developmental initiatives and programs help fulfill the specific needs and aspirations of society. When a strategy aligns with society's culture and incorporates its considerations, its impact on development efforts becomes substantial. These endeavors will succeed when they are carefully tailored to the needs and priorities of the respective societies.

Utilizing culture as a key tool for economic development promotes inclusivity and empowers societies to take ownership of their developmental journeys. Culture can be a strategic asset for a society's progress. It shapes a society's identity, fosters individual creativity, and creates a sense of belonging among its members. It encourages social responsibility and a spirit of cooperation. There is no doubt that a society rich in culture and grounded in its identity and history, even if its progress is gradual, will achieve effective and sustainable results in the long run.

Cultural values play a crucial role in economic development by shaping human behavior, institutions, and social customs. For example, technological advancements in countries such as China, South Korea, and Singapore, which emphasize Confucian values such as intelligence, education, and self-improvement, are not coincidental. Similarly, Japan has achieved a high level of sophistication, not despite but partly because of its collective culture, which fosters values such as group responsibility, company loyalty, and interpersonal trust. Cultures that promote a strong work ethic and discipline, such as Germany and Nordic countries, tend to be wealthier. Cultures that encourage openness, creativity, and risk-taking pave the way for technological innovations, as demonstrated by South Korea's success.

Nations that invest in education and human capital development succeed in unlocking their people's potential. Countries that prioritize the rule of law and institutional integrity attract investment and build trust. A collective culture fosters solidarity among its members. Societies that promote gender equality and inclusiveness harness the technical potential of their entire population. However, the changes we implement must be deeply rooted in our cultural and historical foundations, which we must strive to uphold. This is because development that is disconnected from its origins is not advantageous.

While the positive cultural values mentioned earlier foster growth, certain cultural values in developed countries can hinder progress. These include resistance to change and innovation, rigid hierarchical social structures (such as the enduring caste system in India), gender inequality, belief in witchcraft and other superstitions, excessive reliance on individuals rather than institutions and institutional processes, corruption and discrimination, a poor sense of time, and skepticism or resistance to new ideas. If not properly addressed, these issues can become significant barriers to social and economic innovation.

The Eritrean people and the cultural values they uphold

The Eritrean people are deeply connected to their nation, with a strong sense of identity that embodies resilience and patriotism, and they have a rich history. Their victory in 1991 over the Ethiopian regime and its global allies was fundamentally the result of the sacrifices made over the preceding thirty years. Throughout the armed struggle, despite numerous challenges, the Eritrean people remained united, fighting, communicating, and speaking with one voice regardless of ethnicity, region, religion, or gender. The foundation of its unity was the peaceful political efforts of the forties and fifties that the Eritrean people exerted to secure self-determination. Their history is marked by the remarkable contributions of its heroes, and it is our responsibility to document their history and names, speak of their contributions, immortalize them, and build monuments in their honor. Patriotism is one of the defining characteristics of the Eritrean people.

The Eritrean people are renowned for their hard work and intelligence, characterized by humility and integrity, enriched with traditions, and distinguished by good governance. They invented the alphabet in ancient times, and their governance systems have been documented in writing. Their culture is rich in proverbs, metaphors, poetry, songs, dance, folktales, and oral histories. They have preserved traditional organizational systems in areas such as land administration, farming, land distribution, family, livestock, dispute resolution, relationships with neighbors, and environmental management. They are a humble people who engage in discussions under the shade of a tree (Daa'ero), practicing conflict resolution through dialogue and forgiveness, keeping their promises, staying true to their word, and advising, "Do not betray people who trust you, lest your Creator betray you." The Eritrean people are humble and express warm hospitality.

The Eritrean people boast a rich history of civilization. The regions now known as Eritrea and Tigray were once the cradle of a unique civilization — the Axumite Civilization - distinguished by its culture, technology, and art. This advanced society used gold, silver, and bronze coins for trade and maintained connections with other regional civilizations of the time. Historical researchers note that this civilization, centered in Axum and the ruins of present-day Eritrea, flourished through its sea outlets of Adulis and Zula, inspiring others and expanding its reach, at one point extending as far as Meroe (modern-day Sudan). It developed its own alphabet and script, documenting significant events, including military campaigns, in inscriptions (epigraphs). Sites such as Metera, Qohaito, Adulis, and Zula in present-day Eritrea are remnants of this civilization. With the advent of peace and the commencement of modern archaeological research, the secrets of this civilization will be unveiled to the fullest extent.

Italian historical researchers, such as the late Alberto Pollera and Conti Rossini, conducted comprehensive studies on the Beja kingdoms, also known as the Belew-Kelew era, which spanned the 8th to the 13th centuries AD. They explored the Chaluk, Faluk, and Maluk traditions, the traditions of the Twelve Tribes of Israel, the story of Maryu and Manshu, the traditions of the Land of Nagran (Najran), the Bilen traditions, and so on. These heritages and artifacts are historical treasures with which our people are endowed.

The Eritrean people embraced Christianity and Islam early in their histories. The translation of the Holy Bible into Ge'ez, supported by its nine saints, stands as a legacy that spans several centuries. Above all, the Eritrean people have lived and continue to live in coexistence and mutual acceptance, regardless of their religious differences. Eritrea is adorned with churches, monasteries, and mosques that reflect its deep-rooted religious faith. Another defining feature of the Eritrean people is their value system, characterized by integrity and reverence for God. They have maintained customs and laws that emphasize community solidarity, cultivated over a long period. Their respect for the rule of law is one of their admirable defining characteristics, marked by mutual cooperation and respect for the law.

The Eritrean people boast a long-standing tradition of harmonious living and tolerance toward one another. They continue to address issues through customary practices and regulations, such as the 'Indaba' laws, which facilitate the resolution of disputes before they escalate to the courts. When disagreements or conflicts occur, they consistently employ reconciliation techniques that satisfy all parties involved.

The Eritrean people have developed a strong sense of resilience and perseverance, enabling them to face challenges and difficulties with patience and fortitude.

They are diligent and resourceful, armed with intelligence and experience. Their faith in God nurtures their patience, confidence, and resilience.

Additionally, they maintain a culture of reaching consensus through the wisdom and advice of knowledgeable and experienced elders.

Any changes considered or implemented in Eritrea must be grounded in these values and built on these strengths to ensure sustainability. Development programs and strategies that have succeeded in other nations have effectively harnessed strong cultural elements and adapted them to the local context. By strategically utilizing culture, we can leverage it for further development.

The historical and cultural foundations mentioned above, which are the people's assets, drive economic development. We must utilize them.

Negative cultural practices persist in Eritrea

In Eritrean society, as in others, there is a blend of harmful and beneficial, destructive and constructive, negative and positive, and progressive and regressive cultural practices. This is typical of societies on the path to development. For instance, resistance to change, regionalism, gender discrimination, belief in witchcraft and other superstitions, disdain for manual crafts (such as blacksmithing, goldsmithing, silversmithing, and ironworking), corruption and nepotism, a poor concept of time, and skepticism towards new ideas are prevalent. The negative impact of these factors on social creativity is thus evident.

Since 1991, highly destructive cultural practices have persisted in the country. These practices have been developed and continue to be developed for various reasons, despite not being part of our historical traditions. They have managed to take root and endure through generational transitions. These factors play a significant role in hindering progress. Below, we highlight some undesirable cultural elements.

The failure to distinguish between the government, the PFDJ, the nation, and the leader: Within the PFDJ framework, there has been a continuous effort to obscure the distinctions between the government, the ruling party (PFDJ), and the nation. It is frequently asserted that there is no separation between the government, the PFDJ, the nation, and the president. A narrative has been promoted that equates the PFDJ with the government, the government with the nation, the nation with the PFDJ, and the nation with Isaias Afewerki. From this perspective, any citizen who does not support the PFDJ, the Eritrean government, or Isaias is considered unpatriotic and labeled a traitor, Woyane, mercenary, collaborator, or even a CIA agent. This unwavering loyalty to a single political party and leader fosters a dangerous political culture. This may be linked to a subservient tradition that venerates any king who rules a country. However, it is not unreasonable to suspect that it was deliberately crafted for a specific purpose. This phenomenon warrants further investigation.

Lack of accountability: The absence of accountability erodes the trust that should be inherent within institutions, breeds suspicion and opacity in operations, encourages the abuse of power and corruption, and undermines ethical conduct and responsibility within institutions. In Eritrea, it is not an exaggeration to say that power is concentrated in a single individual. Unlike other countries, there are no government branches—legislative, judicial, or executive—that hold each other accountable and provide checks and balances. The use of state resources is opaque, with no mechanism to oversee the formulation, implementation, and monitoring of government policies. Government officials are not accountable to the people for their actions and are not open to being audited.

On the one hand, government entities, such as ministries, which have defined mandates and responsibilities, are hindered by micromanagement from the PFDJ and the President's office. Budget constraints further impede their ability to fulfill their mandates. As the government does not operate under the constitution, it is not bound by the laws. There is no enforced code of conduct to ensure professional integrity or ethical behavior, nor is there a system to hold underperformers accountable. There are no clear metrics to evaluate outcomes, such as economic progress, service delivery, public satisfaction, the quality of education, and the country's diplomatic relations. Yet, these questions remain unanswered. Corruption, shrouded in excessive secrecy, has become deeply embedded in the system. Crimes are committed and continue to occur with impunity.

Lack of institutions and institutional processes: In Eritrea, the persistent lack of institutions and institutional processes has been a major source of frustration and has significantly contributed to delays. Eritrea's system is marked by unclear mandates and authoritarianism. This lack of accountability has resulted in a fragile governance structure characterized by opaque institutions and corruption, undermining national unity. Consequently, a sense of hopelessness and distrust has developed among the populace. This fragmentation and weakening of institutions have also impacted the legislative and judicial branches of the government. The legislative body, referred to as the National Assembly, has not convened for more than twenty-two years. The centralized system marginalizes institutions, especially government entities with specific mandates and policies. Cabinet meetings are not held regularly, and when they do take place, they are conducted in secrecy, leaving the public uninformed. The system in Eritrea has effectively hollowed out institutions, making them ineffective and unaccountable to the public. This has inevitably led to a decline in trust in these institutions.

Lack of transparency: Transparency serves as both a structural framework and a tool that facilitates the dissemination of precise, beneficial, dependable, and prompt information to the public. It encourages public involvement, guarantees accountability, elucidates government policies for citizens, offers feedback, establishes a platform for citizens to question the government, and deters secretive government practices.

In Eritrea, topics such as the budget (revenue and expenditure), recurrent and capital budget, declarations of war, the execution of development programs, national security matters, revenue from mining, the 2% and other funds collected from the diaspora, annual economic growth rates across various sectors (agriculture, industry, services) (GDP), state revenues from taxes, the finances of companies operated by the PFDJ (party-owned enterprises), foreign exchange rates, and so on, are not part of the system's lexicon. A culture of excessive secrecy has fostered a secretive and non-participatory system that excludes people from the decision-making process. Wars are declared and conducted in secret, Eritrea's international relations are handled opaquely, commercial contracts are signed in secrecy, and a system that encourages the abduction of thousands of citizens, whose whereabouts remain unknown, is sustained.

Political polarization: Fostering a culture of Eritrean political discourse that promotes constructive dialogue rooted in reason and provides a platform for resolving differences through civilized means is crucial. Opposing views should not only be tolerated but celebrated, as diversity is the source of unity and strength. Unfortunately, media outlets representing the government or the diaspora, especially YouTube channels, often fail to fulfill their roles with the necessary responsibility and caution. They spread falsehoods, disseminate unverified or false news, and use harsh and indecent language to attack others.

Moreover, divisive agendas that incite political hatred and division, along with social media influencers (both pro-government and opposition) who prioritize personal attacks over substantive issues, are prevalent. Perhaps the most concerning issue is the time and energy the diaspora community spends demonizing each other. A "you are with us or against us" mentality has taken root. This, combined with the legacy of polarization seen in the 1940s and the 1950s between different Eritrean political factions and exacerbated by the hostile approach inherited from the armed struggle period between competing organizations, has led to internal strife in Eritrea. However, this was not expected to occur. Learning from the past is important for the future.

Militarization of the entire society: For three decades, the government has systematically worked to militarize Eritrean society, embedding this approach deeply into the nation's culture. People's lives are structured and governed by military norms and priorities, which effectively become cultural norms. Through indoctrination, "national security" has become a constant justification and convenient excuse for suppressing dissent. The defense budget has soared at the expense of other social services, and the glorification of wars and war heroes has reached monumental proportions.

This propagandistic effort manipulates the sacrifices made during the struggle for independence, dressing the victories in battles like Nadew, Wqaw, Mebreq, and Fenqel, as well as various fronts against Ethiopian forces, in honor and presenting them as legendary triumphs, thereby exploiting them for political purposes. Additionally, the narratives of the first through eighth Ethiopian offensives, particularly the one culminating in a futile war of attrition, are recounted ad nauseam. There is nothing wrong with glorifying victories; however, using them for narrow political purposes is unacceptable. It also becomes a tiresome exercise.

It has become increasingly common for elderly individuals to be forcibly compelled to participate in military training. Citizens have aligned themselves with the government, fearing retribution from the government. Meanwhile, the 'enemies of the nation' are demonized. This culture fosters a society that is subservient to the military apparatus, stifles professional pursuits, and devalues family time. Instead of focusing on their studies, children are immersed in the military culture.

The education system, rather than promoting critical thinking and inquiry, instills blind obedience and servility in students. This environment creates a social and intellectual vacuum that suffocates democratic values. Above all, it subordinates professions to the military, making them serve its interests.

The militarization of a significant portion of society was evident during the Italian colonial era. The renowned Italian historian Alberto Pollera confirmed in his book, "The Indigenous People of Eritrea," that at one time, thirty thousand Eritrean youths were conscripted by the Italian colonial power. At that time, the population of Eritrea was estimated to be around six hundred thousand (Pollera, 1935). This is a significant figure by any measure. However, it is incomparable to the situation and political repression seen today under the PFDJ

Regimentation of society's thinking into a single mindset and mood: In Eritrea, a culture that stifles diverse political opinions has taken hold, characterized by severe polarization and harsh measures to quash dissent and forcibly silence differing views. The PFDJ's existence hinges on maintaining absolute control and perpetuating it without interruption. Under the PFDJ, the youth are subjected to strict surveillance, molded as part of a social engineering project to create a 'new person.' This involves mandatory participation in the 'National Service' program, initially intended to last 18 months but extended indefinitely.

The aim is to continually shape the youth in the image of freedom fighters. This indoctrination seeks to compel the youth to think as the PFDJ desires, ultimately bringing their thoughts and freedom under the complete control and influence of the PFDJ.

The PFDJ has consistently used fear as a political tool to maintain the continuity and legitimacy of its rule. By amplifying external threats, it instills a pervasive sense of fear among the population. Leveraging this indoctrination, it has indefinitely postponed critical national priorities such as constitutional implementation, national service, development programs, and the resolution of human rights issues.

Eritrea's annual calendar is filled with commemorative holidays, notably Independence Day, Fenqel, Martyrs' Day, Women's Day, Workers' Day, and September One, marking the start of the armed struggle. Additionally, commemorative events for the battles of Wqaw, Nadew, and Mebreq are celebrated annually. From summer until September, nationals are engaged in festivals, both domestically and abroad, with endless parades and dances performed. Observing these holidays is not unusual, but their intent is clear. This is politically motivated—a deliberate strategy to distract people from contemplating pressing issues.

Sub-national allegiances: Within Eritrean constituencies, sub-national allegiances are often fueled by internal and external forces for political gain. These allegiances may stem from regional, ethnic, and religious identities. Regardless of their origin, they ultimately serve those seeking political advantage and are detrimental to society. Such allegiances undermine national unity, weaken social cohesion, erode the patriotic spirit, and corrupt the nation's social fabric. They also impede growth and development.

Conformism: In Eritrea, the primary catalyst for conformism is the fear of punitive consequences or reprisals faced by citizens. Often, individuals, whether out of necessity or coercion, align themselves with the prevailing system to ensure their own safety and that of their families. Some adopt this alignment as a strategy for self-preservation. When voicing grievances can lead to severe repercussions, adopting such a stance becomes a fundamental survival strategy rooted in human nature. Moreover, authoritarian systems typically exert strict control over information and suppress alternative media and viewpoints. This limitation on access to diverse perspectives can lead people to accept the system's narrative as the sole truth. This phenomenon is also linked to the pervasive mentality in society of "either comply or face the consequence of your action."

Mutual distrust: The authoritarian regime in Eritrea has created a profound political divide within society, centered on power, ideology, and the control or exploitation of national resources. This situation necessitates addressing power struggles and reconciling differing views in a manner that does not compromise national security or unity. The distrust that has been sown during the dictatorship has the potential to persist, eroding social trust and undermining national cohesion.

Politicization of everything: In Eritrea, social, cultural, art, and economic issues have assumed a political dimension, leading to social fragmentation. An "us versus them" mentality has taken hold, eroding trust in institutions, such as the media, as they are perceived through this lens. This phenomenon is a powerful driver of prejudice, as certain groups in society may become economic beneficiaries because of their political allegiance to the government.

Erosion of traditional citizen names: Traditional names carry profound cultural, historical, and spiritual significance. They embody meaning, identity, and ancestral wisdom, which have been passed down through generations. These names are undeniably part of the cultural heritage that deserves preservation. However, a pressing issue has emerged concerning the names that parents choose for their children. The custom of bestowing traditional names is being supplanted by a trend favoring modern names, with a growing tendency to create new names by merging two existing names into one. If this trend is not addressed, it could lead to the erasure of history and the stripping away of identities. This is a matter of concern for the future. The superficial cultural trend that has taken root in Eritrea poses serious consequences for our society, and future generations are likely to bear a significant burden of this trend.

Conclusion

For a nation to achieve sustainable economic development, improve its citizens' standard of living, enhance its security, secure the future for upcoming generations, preserve cultural wisdom, and strategically utilize its cultural assets for prosperity, it must first restore its foundational elements. This involves a systematic and deliberate approach to identifying and promoting the cultures and values that drive economic growth, while simultaneously uprooting and discarding superficial cultures that may hinder this growth.

As economic growth inherently demands the dynamic cultural characteristics previously mentioned, the potential for culture to evolve into a more productive stage increases with economic expansion. This symbiotic relationship positively impacts the economy, as they complement and support each other and develop in tandem. Economic integration can also be a significant catalyst for cultural renaissance.

A cultural renaissance cannot be achieved through words alone; it requires effort and time for nurturing. To realize this, an educated populace, skilled human capital, and robust infrastructure, including land, sea, and air transport networks, are essential. Additionally, efficient institutions, such as sophisticated financial and service-providing entities, and dynamic economic and trade relations with regional and international communities are crucial. Such an economy encourages citizen interaction, strengthens integration, and provides a platform for exchanging experiences, ultimately leading to economic prosperity. It cultivates cultural champions, thought leaders, entrepreneurs, and investor-citizens. As the saying goes, "capital has no boundaries," allowing citizens, regardless of their background, to collaborate and benefit from their collective efforts.

However, our culture has not been fully documented. Not all customs have been recorded in writing. The oral traditions of our historians and elders, with their nuances, have not been thoroughly passed down to the younger generations. Our manuscripts remain uncollected, and our literature has not reached the desired level. Nonetheless, efforts have been made to standardize the language, with dictionaries written in Eritrea's various languages serving as living testaments to this endeavor.

People who are proud of their identity and history are always ready for a better and brighter future. Their ambitions are boundless, and they face no difficulties in reclaiming a bright future and securing their place in the world. This is the foundation of economic growth.

Chapter 8

Harnessing the Tide: The Eritrean Diaspora's Role in National Change

I will begin with the following hypothesis:

> "Like Diasporas everywhere, the Eritrean Diaspora is dispersed and will continue to spread across various continents in the future. This group constitutes a substantial portion of Eritrean society, spanning three generations, and is significant in size. If effectively organized and mobilized, it has the potential to make a significant contribution to nation-building."

Therefore, this chapter seeks to explore the contributions the Eritrean diaspora can make to support nation-building both before and after regime change in synergy with the ever-evolving situation.

Introduction: Diaspora relationship with its home country

Tens of millions of citizens from various countries live outside their homelands for multiple reasons. Among these distinct diaspora communities are

Indians (32 million), Mexicans (22 million), Chinese (20 million), Russians (15 million), Syrians (13 million), Egyptians (5 million), and Nigerians (4 million).

Regardless of the continent where these diaspora communities reside or how many years they have spent in exile, most maintain a connection with their homeland. This connection manifests in various ways. One significant form is remittances sent back home, which serve as a primary source of foreign exchange and contribute to the country's economic stability. This is evident among Indians, Filipinos, Nigerians, Egyptians, and Ethiopians, who are spread across different continents worldwide.

Additionally, diaspora communities invest in their home countries through real estate, infrastructure, and business ventures. They also provide financial support to needy family members. Beyond this, they transfer the skills and knowledge acquired in exile to their home countries. Across various continents, diaspora members, such as doctors, engineers, and business investors, return to their homelands to engage in partnerships with domestic institutions, thereby participating in the development of their nation's human capital. In summary, they contribute to the economic development of their home countries. Diaspora communities can influence their host countries' policies, transforming them into benefits for their homelands. This dual relationship is often bolstered by lobbying efforts, with the Jewish diaspora being particularly noted for its impact in this area.

Diaspora communities engage in organizing festivals, establishing language learning centers, and creating media outlets to preserve their identities, experiences, and cultures. These activities not only maintain the community's connection to its homeland but also promote it on international platforms. Additionally, diaspora communities are known for providing substantial aid during natural disasters.

For instance, the approximately thirty-two million Indians spread across various continents contribute to the growth of their homeland's technology industry by sending remittances and engaging in political lobbying. The Jewish diaspora is exceptional in its advocacy and investment in its homeland. Filipinos abroad send significant amounts of foreign exchange back home as remittances to their families. According to World Bank reports, in 2023, Filipinos sent $39 billion in remittances, accounting for up to ten percent of the country's Gross Domestic Product (World Bank Group, 2023). In the same year, remittances from other countries were as follows: Thailand, $9.6 billion; Egypt, $19.5 billion; Morocco, $11.8 billion; Bangladesh, $22.2 billion; Pakistan, $26.6 billion; Nigeria, $19.5 billion; Kenya, $4.2 billion; and Senegal, $2.9 billion.

In brief, the relationship between the diaspora and their homeland evolves with changing opportunities and challenges. However, astute governments have developed and implemented policies to engage their citizens abroad, ensuring their contribution to their homeland's economic development. The Diaspora Bond is one such strategy. Another approach is to establish a Ministry or Commission dedicated to diaspora affairs, such as the Commission for Nigerians in the Diaspora.

Eritreans in the diaspora represent one of the most distinct African communities abroad, notable for their numbers and voices. Their narrative stands out when compared with other diaspora groups. One major reason for the Eritrean exodus was the prolonged conflict in their homeland, particularly Ethiopia's attempts to forcibly annex Eritrea and the ensuing protracted armed struggle in response to this annexation. Political repression and persecution that persisted during Ethiopian rule and later under the PFDJ system, spanning a continuous thirty years, mark the second chapter of their story. Prolonged wars with neighboring countries, political despair, and a weak economy have prompted hundreds of thousands of Eritreans, especially the youth, to seek refuge in other countries.

History also notes that during the Italian colonial period, a small number of Eritreans—students, workers, and those recruited into the Italian military—migrated to Italy for various reasons. Even before the 1930s, a few Eritreans moved to Sudan, Ethiopia, Egypt, and various Middle Eastern countries for various reasons.

The thirty-year-long war for independence resulted in mass population displacement. Hundreds of thousands of Eritreans have sought refuge in Sudan. From there, some dispersed to Europe (Germany, Sweden, Italy, and Great Britain), North America, and the Middle East, where they eventually settled. Consequently, the Eritrean diaspora now spans three generations.

After Eritrea gained independence, political developments led to a mass exodus of its citizens. Instead of reaping the benefits of freedom, the people found themselves under the oppressive and despair-inducing rule of the PFDJ. Thirty-four years later, Eritrea is in a precarious condition. The potential of two generations has been squandered, the social structure deliberately dismantled, and the rich, diverse culture that had been nurtured over time has been eroded or destroyed. Unjust interference and control over religion and religious institutions have become commonplace, the rule of law has been undermined, lawlessness has been institutionalized, and dissenting voices have been suppressed through force or through intimidation.

The youth are caught in an endless cycle of national service and forced labor, with no escape from being conscripted. Violations of fundamental human rights have become routine, and veteran freedom fighters have been marginalized. Furthermore, manipulation, coercion, and fear have been systematically employed to ensure that the system's interests dominate all aspects of life. Eritrea has become isolated from its neighbors and the international community. The 1998 conflict with Ethiopia significantly exacerbated this problem. The ongoing national service, coupled with forced labor and the constant threat of war, has driven hundreds of thousands of young and middle-aged Eritreans to flee their homeland in search of refuge elsewhere.

The Eritrean diaspora and its nature and activities

Despite their collective grievances and other differences, Eritreans in the diaspora do not see themselves as separate from the national struggle for independence. For three decades, from the 1960s to the early 1990s, the Eritrean diaspora consistently supported the movements that fueled the independence struggle, namely, the Eritrean Liberation Front (ELF) and the Eritrean People's Liberation Front (EPLF). Beyond being a major source of funding, the diaspora also offered steadfast political support for the independence movement. Through public diplomacy, it acted as the voice of the Eritrean people on various international and regional political platforms, making a significant contribution to Eritrea's independence struggle.

According to United Nations documents, as of 2024, an estimated 663,085 Eritreans are living in exile (UNHCR, 2023). The primary host countries include Sudan, South Sudan, Ethiopia, Germany, Sweden, Switzerland, Norway, the United States, the Middle East, Canada, Israel, Australia, and Uganda.

Due to hopelessness and economic collapse in the country, the number of Eritreans in the diaspora continues to grow. The younger generation, which is spread across different continents, is actively demanding change.

The Eritrean diaspora invests in various economic activities, including professional services, trade, academia, and other ventures to sustain their daily livelihoods. The number of Eritreans living in refugee camps is also significant.

Eritrea's economy heavily relies on diaspora remittances, which serve as the primary financial source for most Eritrean families. Additionally, the well-known 2% tax, which is compulsorily levied on the Eritrean diaspora, is the government's main source of foreign exchange.

Since gaining independence, Eritrea's embassies have consistently and persistently collected substantial funds from the Eritrean diaspora through a 2% tax, remittances, and requests for donations for various purposes. These include supporting the fight against the Woyane (TPLF), aiding disabled veteran fighters, funding war memorials and statues, assisting the families of martyrs, and financing medical supplies, school construction, and hospital or health center projects. A requirement for this is that diaspora members must regularly obtain permits to access government services, which allow them to acquire birth and wedding certificates, land ownership rights in Eritrea, business work permits, and exit visas for their elderly relatives.

This approach, often termed "milking the diaspora," enables the regime to gather hundreds of millions of dollars each year, which it uses to maintain its coercive apparatus. Unlike most diplomatic institutions globally, Eritrea's embassies often prioritize extracting money from the diaspora, spying on their own citizens, and engaging in transnational repression, well above the typical functions of an embassy. The regime's arbitrary control and manipulation of the official foreign exchange rate further worsened the situation, as it was well below the international market.

Some diaspora members are apprehensive about the regime because they own property in Eritrea and cannot afford to express dissent. Others, having been away from their homeland for years, long to visit their elderly parents, siblings, and close relatives; thus, to preserve this opportunity, they choose to comply. Many fearing being labeled as traitors or Woyane [TPLF] supporters and risking ostracism from their community opted to remain silent. They attend annual festivals organized by the PFDJ, as these events allow them to connect with their compatriots, reminisce about their homeland, and express their nostalgia. Additionally, these gatherings provide a chance to socialize through traditional Eritrean dances, engage in conversations, enjoy injera (local bread), wear traditional clothing, and celebrate. It also serves as a significant opportunity for different generations to come together.

The Eritrean diaspora and its future - Harnessing the potential of the diaspora, integrating the diaspora into national reconstruction

It is essential to remember that the diaspora played a pivotal role, made significant contributions, and endured numerous sacrifices during Eritrea's struggle for independence. Both the Eritrean People's Liberation Front and the Eritrean Liberation Front, after being isolated from major global political powers (the Western nations led by the United States and the socialist bloc led by the Soviet Union), rallied the diaspora community as a crucial political support base and primary source of financial backing.

Reflecting on the period following independence, the Eritrean government might have chosen a different path and found a more effective way to engage the diaspora in national projects. Instead of imposing a 2% tax on their income, it could have encouraged and incentivized them to invest in their homeland. This approach might have attracted substantial foreign capital to the country, potentially setting it on a path of healthy economic development. Furthermore, the Eritrean government could have laid the groundwork for establishing an inclusive government based on national consensus by involving various political groups, civic organizations, religious bodies, and strong networks formed by the Eritrean diaspora.

Regrettably, what unfolded after independence was a climate of political exclusion, mistrust, and division fostered by the PFDJ among the diaspora. Currently, we are witnessing unprecedented conditions that do not encourage diaspora engagement in their home country's affairs.

Young Eritreans are beginning to come together and express their opinions. They have established branches across various regions, including Europe, the Middle East, North America, and Africa. This movement comprises Eritrean youth who have encountered significant challenges in their lives. Some were shot and injured while trying to escape to Sudan and Ethiopia to avoid national service; others suffered forced labor and abuse while traversing the Sahara Desert in search of safety; and others risked their lives crossing the Mediterranean Sea, among other hardships. These young individuals feel resentment towards the system that has ruined their youth. They experience frustration and anger, believing that they have been let down by the system. They are politically conscious and committed to initiating changes. But they lack organization and foresight.

To enhance its influence, this movement must clearly define its goals, broaden its support network, and expand its membership. Its strategy needs to be well-articulated to effectively counter the deceptive tactics of the Eritrean regime, which aims to dismantle it from within. Focusing on building wider organizational capacity is crucial to counteract the regime's attempts to manipulate Eritreans in the diaspora through false nationalism and fear. The movement must develop a more sophisticated strategy that surpasses the regime's outdated approaches and ensures the active participation of youth.

What needs to be done – Some recommendations
Pre-change

There is an emerging consensus among Eritreans on the need for change. Furthermore, there is widespread support for establishing a constitutional government following this change, starting with a transitional phase.

The government should embody accountability, transparency, and adherence to the rule of law. From the outset, various opposition groups engaged in discussions about the defining characteristics of a transitional government. However, the justice-seeking Eritrean diaspora must clarify its position on this issue. A shared understanding of the mission, strategy, and approach is crucial to achieving this goal. To this end, creating a common political platform or space that can serve as a political alternative to effect tangible change is essential. This can also be expressed as forming a united front. It is not necessary to unite under a single political platform; it could also manifest as two or three initiatives, provided that they are willing to collaborate. The objectives of the united front may include the following:

First, the Eritrean diaspora's contribution to efforts for change depends on its integration and alignment with similar movements in Eritrea. Achieving this requires an agreement on a minimum program. It is imperative for all political organizations, civic associations, justice-seeking entities in the diaspora, and other activists desiring change to form a coalition or a united front built on the following three fundamental objectives:

- Ending the one-man dictatorship;
- Establishing a transitional government that includes all Eritrean stakeholders based on inclusivity, the rule of law, accountability, and transparency; and
- Transitioning through the establishment of a constitutional government, national reconstruction, and sustainable development.

These objectives can also serve as foundations. And for these objectives to materialize, the following priorities are proposed: -

A. *Formulating and implementing outreach strategy:* To achieve the objectives outlined above, it is essential to develop and implement a communications strategy that effectively challenges the regime's propaganda machinery. This strategy should primarily aim to capture the attention and sympathy of the Eritrean people, affirming the existence of a credible movement dedicated to seeking justice and driving change. Once its credibility is established, the movement can call upon the army, security forces, veterans, national service members, parents, religious and traditional leaders, and others to join the cause for change.

B. Conducting coherent and smart diplomacy: Diplomatic initiatives should be rooted in partnerships with host governments and regional and international bodies. This engagement must not only address the country's situation and the suffering of its people but also emphasize the potential benefits of change and its aftermath for all parties involved.

Diplomacy often serves to advance one's interests. A decisive action the diaspora can take is to diplomatically isolate the regime in Asmara and denounce the atrocities it commits against its citizens. This can significantly help ensure that the suffering of our people is acknowledged by the international community. It is also essential to communicate complaints and grievances to foreign governments, international organizations, and major media outlets in an organized way. Through these efforts, pressure can be applied to the PFDJ regime to stop interfering in the lives of its citizens, uphold the rule of law, respect human rights, release political prisoners, and, if it persists, implement changes to its agenda (though regrettably, this is not anticipated).

The diplomatic initiatives undertaken by the Eritrean diaspora can provide vital support to Eritrean refugees scattered worldwide and help secure favorable international legal frameworks for them. These efforts include diplomatic statements, conferences, and information dissemination through major media outlets. Such actions will undoubtedly raise international awareness of the calamity facing Eritrea. As global awareness grows, it will contribute to exerting additional pressure on the dictatorial regime. These efforts must be meticulously planned and executed to increase their intensity to a higher level.

The majority of the diaspora usually stays aloof from the politics of the host country. This is often not a smart strategy. It is to their distinct advantage to be part of a wider political network, as understanding and engaging with the system helps them navigate it effectively. Such engagement allows them to raise a political agenda that can directly improve the lives of their communities and even create channels for their countries of origin to benefit from strengthened bilateral ties. But although integration is a common achievement, ascending to the highest level of civic engagement—political office—is a rare feat. The diaspora communities need to work on this.

C. *Organizing the diaspora community by professional status:* Organizing the diaspora community according to their professions and capabilities can significantly enhance their contribution to the change effort and maximize potential benefits—political, economic, and social—wherever feasible.

D. *Drafting post-change policy documents:* A key objective is to draft policy documents that will guide the post-change period across various domains. These drafts can play a pivotal role in directing an interim transitional government. These, among others, may include: draft National Charter, draft National Development Strategy, draft Refugee Resettlement Policy, draft Policy on Transitional Justice Framework, draft Policy for Building a Professional Army, draft Foreign Policy, and a draft Policy on the Resettlement of Displaced Persons.

Regardless of how extensive and profound the diaspora's efforts for change may be, the ultimate validation of change will emerge from within the country and its inner circles. Nonetheless, the diaspora must consistently recognize and remember that Eritreans fighting for justice within Eritrea—whether in the regime's military or security apparatus or in the civil service, including PFDJ members—are its true allies and partners in the quest for change. Therefore, the diaspora's strategy should also focus on building bridges with the forces for change inside Eritrea. Strengthening collective efforts aimed at change and providing moral support and encouragement to movements striving for change in Eritrea is essential.

Second, the diaspora should nurture a culture of tolerance, embrace diversity, and instill a spirit of sacrifice in the younger generation to champion the causes of justice they believe in. To resolve differences constructively, it is crucial to cultivate a political culture that encourages civil debate and discussion alongside a diaspora political culture enriched by diverse political experiences. It is important not only to tolerate opposing views but also to respect and appreciate them. Our differences are a source of unity and strength. The key is to create a shared space that serves as an alternative to collective efforts. Although this requires patience and persistent effort, it is achievable. In this endeavor, we must remember that many foreigners who are friends of the Eritrean people support the Eritrean people and are willing to collaborate.

Third, media outlets representing the diaspora have a duty to operate accurately, carefully, and responsibly. Some social media platforms promote division and political hatred, prioritizing personal attacks over fundamental issues. This must cease. It is also crucial to avoid inflammatory language and insults.

Fourth, Young Eritreans need to refine their goals and strategies to achieve them. Beyond the justice-seeking movement's objectives mentioned earlier and listed below, this also involves actions such as boycotting the 2% tax, avoiding festivals that glorify the regime, and encouraging others to abstain from participating in these activities. Justice-seeking youth in the diaspora must assume leadership of this struggle.

Fifth, many Eritrean diaspora members face challenges related to identity and integration. Eritrean community associations play a vital role in addressing these issues in host countries. They can offer counseling or support to those who experience pressure, isolation, or discrimination. By leveraging various social opportunities, they can help individuals build a sense of identity and claim the rights and benefits available to the diaspora in their host countries. The diaspora can also engage in the politics of the host country and, by collaborating with governmental institutions, articulate their demands and advocate for their causes in the host country. Engaging in the political landscape of a host country does not mean forsaking one's roots; rather, it is a powerful strategy to elevate them, ensuring that the diaspora has a voice and a champion where it matters most.

Additionally, diaspora communities can support new refugees. This includes assisting them in finding housing and employment, providing resettlement aid, and ensuring that they receive high-level orientation on issues related to the host country's laws and immigration. Diaspora members can also organize courses or training sessions to help them integrate into the host society.

Sixth, Eritrean community centers and associations can facilitate networking and provide various forms of support to help Eritreans invest in businesses and projects, thereby enabling them to leverage local resources to their advantage. They can conduct financial literacy workshops to empower members economically and help them reap the benefits. Additionally, they can encourage Eritrean participation in local initiatives to contribute to host communities. These centers can also play a crucial role in preserving the mother tongue for future generations by developing resources such as books, websites, and apps. By organizing cultural events, festivals, and workshops, they can maintain and pass on cultural traditions to younger generations. Cultural centers can also build a bridge between the diaspora and the host country showcasing history, art, and cultural experiences to host societies.

Seventh, Diaspora communities can utilize media centers established within them, particularly social media platforms, to connect with and mobilize members globally. They can offer legal support and information on immigration, citizenship, and other legal issues, advocate for equitable immigration policies, and assist those facing legal challenges.

2. Post-Change?
Let us revisit the hypothesis initially proposed.

> Similar to diasporas worldwide, the Eritrean diaspora is dispersed and will continue to spread across various continents in the future. This group represents a substantial portion of Eritrean society, spanning three generations, and is significant in size. If effectively organized and mobilized, it has the potential to make a meaningful contribution to nation-building."

Given the high potential of the diaspora community, it is not an exaggeration to predict that they will play a role in nation-building. To harness this potential for nation-building, a well-thought-out policy and strategy will be needed after the change that could include the following: -

Establishing a diaspora affairs commission
The first objective is to establish a body (or commission) to handle diaspora affairs. This institution will serve as a bridge between the diaspora and the government and conduct in-depth studies on the diaspora's conditions. This lays the groundwork for the contributions that the diaspora can make to nation-building. It will encourage and advise the diaspora to invest in various sectors of the economy, promoting contributions in areas such as housing, construction, and infrastructure. It will facilitate the investment of capital needed to start businesses and trade. In general, it advocates for investment initiatives to ensure that the diaspora community participates at a higher level in building their homeland without severing their

connection to it. The contributions of the Chinese, Egyptians, Filipinos, Turks, Nigerians, and Pakistanis in the diaspora to their home countries' economic development can be cited as examples.

The transitional government that will be established in post-change Eritrea will be responsible for facilitating diaspora participation in all spheres of life, including the economic, political, and social. The diaspora community can also play a major role in supporting the drafting of the constitution and other relevant national policies.

The financial potential of the diaspora in driving national economic growth and development

A significant financial resource for Eritrea is the remittances sent by Eritreans living abroad. This contribution is substantial by any standard. For instance, we have already mentioned about the Vietnamese diaspora, which numbers approximately five million globally, and sends approximately $16 billion annually to the country. Similarly, with an Eritrean diaspora of about one million, it is plausible to estimate that remittances to Eritrea could amount to $3 billion per year. The Eritrean government, once established after the transition, should be keenly interested in leveraging this potential for further development of all sectors of the economy, including the tourism sector.

Enhancing technology transfer

In addition to the financial capital mentioned, the skills and education that members of the Eritrean diaspora bring back to their homeland are invaluable. These individuals have significant potential to facilitate technology transfer.

Enhancing lobbying capacity
Members of the diaspora community can form influential lobbying groups, promote their homeland internationally, facilitate cultural exchanges between their homeland and host countries, and build beneficial relationships with these institutions. These efforts can create opportunities for substantial contributions to a country's development.

Promoting domestic tourism
Tourism is a crucial source of foreign exchange. If the Eritrean diaspora, numbering in the hundreds of thousands, begins visiting their homeland, Eritrea's tourism sector will grow substantially. This influx will create job opportunities for Eritreans and help stabilize the country's financial situation.

Organizing social events
There is no reason why the diaspora cannot leverage the same networks currently used by the Eritrean government to engage with it. These networks include festivals, national holidays, and other similar events. However, the focus should not be on raising funds or "milking" the diaspora but rather on fostering a unified organization, spirit, momentum, and objective that unites all Eritreans under one banner.

Organizing professionals
When organized into various professional associations, the diaspora community has the potential to invest in technology transfer or collaborate with academic institutions. This collaboration will undoubtedly enable the country to benefit from technology and advance to the level of global progress required. Establishing

Establishing language centers

The diaspora community can establish and manage educational centers where children can connect with their native languages. This initiative will also help preserve the connection between the generation born abroad and their home country.

Conclusion

Decades of war, followed by years of harsh rule under the PFDJ, have driven the Eritrean exodus. Over time, hundreds of thousands of Eritreans have settled in host countries. Some have advanced their academic standing by attending higher education institutions, while others have directly entered the workforce to build their lives and support their families. Over time, they established families, acquired property, and became managers and investors in various businesses. Today, an Eritrean diaspora community spanning three generations has emerged.

Similar to other diaspora communities, the Eritrean diaspora has continued to integrate and adapt to the cultures, norms, and systems of their host countries. Their outlook on life has also evolved. As their livelihoods stabilized, their assets and management roles grew, and their children began attending educational institutions in host countries, the prospect of returning to their homeland gradually diminished in their minds. However, their connection to their homeland remains intact, as most have not stopped visiting it.

The Eritrean government has no choice but to tap into this immense potential for national development. If properly harnessed, this potential offers all the benefits mentioned above. To achieve this, the transitional government of Eritrea or the constitutional government to be established must formulate sound policies that benefit the country and devise strategies to support their implementation.

Chapter 9

The Case for a Deterrence-Centric National Defense

ERITREA, A SMALL nation located in the Horn of Africa, is bordered by Sudan, Ethiopia, and Djibouti, with the Red Sea along its coast. This strategic location offers significant potential for influence from both global and regional geopolitical forces.

In my previous book, "Eritrea's Hard-won Independence and Unmet Expectations," I explored how the Red Sea, stretching from the Bab el-Mandeb Strait at its southern entrance to the Suez Canal in northern Egypt, serves as a crucial maritime trade route of considerable economic significance. This significance is shared by Eritrea's neighboring countries. I emphasized that the Red Sea's role is underscored by the fact that it handles ten percent of global trade, leading to the conclusion that Eritrea occupies a strategically important position.

Additionally, I outline several potential threats that Eritrea may face in the future. To mention some: - The Red Sea's importance to both Western and Eastern nations, as well as the international community as a maritime corridor; Ethiopia's strong interest in gaining access to the sea; political instability in the Horn of Africa due to historical issues and unresolved political conflicts; and the risk of proxy wars.

A distinct issue from the previously mentioned factors is Ethiopia's persistent and intense ambition for a sea outlet, particularly the Red Sea. Consequently, there are loud and clear calls for Eritrea to return to its "legal motherland," Ethiopia, based on historical claims. This policy has been extensively upheld since the reign of Emperor Haile Selassie. The federal arrangement for Eritrea, decreed by the United Nations in 1952, underscores this fact. Until the Eritrean people affirmed their independence through a lot of sacrifice and a referendum, Eritrea remained under two Ethiopian regimes against the will of its people. The political ambitions expressed today by Ethiopia's current ruling party continue to reflect these enduring sentiments. These ambitions are persistent, and it appears it is likely that they will be raised over and over again by Ethiopian politicians.

This phenomenon has caused significant divisions in the region. If this renewed political rivalry persists, it could threaten regional security. With the addition of geopolitical dynamics and resulting proxy wars in our region, the evolution of these factors over the coming decades remains an unwritten story.

Given this potential political turbulence, Eritrea must define its position and consider the steps it must take to establish itself as a significant player in the global political and economic systems while maintaining its legitimate right to defend itself from foreign aggression.

What does Eritrea's positioning mean?

Eritrea's positioning fundamentally involves its capacity to anticipate and prepare for potential threats to national security. The first step in addressing this challenge is to acknowledge the existence of these threats. At the heart of this issue is the identification of internal and external threats that may arise in this region. Additionally, it is crucial to consider the causes of these threats and explore potential solutions to address them.

The world is keenly interested in the role Eritrea will play, not only in maintaining its internal security but also in its interactions on the global political stage. This is a complex issue because Eritrea's actions could conflict with the interests of the global community, potentially endangering its national security. Such a scenario might lead powerful nations to impose and enforce political, diplomatic, and economic measures against Eritrea.

In the eyes of the global community, Eritrea must strive to establish itself as a stabilizing and peaceful nation. Strong diplomatic efforts are crucial to demonstrate Eritrea's commitment to peace and regional stability while countering the perception that Eritrea is part of Ethiopia. Therefore, Eritrea's national security policy should be understood in this context:

What is deterrence?

For small nations, the idea of establishing and maintaining large standing armies is daunting because of their limited resources and capabilities. Moreover, they face the risk of engaging in conflicts with threats that far surpass their military and economic capacities, which presents a significant constraint. Consequently, the only viable option is to rely on a credible deterrent that aligns with their realities. One such option is adopting deterrence as a policy tool, which requires careful consideration and discussion of measures related to its implementation.

What does deterrence entail? Deterrence is a method that enables the proactive prevention of potential threats by acquiring predictive intelligence. It serves as a tool to avert anticipated military aggression by adversarial forces.

The use of deterrence as a policy in the national strategy of a small country is not a novel concept. Typically, this is achieved by emphasizing the advantages of peaceful resolutions rather than engaging in an arms race with aggressive strategies. Additionally, it is not uncommon for a country to adhere to a deterrence policy that employs high-impact defensive strategies. This includes training special forces, adopting missile defense strategies, and investing in areas such as drone technology, among others. For instance, Singapore relies on technology-enhanced compact armed forces.

Another effective deterrence tool for ensuring security and stability is the potential to join powerful military alliances such as NATO. Membership in defensive military alliances presents a valuable opportunity for smaller countries to defend themselves from aggression. The Baltic states, for instance, exemplify the security stability gained from NATO membership, with their contribution to security being evident. Similarly, the mutual defense treaty between the United States and the Philippines serves as another example.

Small countries can enhance their deterrence strategies by modernizing their defense capabilities. This can be achieved by acquiring advanced weapons systems or ensuring that their arsenal includes high-impact, low-cost weapons through arms procurement. Additionally, conducting joint military exercises with allied forces or treaty partners supports this strategy.

Forming strategic partnerships with major world powers is another option. Beyond tactical advantages, such alliances guarantee the security of smaller nations and facilitate access to intelligence from major nations. The extended deterrence support provided by the United States to South Korea illustrates this point, as do the relationships that countries such as Qatar and Kuwait maintain with the US.

Small nations employing deterrence as a defensive doctrine also focus on building credible and robust defensive forces to deter aggression. By reinforcing this with continuous military exercises, they effectively demonstrate their strength. Within the limits of their economic capacity, they also invest in acquiring strategic weapons that bolster deterrence, such as missiles, drones, and cyber defense, and in developing and training long-range special forces.

A strong, modern, and efficient national infrastructure, along with the establishment of civil defense capabilities, as seen in Switzerland and Finland, can significantly bolster a nation's deterrence policy. Ensuring that critical infrastructure, such as dams and communication networks, is safeguarded against threats is a crucial challenge. In today's technologically advanced world, where cyber-attacks pose significant risks, prioritizing cybersecurity is essential.

A successful deterrence strategy requires sending clear and unequivocal messages to adversarial countries. It is vital that adversaries understand the red lines small nations uphold and the national stability guarantees they have established. In situations similar to Eritrea's, issues of national sovereignty and territorial integrity are non-negotiable.

Deterrence demands both political and economic strength, along with resilience against potential vulnerabilities, such as those affecting dams and trade. To deter aggression, enhancing internal stability by establishing a robust governance system that secures a strong social foundation is crucial. This effort also involves employing outreach strategies to win the hearts and minds of the population.

Moreover, deterrence requires the development of advanced surveillance and intelligence capabilities and robust information exchange networks. Establishing an institution with predictive analytical capabilities that utilizes this information system is essential for taking preemptive measures against unforeseen threats and countering disinformation and political smear campaigns.

Deterrence necessitates both prioritization and adaptability to changing circumstances, laying the groundwork for a comprehensive understanding of the ever-evolving security landscape, its analysis, and subsequent proactive measures. Deterrence strategies must also adapt to technological and geopolitical shifts.

Diplomacy is a vital component of deterrent strategies. For smaller nations employing sophisticated diplomacy, the chance of securing allies or treaty partners during a crisis is substantial. By leveraging diplomacy, they can better prepare for potential threats to their national interests and security. However, it is crucial to maintain a balance between deterrence and diplomatic efforts. Deterrence should be demonstrative; it fulfills its purpose when supported by a credible threat of force and is paired with peaceful and discreet conflict-resolution efforts.

Countries that utilize deterrence as a strategy include:

- Singapore: Adheres to a deterrence policy known as the "Poisonous Shrimp Strategy," which emphasizes a small yet formidable force, bolstered by strong alliances.
- Switzerland: Employs armed neutrality, civil defense, and expertise in mountainous terrain as components of its deterrence strategy.
- Israel: Regularly implements layered deterrence, preemptive strikes, and a cyber warfare doctrine.

The national defense doctrine pursued by the Eritrean Government

Building a robust and professional defense capability is crucial for safeguarding a nation's sovereignty and territorial integrity. The formation of a professional military should not be intended for aggression or for resolving misunderstandings with neighbors through hostile means. Instead, it serves as a shield or deterrent, thereby enhancing national security. A capable and professional military enables a nation to confront threats and earn the respect and esteem of its neighboring countries.

Hostile standoffs between sovereign nations should be resolved through peaceful negotiations and diplomacy whenever possible. The brutal nature of war spares no one, and its consequences adversely impact everyone. The most effective way to prevent such conflicts is through the discreet resolution of these diplomatic tensions. For these reasons, diplomacy is fundamentally a tool of deterrence in international relations.

Substantial evidence indicates that the Eritrean government's defensive doctrine is not primarily focused on deterrence. The regime's national security strategy appears to draw from the obscure philosophy of "create facts on the ground, then negotiate." This approach does not view war as a last resort or as a measure to be taken only after exhausting all peaceful options. The military confrontations the regime has engaged in over the past thirty years with its neighbors—Yemen, Ethiopia, Djibouti, and Sudan—speak volumes about its behavior. As indicated in Chapter 6, there is also the pattern of meddling in neighboring countries, often times quite publicly.

The Eritrean government's defensive doctrine does not prioritize diplomacy or discretion. Moreover, since securing its sovereignty, Eritrea has been entangled in continuous hostile standoffs that have drained its human and economic resources. Consequently, Eritrea is economically strained and isolated from the global economy. Therefore, Eritrea's national defense philosophy must be reformed.

What is to be done?
As previously mentioned, Eritrea's strategic approach hinges on its capacity to anticipate and prepare for potential threats to national security. The first step in addressing this issue is to identify these threats, as noted above. Central to this is the recognition of both internal and external threats that may arise in this context, and to analyze the causes and

explore potential solutions to this problem. The Eritrean government's defense policy should include the following:

First: Becoming a hub of peace and stability

Eritrea must acknowledge the sensitivity of its position in the international political arena. Any actions or policy changes that conflict with the interests of the global community could have significant repercussions for Eritrea's national security, potentially prompting influential countries to impose political and diplomatic measures against Eritrea. Eritrea can adopt several strategies to defend against such potential threats.

Eritrea should strive to establish itself as a nation that promotes regional and global stability and peace. Strong diplomatic efforts are essential to demonstrate Eritrea's commitment to peace and regional stability and affirm its role as a security cornerstone in the region. Eritrea must recognize that the stability of Ethiopia and its surrounding areas is in its own and the region's best interest, and fostering relationships based on mutual interest and cooperation with neighboring countries should be a top priority. Consequently, it should demonstrate goodwill in addressing Ethiopia's as well as other neighboring countries' security concerns and propose solutions that adhere to international standards and principles, benefiting both countries. The only viable solution is one achieved through peaceful, discreet, as well as overt diplomatic channels.

Second: Building a modern and professional military as a deterrence mechanism

Establishing a compact, agile, and well-equipped modern military is crucial to Eritrea's deterrent strategy. It is not an exaggeration to say that the Eritrean military currently lacks professional attributes. This observation may seem disparaging, but that is not the intention. This should not be understood as an attempt to downplay the size, dedication, history, or military culture of the army. It is also important to note that some characteristics discussed regarding the Eritrean military may not apply to certain branches, such as the naval force, air force, and mechanized units.

A professional military is distinguished by its high level of discipline, training, and teamwork, which are critical traits that set it apart from a reserve army or conscript-based army. It is challenging to assert that the Eritrean military meets this standard.

A professional military is characterized by superior training, capability, and skill. It engages in rigorous physical and tactical training and is committed to expanding its expertise on weaponry. Continuous professional training, advanced courses, and specialized training, including airborne, commando, and urban warfare training, are integral components. Joint procedures and exercises with allies exemplify this collaboration. While the Eritrean military may have benefited from such training, it is difficult to claim that the training provided was adequate.

A professional military is distinguished by its strong discipline and a clearly defined chain of command, featuring officers with explicit rank structures and lines of responsibility and accountability. This framework is invaluable for enhancing decision-making and its implementation. However, it is challenging to assert that Eritrea possesses a military structure that adheres to this chain of command.

The Eritrean military suffers from a lack of institutional cohesion, with all units reporting directly to the President. These units are often discouraged from collaborating and are kept isolated to prevent any potential coup d'état or organized opposition to the regime. In its efforts to avert challenges to the government, the system actively takes steps to weaken and sow seeds of division in the military forces. Former Minister of Defense Mesfin Hagos notes that this weakening was achieved through inadequate training, the supply of outdated weapons, and the establishment of alternative military institutions, such as the reserve army, designed to diminish the regular army's power. Sources within Eritrea confirm that the President systematically undermined the military from playing its legitimate role right from the beginning and also displayed a lack of political will to build a professional army. This is known as "coup-proofing" in academic literature. Instead of fostering development, he suppressed it. Moreover, when a large number of fighters were demobilized, there was no policy to reorganize, restructure, or transform the military into a professional army (Hagos, 2023).

A professional military is governed by military law and is held accountable at every level, a standard not fully realized in Eritrea.

A professional military is equipped with modern tools, including weapons, machinery, drones, and communication devices, and relies on reliable supply lines for ammunition, fuel, food, and medical supplies. Even if the Eritrean military aspires to possess such equipment, it is difficult to claim that Eritrea's economy can adequately support this.

A professional military operates on a merit-based career ladder system that encourages its members to remain in the profession for extended periods. This system is crucial for deciding whether to pursue a lifelong military career. However, in Eritrea, various sources indicate that military ranks have remained stagnant for nearly thirty years, with promotions being rare.

A professional military upholds a robust ethical code and adheres to the laws of war, fostering camaraderie and trust among its members and reinforcing their confidence in its mission. Unfortunately, this characteristic is not fully apparent in the behavior of the Eritrean military. It is easy to understand how the morale of conscripts can wane during an indefinite national service period.

Another crucial aspect is that a professional military is subordinate to a legitimate civilian government elected by the people and serves the constitution, remaining impartial to domestic politics. In contrast, the Eritrean military is not subordinate to any legitimate civilian government but serves a single individual: the President. It lacks impartiality in the country's domestic politics, with most middle- and high-ranking officers being members of the ruling party (PFDJ).

A professional military adheres to well-defined recruitment standards that emphasize physical and mental qualifications. Members of such a military enjoy comprehensive benefits, including health insurance, leaves, and pensions. In contrast, Eritrea's military lacks clear recruitment criteria and comprises national service members and a reserve army. These army members are not salaried employees and do not receive any benefits. Moreover, they do not view military service as a career choice.

Considering the factors mentioned above, it is difficult to claim that the Eritrean military possesses the attributes of a professional army. Therefore, Eritrea should prioritize the development of a strong and well-equipped defensive force. By supplementing this with regular military exercises, the country can further enhance its reputation. As Eritrea achieves higher economic levels, it should also aim to acquire strategic weapons that strengthen deterrence, such as missiles, drones, and cyber defense systems, while establishing and training various special forces to achieve its national security goals.

Infrastructure development and enhancement of civil defense capabilities can further support deterrence strategies. Ensuring the resilience of critical infrastructure against threats is vital to national security. In today's technologically advanced world, where cyberattacks pose significant risks, prioritizing cybersecurity is essential.

One of the Eritrean government's primary responsibilities is to ensure internal stability, defend national sovereignty, and enhance citizen security. This is a top priority, drawing on the rich experiences—both positive and negative—accumulated over the past decades and considering the commitment and goodwill of its members and citizens to build an agile, modern, merit-based, and professional army capable of safeguarding national security. Embarking on security-sector reform should thus be crucial or a priority of a transitional Eritrea.

Third: Establishing a military academy

With over thirty years of accumulated experience and the commitment and support of its citizens and members, the Eritrean government was uniquely positioned to develop a modern, efficient, and professional military force to safeguard the nation's security. Establishing a military academy focused on teaching contemporary military theory and practical skills relevant to Eritrea would have produced a core group of military officers or a military elite dedicated to lifelong professional excellence in the service of the country. Additionally, the military academy could have functioned as a significant research and documentation hub for the military history of the Eritrean Liberation Army (ELA) and the Eritrean People's Liberation Army (EPLA), preserving their rich heritage for future generations.

There was a significant opportunity to establish a military academy aimed at developing a professional military. However, the leader undermined the regular army by implementing the "National Service" program. This policy was crafted to prevent the military from functioning as an institution, whether intentionally or not. No one can explain better than Mesfin Hagos, the former Minister of Defense, how the military was transformed into the personal property of a single individual, the President. Mesfin, a member of the G-15 group, served in Isaias's cabinet. In his 2023 book, "The African Revolution Reclaimed," he details how Isaias dismantled the army and turned it into his personal tool. According to veteran fighter Mesfin Hagos, Isaias treated the military as his own property: after approving the budget, instead of granting the Minister some operational freedom, Isaias would manage things himself or dictate actions without consultation. Mesfin further elaborates on how such failures—weak institutionalization and professionalism, coupled with excessive presidential interference—have weakened the military as an institution and harmed the country. Mesfin does not stop there; he describes how the President of the State of Eritrea consequently dismantled his ministerial position and the ministry as an institution: "The ministry's key departments were gradually eroded, creating confusion and conflict among them, damaging their personal and professional relationships. The tragedy was reflected in five institutions: the Air Force, the Naval Force, the National Service, the Ground Force, and the Office of the Minister. (Hagos, 2023)."

This operational approach has damaged the Eritrean military. It is also crucial to note that this is one of the factors contributing to Eritrea's weakness as a nation. Furthermore, it should be mentioned that undermining the Ministry of Defense weakens civilian control of the military.

Fourth: Establishing a robust governance system

To mitigate aggression, Eritrea must build a strong social foundation by implementing a governance system grounded in the rule of law and accountability that garners widespread support from the people. A governance system weakened by corruption fails to earn public trust, leading to a deterioration of the relationship between the people and their government. This erosion of trust poses a potential threat to national security.

Fifth: Membership in military alliances or pacts

Given Eritrea's relatively small size and limited resources, the government should consider developing strategies to counter potential military imbalances by forming alliances with major and powerful nations. Such alliances play a crucial role in deterring external threats to the state. Moreover, Eritrea should explore the possibility of aligning itself with major world powers through strategic partnerships. Beyond offering tactical advantages, these partnerships bolster national security. The primary aim of such alliances should be to enhance Eritrea's security and that of the surrounding region.

Sixth: Pursuing smart diplomacy

Sovereign nations function as nation-states in the diplomatic arena to negotiate, advance their interests, and form various alliances. Globalization has ushered in unprecedented levels of interdependence worldwide, making nation-states reliant on one another. This interdependence creates a scenario in which the survival, let alone the development, of individual nations hinges on their integration into the global community. To thrive in an interconnected world, countries must understand the rules of engagement with other nations. Failing to do so increases the risk of weakening and isolation. It is undeniable that acquiring a comprehensive understanding of the global system's rules and the wisdom to navigate them is essential. The common global practice, even if not universally followed, is to pursue national interests without causing harm or aggression to others. In international diplomacy, this means creating conditions in which all parties involved find a win-win solution.

By understanding and respecting certain international norms and creating and utilizing common ground, countries can ensure regional peace and stability, promote growth and development, learn from each other, and coordinate effectively. Sovereignty serves as a tool that allows a nation to determine its political role without being confined to any single bloc.

Fostering warm and genuine relationships with neighboring countries, grounded in respect for sovereignty and territorial integrity within a framework of partnership, mutual respect, and trust, is crucial for any nation seeking respect from its neighbors. Beyond bolstering national security, this approach can lay the foundation for countries in the region to build a stable and prosperous future for themselves. In regions marked by instability, additional efforts are necessary to develop the capacity to regulate, manage, improve, and resolve these situations. Sovereignty is a vital principle that opens up opportunities to form strategic partnerships with other sovereign nations.

Therefore, Eritrea should prioritize broadening its perspective on global and regional conditions and formulate and implement a foreign policy aimed at fostering regional peace and stability, which would help avert potential conflicts.

Military standoffs between Eritrea and its neighboring countries (Yemen, Djibouti, Ethiopia, and, to some extent, Sudan) were not entirely unavoidable. Even if each of these events had its own triggers, there was no inherent reason for them to begin or end with hostility.

Eritrea stands to gain from policies that adhere to these principles. It also had the opportunity to leverage its sovereignty to its advantage. However, Eritrea has now crafted a foreign policy that has isolated it from the world, rendering it a pariah state without partners or allies. This situation has significantly endangered the country's sovereignty.

Eritrea's outreach strategy should project the image of a peaceful and stable nation. However, as a sovereign nation, it also has a duty to clearly articulate its non-negotiable red lines.

Seventh: Building a strong economy

National defense is rooted in a strong economy. Maintaining a military equipped with 21st-century technology, preventing obsolescence, and ensuring a reliable logistics supply chain is inconceivable when based on a subsistence economy. Sustaining a deterrence strategy in a fragile economy is challenging, especially one that relies solely on remittances and subsistence economies. Wars deplete economies and bring destruction, a reality that seems to be overlooked in Eritrea. Eritrea must develop a robust economy that can withstand such crises. A strong economy supports investments in building a modern military, which involves crafting sound economic policies, enhancing domestic production capacity, fostering an investment-friendly environment, and expanding human capital. To unlock its economic potential, Eritrea must leverage appropriate technologies and investments.

Eritrea possesses untapped potential that could lead to a thriving economy in the future. To harness this potential, it must focus on harmonizing domestic policies and adopting strategies that attract foreign investment and technology. This approach can fully unleash domestic production capabilities. By pursuing bilateral trade agreements, Eritrea can foster mutually beneficial trade and economic partnerships with various regional and global partners. It is essential to eliminate policies that deter investors and to implement policies that encourage and attract them. Another asset is Eritrea's diaspora, which, if properly engaged, could significantly contribute to economic growth and enhance national security.

Eighth: Acquiring strong and advanced surveillance and intelligence capability

Eritrea must develop advanced surveillance and intelligence capabilities, complemented by robust information exchange networks. Establishing an institution with predictive analytical capabilities through this information system is essential for effective deterrence. This approach enables preemptive measures against unforeseen threats and counteracts the spread of disinformation. Additionally, it facilitates a thorough understanding of the ever-changing security landscape, allowing for analysis and proactive measures. Eritrea's deterrence strategy must adapt to technological and geopolitical shifts.

In an interview with Muza TV on March 30, 2025, Colonel (Engineer) Biniam Tewelde, then a member of the Ethiopian National Intelligence and Security Service (NISS), highlighted the Eritrean government's vulnerability to digital attacks. The NISS revealed that since Hagos Ghebrehiwet

(Head of Economic Affairs for the PFDJ) email was completely compromised, they had access to all information regarding Eritrea's relations with China. Furthermore, the Ethiopian institution claimed to have obtained information from the cyber department of the Eritrean Ministry of Defense regarding the weapons Eritrea was purchasing from Russia. Similarly, they monitored communications between the offices of the president of Eritrea on the one hand, and Qatar, and Saudi Arabia on the other. Eritrea must take significant steps to prevent such threats and build resilience against cyberattacks.

Conclusion

The challenge of direct defense due to limited resources underscores the strategic significance of deterrence in ensuring national security. Within this framework, it is essential to adopt policies and strategies that are effective and cost-efficient. Establishing a professional army is crucial, and cybersecurity plays an indispensable role. Alliances bolster security by providing multiplier effects, whereas earning the respect of adversaries can be achieved through astute diplomatic efforts.

Small nations with strong economies and social structures typically encounter fewer security challenges. Therefore, the Government of Eritrea should prioritize building a robust economy. Shifting from a subsistence economy to a diversified economy can reduce vulnerability to aggression. A small country should also focus on influencing its adversary's perception. Employing effective communication channels, propaganda, and cyber techniques is essential for shaping and manipulating an adversary's mindset. Countering enemy propaganda is vital for maintaining domestic morale and preventing vulnerabilities.

Chapter 10

The Pursuit of Smart Diplomacy

DIPLOMACY SERVES AS a fundamental political instrument for sovereign states, aiming to manage bilateral relations and connections between these territorial entities while facilitating legal activities. The Westphalian principles of sovereignty and territorial statehood, established in the mid-seventeenth century, underpin the contemporary multilateral diplomatic system.

Recently, globalization has emerged as a phenomenon that brings countries with varying levels of economic development and political systems closer. This process shifts the focus from national characteristics to international ones, encompassing interdependence, production and distribution systems, and market integration. Since the emergence of this phenomenon, the world has witnessed structural changes that were previously nonexistent. These changes include the free movement of capital and people, qualitative and quantitative expansion of financial activities, rapid development and enhancement of communication networks, swift dissemination of knowledge, mutual dependencies, and increasing inequality among nations.

Another notable aspect of globalization is its significant contribution to boosting productivity. This process, which has taken centuries to reach its current stage, represents deepening economic integration from an economic perspective. It includes an internationally organized free exchange of capital, services, technology, and labor in the global market. Moreover, the promotion of free market liberalization and the facilitation of communication technology have accelerated globalization.

Globalization is said to create opportunities for developed countries, allowing them to leverage their economic and technological superiority to exploit these opportunities. In contrast, some scholars suggest that developing countries have not sufficiently benefited from globalization. Low educational levels, unskilled human capacity, inadequate technological capabilities, and the presence of underdeveloped institutions are cited as hindrances.

Diplomacy has undergone a significant transformation with the emergence of multilateral organizations. Beyond nation-states, various multilateral organizations, international non-governmental organizations, and other private actors or stakeholders have begun to engage in diplomacy, actively shaping its form in response to the rapidly changing global political, economic, and social landscapes. This evolution has led to multilateral diplomacy involving multiple stakeholders and participants. In his book "Modern Diplomacy," Barston describes what he terms "New Diplomacy" as follows:

> In the diplomacy conducted at the United Nations, a single diplomat's mandate typically encompasses the following objectives: formal representation of their country, gathering information, conducting discussions or studies that form the basis for policy or other objectives, promoting reconciliation between nations, and participating in the amendment of regulatory laws (Barston, 2006).

The manner in which nation-states conduct diplomacy varies by nation. Some are small, whereas others are large. Some have centuries of diplomatic experience, whereas others are newcomers. Some are on the path to development, while others are already economically advanced. Their political systems also differ significantly from one another. Although diplomacy is often conducted openly, the world also witnesses secret diplomacy or a combination of both forms. The sophistication of diplomacy varies according to each country's conditions, too. Despite this, one truth remains: regardless of the form or type of diplomacy, the ultimate goal is the pursuit of national interests. In other words, diplomacy is the means by which a country pursues its strategic interests externally as a continuation of its domestic policy.

The diplomacy practiced by the United States and other economically developed countries is both diverse and complex. The skills required by diplomatic institutions vary, and their focus on trade and other commercial activities is significant.

Currently, all diplomatic missions and interest sections prioritize economic and political activities. In other words, the art of diplomacy must consider all the factors mentioned above. Economic diplomacy is one such tool that can be used.

Global Interdependence

We live in a constantly evolving and interconnected world. Technological advancements and globalization have intensified interactions among governments, and the rapid flow of information has shaped people's worldviews, empowering them to make informed decisions about their futures. When effectively harnessed, this information offers opportunities for further development. However, our world faces environmental threats, a widening gap between the North and South, persistent nuclear threats, and domestic conflicts aimed at regime change. Additionally, entities with sophisticated political agendas operate within this landscape.

Diplomacy has established channels and platforms to address these challenges, aiding in the resolution of various global security threats, including nuclear dangers, international conflicts, and famine-related issues. The comprehensive nature of diplomacy underpins the existence of an international system, despite its complexity, and plays a crucial role in managing global changes.

Enhancing universal security is a critical function of diplomacy, encompassing both political and economic dimensions, as economic security is a fundamental human right. This enables people worldwide to live with dignity and peace and fosters a prosperous world through collective efforts. Engaging in diplomacy that includes all members of the global community—politicians, business leaders, non-governmental organizations, religious institutions, artists, celebrities, academics, research institutions, government officials, ordinary citizens, women, other concerned groups, and trade unions—strengthens collaboration between governmental and nongovernmental stakeholders.

Fundamental tenets of small states' foreign policy

Multilateralism as a Core Strategy: Small states actively engage with international organizations to amplify their voices on the global stage. Advocating for international law is another crucial belief, as they strive to contribute to the United Nations' structure without exclusion and aim to curb the dominance of powerful nations. They also need to promote the necessity of building coalitions, leveraging diplomatic strength, and increasing their political weight. These coalitions can be formed around various themes, with the fight against climate change serving as a prime example.

(Active) Neutrality is another essential tool, yet it is preferable to demonstrate flexibility, dynamism, and adaptability in its application. Avoiding burdensome blocs can be seen as a means of maintaining neutrality. Membership in protective frameworks that guarantee security is also crucial, as evidenced by Latvia's beneficial membership in the North Atlantic Treaty Organization (NATO), which includes other Baltic and Nordic countries.

Pursuing regional integration is another important strategy for accessing benefits that are unavailable within one's own country. It facilitates comprehensive collaboration and consultation, sometimes creating opportunities for neighboring countries with shared interests to engage in joint diplomatic training and experience exchanges. They also share available information. The Intergovernmental Authority on Development (IGAD) serves as an example, although its effectiveness depends on proper utilization by member states.

Enhancing visibility necessitates conducting or organizing international events and the deployment of tools such as public diplomacy. The practice of diplomats rotating between countries over time also broadens their experience. Neutrality is inherently advantageous, and public diplomacy is crucial to maintaining it. For instance, Rwanda sponsored the English football club Arsenal to change the global perception of the nation.

As detailed in Chapter 8, engaging with the diaspora is another diplomatic tool used to connect a country with host nations.

Being a small country can be challenging, but it does not impede creativity or innovation. In fact, it fosters ingenuity and innovation. Small states must be resourceful in transforming challenges into growth opportunities. The Baltic states, Austria, Switzerland, Singapore, and Nordic countries have become significant international stakeholders by adding value and seizing favorable opportunities, despite their size. Singapore's pragmatic policies and strong alliances forged through diplomacy exemplify this phenomenon.

Challenges of small states

Small states encounter distinct challenges that can influence their foreign policies. Notable examples include limited resources, geopolitical vulnerability, and the inequitable structure of the global system. The evolving global landscape and its implications often exacerbate these disadvantages. However, this does not mean that there are no strategic tools to overcome these limitations. Some of these include:

The dominance of major global powers, especially in international forums, often sidelines smaller countries. These dominant forces frequently use their economic and other forms of influence, including veto power, to pressure smaller states to adopt specific political stances or maintain neutrality in the marketplace of ideas. To counteract this, forming coalitions with other similar small states is essential, as it can bolster their collective bargaining power and amplify their individual voices.

Resource scarcity hinders the establishment of a global presence. To address this, strategies such as reducing the number of embassies, establishing embassies that represent multiple small states, or appointing a single diplomat to represent several countries should be considered. Additionally, some countries commonly house their embassies within other friendly embassies in host nations, which helps them utilize resources efficiently.

Small states may find themselves reliant on powerful nations in specific trade sectors, often due to historical factors such as colonialism or geopolitical conditions. Diversifying their trade partners offers a solution, providing opportunities for alternative approaches and the potential to gain leverage in competitive markets.

As outlined in Chapter 9, small states often find the prospect of building and maintaining large standing armies daunting because of their limited resources. Additionally, they may encounter security threats that exceed their military and economic capabilities. For these states, the judicious use of neutrality as a strategic tool is crucial to their survival.

To bolster this approach, engaging in collective security agreements and participating in joint military exercises are essential. Qatar, the UAE, Djibouti, and the Baltic states serve as examples. Furthermore, the potential for membership in powerful military alliances represents another facet of neutrality that can ensure the country's security. Mastering conflict resolution is also a vital diplomatic tool.

In geopolitics, powerful nations can compel small states to take sides. In such scenarios, employing neutrality as a tool proves advantageous, as evidenced by the consequences of abstaining from the vote. It is a common diplomatic practice for small states representing diverse interests to adopt such positions when caught in political turbulence. The following examples are considered:

Singapore: This nation has evolved from an impoverished island into a global hub. A key aspect of its foreign policy is delicately balancing its relationships with the United States and China. Singapore maintains favorable ties with both nations, treating them equally and reaping the benefits of its agreements with each country. This long-standing strategy underpins its neutrality.

Rwanda: The 1994 genocide against one ethnic group in Rwanda shocked the world. Since then, Rwanda has diligently worked to restore its tarnished reputation by focusing on post-conflict resilience building initiatives. It promotes itself on the global stage with the slogan "We are building the 'Singapore of Africa'." Rwanda has established a diplomatic academy to cultivate skilled diplomats, thereby highlighting the significance of diplomacy.

In general, for small states, demonstrating flexibility to turn disadvantages into advantages, investing in human capacity development, and anchoring their politics to international law are crucial for their survival. These states ensure their existence not by striving for power but by consistently practicing astute diplomacy.

Eritrea's foreign policy

Eritrea's foreign policy is a complex interplay of regional dynamics, historical injustices against the nation, and the characteristics of its internal domestic situation. To comprehend Eritrea's foreign policy, one must examine its relationships with neighboring countries, its perception of external threats, and the nature of its political system.

Historically, Eritrea has been embroiled in a political and armed struggle for fifty years (1941–1991). For over thirty years following independence, it has been entangled in low-intensity political and diplomatic conflicts. This situation is further complicated by the war between Eritrea and Ethiopia from 1998 to 2000 and the subsequent 'no war, no peace' state, which has contributed to the region's tense political landscape.

In the 1940s, when the question of Eritrea's fate arose, unlike other countries under Italian colonial rule, Eritrea was federated with Ethiopia and was later annexed. This decision was made to serve the strategic interests of Western powers, causing significant resentment among Eritreans who supported independence.

Between 1961 and 1991, Eritrea faced an unfavorable global political climate in its quest for independence from Ethiopia. Positioned between two opposing blocs and lacking support, Eritrea remained steadfast in its pursuit of victory despite overwhelming odds. After a hard-fought war for independence, marked by numerous sacrifices, it achieved an unparalleled victory. The West, due to its policy shift regarding Eritrea in the 1940s, continued to act as a partner for Ethiopia.

With the political changes in Ethiopia in 1974-75, the socialist bloc, led by the Soviet Union, sided with the Derg regime, offering political, diplomatic, economic, and military support to expand its sphere of influence in Africa. Additionally, the Organization of African Unity (now the African Union) maintained a biased stance toward Eritrea. Under these circumstances, Eritrea had no choice but to rely on its own resources, thus embracing self-reliance in the process.

In addition to its self-reliance, Eritrea has significantly benefited from the support of Arab countries, although this support was not always consistent. The backers of the Eritrean cause varied in their levels of assistance and motivations, including Egypt, Sudan, Iraq, Syria, Yemen, Algeria, Saudi Arabia, Kuwait, and Qatar.

Another strategic decision for Eritrea was to forge an alliance with the opposition forces in Ethiopia. Despite the challenges faced along the way, this alliance achieved its intended purpose. The overthrow of the Derg regime by the Eritrean People's Liberation Front in Eritrea and the Ethiopian People's Revolutionary Democratic Front (EPRDF) in Ethiopia, leading to the establishment of new governments in both countries, clearly demonstrates the success of the collaboration of these two forces.

The Eritrean Nationalist Movements, namely the EPLF and ELF, forged robust alliances with progressive movements active in the West. These connections were instrumental in aligning their struggles with the people they represented, thereby securing political, moral, and material support.

As emphasized in Chapter 8, recognizing the Eritrean diaspora's rise as a formidable force is essential, given their significant contributions and numerous sacrifices in Eritrea's pursuit of independence. Both the Eritrean People's Liberation Front and the Eritrean Liberation Front, isolated from major global political players—the Western bloc led by America and the socialist bloc led by the Soviet Union—organized the diaspora into mass organizations, utilizing them as a substantial political force and a source of financial support. Members of the diaspora engaged in impactful public diplomacy, linking the just struggle of the Eritrean people with the global community, thereby making an invaluable contribution to the struggle's success and ultimate victory.

Post-Independence

As previously noted, Eritrea's foreign policy is profoundly shaped by its history of independence struggles and the region's political dynamics. Some regional experts assert that Eritrea's foreign policy is rooted in self-reliance. Some political analysts argue that Eritrea's approach is defensive, pragmatic, and sovereignty-centered. Additionally, other experts in the area suggest that Eritrea adopt a stance of non-interference, avoid major political blocs, and harbor suspicion towards Western countries. These observers argue that Eritrea perceives Western nations as attempting to undermine its national sovereignty.

The governments of Eritrea and Ethiopia have consistently maintained a relationship characterized by rivalry, despite occasional warmth. Eritrea and Djibouti have ongoing border disputes, whereas Eritrea has fostered positive relations with Gulf countries. Some political analysts contend that the mutual political interest in combating extremism in the region underpins the strong relationship between Gulf Arab countries and Eritrea.

Eritrea has continued to strengthen its ties with China and Russia, focusing on trade and diplomatic support. In the Middle East, its relations remain balanced, with Arab countries on one side and Iran on the other.

Owing to its authoritarian political system and its role in destabilizing the Horn of Africa, Eritrea remains isolated from the international community. The United Nations sanctions imposed on Eritrea from 2009 to 2018 exemplify this isolation, stemming from Eritrea's alleged support for the Somali militant political movement Al-Shabaab.

Eritrea has not fostered good relationships with its neighbors based on mutual respect and cooperation. Establishing such relationships does not appear to be a priority on its foreign policy agenda, however. Sporadic military conflicts between Eritrea and its neighbors—Yemen, Djibouti, Ethiopia, and, to some extent, Sudan—serve as evidence. These conflicts were entirely unnecessary and avoidable. Although each of these events had specific triggers, there was no reason why they could not be resolved through negotiations.

Eritrea's weak ties with regional bodies, such as the IGAD and the African Union, and international organizations, such as the United Nations, have allowed it to distance itself from the international community. Its alignment with countries such as North Korea and Belarus in supporting Russia's war in Ukraine reflects the misguided policies of the Eritrean government. The government's biased stance on the two-state solution to the Palestinian issue is another example.

Eritrea's apprehension towards other political actors is more accurately attributed to its self-imposed isolation. This also mirrors a panicked mindset of "they are coming to attack us." The regime appears resolute in advancing its interests, often at the expense of others. While Eritrea strives to forge strategic alliances with countries such as China, it seems reluctant to take sides. Its influence in the region remains marginal, vacillating between conflict and diplomacy.

As discussed in Chapter 9, the diplomacy practiced by the Eritrean government appears to lack a foundation in a philosophy of neutrality and is not driven by a strategic vision. The regime's national security doctrine is based on the ambiguous principle of "create facts on the ground, then negotiate," as mentioned in previous chapters. This doctrine does not view war as a last resort or as a consequence of exhausting all peaceful options. The Eritrean government does not prioritize engagement in diplomacy or forums. As a result of this flawed policy, Eritrea has been embroiled in continuous conflict since gaining sovereignty, leading to significant human sacrifices and economic decline. Consequently, Eritrea has become economically devastated and isolated from the global community.

As outlined in Chapter 1, the latest evolution in Eritrea-Ethiopia dynamics, following brief cordial relations between President Isaias and Prime Minister Abiy, warrants attention. Ethiopia's pursuit of Red Sea access and control has intensified the strained bilateral ties that have persisted since the 1998-2000 War. As an independent nation, Eritrea is entitled to protect itself against this threat through political and military means. Robust diplomatic efforts are also essential to address these challenges. The Eritrean government must approach major global powers—the US, EU, China, and Russia —and make a well calculated plea for peace and support. This can be argued from a moral standpoint, representing all Eritreans. Action is required to harness regional and international initiatives to address these issues. By speaking with one voice, Eritrea can effectively urge the UN, IGAD and the African Union to move beyond statements and apply diplomatic pressure on Ethiopia to abandon its maritime ambitions and follow international law.

Triggers of Eritrea's foreign policy doctrine

The primary reason for adhering to the aforementioned foreign policy is the lack of understanding of issues related to world order. In today's interconnected world, globalization has fostered interdependence among nations, creating a scenario in which survival, let alone development, is challenging without understanding the rules of engagement. A country must grasp these rules to assert its presence in the globalized world; otherwise, it risks marginalization and isolation from the global community. It is undeniable that a sovereign state lacking comprehensive knowledge or perspective on the world order and the skills to navigate the global system cannot succeed in the modern world.

The global order is also increasingly shifting toward a multipolar structure, driven by several interconnected developments. First, the relative influence of the United States has receded, a consequence of costly overseas engagements and deepening political divisions at home. Concurrently, China has risen to become a formidable peer competitor, wielding substantial economic and military power. Further contributing to this diffusion of power is the renewed assertiveness of Russia, which leverages its military capabilities and energy resources to disrupt the status quo. Economically, the impressive growth of major developing nations—such as India, Indonesia, and Brazil—has expanded their global weight and autonomy. Underpinning all these trends is the engine of globalization, which, by dispersing technology, investment, and knowledge worldwide, has systematically lowered the barriers for new centers of power to emerge.

The prevailing global agenda, even if not apparent to all sovereign states, is to expand national interests without harming others. In international diplomacy, this involves creating conditions for win-win solutions for all parties involved. By understanding and adhering to international norms and finding common ground, countries can foster regional peace, stability, prosperity, and growth. It seems that the Eritrean government has not fully grasped the principles of flexible and smart foreign policy.

The second factor is the spirit of suspicion in Asmara towards other political actors or powers, whether Western or otherwise. As mentioned earlier, Eritrea perceives the West's policy with suspicion and believes it is aimed at undermining its sovereignty. The President of Eritrea's speeches, particularly on Independence Day and in interviews on Eri-TV, reflect Eritrea's foreign policy stance towards the West. This does not mean that Eritrea does not try to appease and improve its relations with the West; however, there is a lack of consistency. To illustrate, here are a few examples.

The ad-hoc foreign policy initiatives that Eritrea tried to project can be summarized by the following examples: -

- In 2003, during the Iraq war, Eritrea demonstrated its desire to contribute on the global stage by expressing its willingness to join the US-led coalition force known as the "Coalition of the Willing."
- Eritrea was also open to allowing the US to establish a military base on the Dahlak Islands. In 2002, The Washington Post highlighted the ongoing

- backchannel communications between the US and Eritrea, facilitated by lobbyists.
- Although the details were not disclosed to the public, the cooperation agreement Eritrea recently signed with Italy serves as another example.
- Recently, President Isaias has displayed his incoherent mental state on various regional platforms, such as those in China, Russia, South Africa, Kenya, and Saudi Arabia. For an observer, it is astonishing to witness a leader who is unable to provide basic living conditions for his citizens yet lectures world leaders about international cooperation and the new world order that he envisions.
- The Eritrean government's recent decision to withdraw from IGAD, made without consulting the National Assembly and the Cabinet, clearly demonstrates its reckless and misguided foreign policy. Eritrea withdrew from IGAD twice: first in 2007 and then again in December 2025 after a brief reactivation in 2023. The country initially joined the group in 1993. While the government cited official reasons for its departure, the underlying cause is widely believed to be President Isaias Afwerki's intolerance for any organization he cannot control.

Third, the Eritrean government's immense ego, particularly that of President Isaias, and their profound disdain for the world are evident. To illustrate this, consider an article I wrote under the pseudonym Tedros Tesfay in 2000.

> The Front (People's Front for Democracy and Justice) believes it alone knows what benefits Ethiopia, Uganda, Sudan, Congo, the region, and the world. Similarly, it claims to understand what is good and what is bad for international non-governmental organizations. The Front fails to recognize that other entities have their own legitimate interests to protect, values to uphold, and ideas to which they are committed. The

Front lacks insight into how others think and does not permit them to be judged. (Tesfay, 2001)

In an article I wrote under the pen name Zeineb Ali, the regime's nature is described as follows:

> The government pursues an aggressive foreign policy, essentially one of brinkmanship. It views bullying others as a strength and political skill. The President's character is not that of a wise leader. In terms of conflict resolution with other countries, the regime disregards international rules or norms, opting for force over diplomacy. Its relationships with Yemen, Sudan, Ethiopia, and Djibouti exemplify this quarrelsome and vindictive nature. Its stubbornness was apparent in the initial efforts to resolve the border misunderstanding with Ethiopia through violence. The regime's adventurous foreign policy was tested in the Democratic Republic of Congo and Somalia, pushing for its national interests at the expense of others. (Ali, 2021)

Fourth, the regime's foreign policy is irrational or inconsistent, suggesting that it is not based on a thorough study or national vision. At times, the President insists on one course of action, only to unexpectedly relent under pressure from powerful external actors. This indicates subsiding stubbornness and yielding to external forces. An authority who wished to remain anonymous for safety reasons provided the following example:

When the dispute between Eritrea and Djibouti was brought before the UN Security Council, it was agreed in principle, without a formal decision, that the global force present would take deterrent measures. Upon hearing this warning, the President of Eritrea became agitated, contacted the Emir of Qatar, and promptly expressed his readiness to fill the gaps in global forces. Qatar immediately dispatched a peacekeeping force within a few days.

According to an anonymous (and reliable) source, the second inconsistency involves the United Arab Emirates' (UAE) efforts to establish a military base at the Port of Assab. Despite no formal allegations against Eritrea for supporting the Houthi militia in Yemen, the UAE succeeded in putting pressure on the Eritrean government setting up a military base at the Port of Assab after bombings in Mai Edaga and the Bisha Mining Company (which it subsequently used against Yemen). If the accusation is true, this event signifies a major shift in the alignment of forces.

Another event concerns the "senseless war" of 1998-2000, declared by the leaders of Eritrea and Ethiopia on various occasions. This peace agreement was slated for implementation after Eritrea accepted the peace initiative led by the international community, with the US and Rwanda at the forefront, following the Ethiopian army's occupation of a significant portion of Eritrean territory. It is worth recalling that Eritrea remained intransigent to the call made by the US-Rwanda delegation once the war erupted.

Conclusion

Nations cannot choose their neighbors, and the destinies of neighboring countries are inherently linked. Changes in one country can significantly impact others, and neighboring nations often face similar challenges. Issues such as climate change, the refugee crisis, the rise of political extremism, and efforts to combat illegal human trafficking, drug trafficking, and other illicit activities are prime examples of this.

Whether divided by borders or other interests, history shows that conflicts between neighboring countries require global attention. Resolving these conflicts necessitates adherence to international laws and regulations, with war being the last resort. Some countries have endured border disputes for decades, yet the process of growth continues even when third-party mediation occurs.

For any nation seeking stability, it is crucial to establish genuine and positive relationships with neighboring countries, grounded in partnership, mutual benefit, and respect for sovereignty and territorial integrity. This approach not only enhances national security but also lays the groundwork for a stable and prosperous future in the region. However, in regions marked by instability, additional efforts are needed to build the capacity to manage, control, and eliminate these conditions.

Therefore, Eritrea should prioritize formulating and implementing a foreign policy that enhances its ability to understand global perspectives and the evolving world order while striving to secure regional peace and avert potential crises.

The war between Eritrea and Ethiopia, which resulted in this unfortunate outcome, was avoidable. Leaders from both nations have acknowledged it as a "senseless war." The conflict extended beyond a simple border dispute, encompassing geopolitical calculations of dominance, influence, and strength in political, economic, and military terms. Factors such as trade exchanges and port usage also contributed to the conflict. Ultimately, resolution was destined to occur at the negotiating table. The inability of both regimes to address this issue with skill and wisdom underscores a lack of vision and maturity. The Ethiopian regime's refusal to accept the UN's fair border ruling was an unforgivable political misstep that worsened the situation. The global community's observation of this development and its silence reveal a profound level of hypocrisy, amounting to an act of betrayal by all accounts.

Chapter 11

Partnership, Not Patronage: Reframing International Development

Assistance as it stands now

The recent withdrawal of foreign aid administered by USAID under the Trump Administration ignited widespread discussion and concern across various platforms in the US. This abrupt cessation halted the flow of critical assistance, significantly impacting vital sectors such as basic health, education, and other essential services. The ripple effects of this decision have not only stirred commotion within the international community but have also caught several governments that rely on this aid off guard. Such a shift in policy is poised to alter the international perception of the United States as a significant player on the global stage. To say the least, the secondary ramifications of this action are severe. Due to the sudden stop in funding, thousands of jobs disappeared in both local and international contexts, leaving many families struggling to survive. The way the Administration labeled the agency (USAID) as a "criminal organization" run by "a bunch of radical lunatics" is also deeply concerning.

In another development, we are witnessing other Western donors cutting back on foreign assistance. The UK is slashing its aid budget by

40% to boost its defense. France, the most generous Western donor after America, will reduce its aid by 35% this year. Germany is also considering similar measures.

This situation invites a deeper exploration of foreign aid and development cooperation. It raises important questions about how developing nations view foreign assistance: Should it be regarded as a perpetual lifeline, or should nations prepare for a future where such support may eventually cease, necessitating a transformation towards more sustainable practices? This challenge could also serve as a wake-up call for countries that have long depended on external aid to rethink their strategies. Rather than relying largely on foreign assistance, should these nations not consider pooling their resources and efforts to foster development more robustly and enduringly? Is it not time to make tough choices? These issues require further deliberation.

In light of these developments, it is crucial to contemplate what this paradigm shift entails and how developing countries can leverage this situation to create opportunities for growth and self-sufficiency.

Understanding development

Development is a dynamic process that empowers individuals to achieve a better life by meeting their basic needs, fostering innovation, and creating opportunities for a better future. It should primarily be carried out within the framework of a nation's developmental policies, which consider the socio-economic architecture of societies and are supported by sound strategies. Development should be a locally driven initiative aimed at addressing local priorities and needs of the people. Effective development occurs when strong institutions and good governance are in place, enabling the meaningful tapping of domestic resources and forging partnerships with development partners who may provide technology, expertise, and financing. However, this external support must not replace the vital efforts and commitment of local communities, with their unique contexts and aspirations shaping their development strategies. Economic growth can be achieved, and foreign assistance works best where governments are already on the right track, establishing priorities, implementing policies, and developing key institutions for their own reasons rather than trying to impress people in foreign capitals.

Foreign aid in practice

Foreign assistance can provide financial support for infrastructure projects, healthcare, education, and other essential services. This can help combat diseases, improve healthcare systems, and provide access to essential medications and vaccinations, thereby enhancing public health on a global scale. Assistance targeting educational programs and training initiatives can empower individuals with the skills needed for the job market. It can be used to promote global development, foster international cooperation, and address pressing global challenges.

Moreover, foreign aid is crucial for alleviating humanitarian crises by providing vital, life-saving assistance to communities, including refugees and internally displaced persons (IDPs) affected by conflicts, natural disasters, and other emergencies. Countries that strategically receive and utilize foreign aid often experience significant benefits, including reduced mortality rates, improved health outcomes, and greater access to education. While challenges such as dependency and misallocation of resources remain, effective foreign assistance—when carefully tailored to the specific needs of the affected populations—can make a difference in alleviating suffering and fostering long-term recovery. However, it is not without its flaws.

While foreign aid can provide immediate relief, its long-term impact on self-sufficiency and development is best promoted when initiatives are designed to increase the probability of achieving these outcomes.

From foreign aid to development cooperation: The way forward

Development partnerships cultivate genuine collaboration among host governments, organizations, and international entities, fostering a more inclusive approach that results in sustainable and impactful solutions tailored to local contexts and grounded in shared values. Furthermore, prioritizing local needs when shaping development agendas ensures that initiatives remain relevant and effective. By concentrating on the specific needs of host communities, development efforts can achieve more successful outcomes and encourage solutions that are driven by local communities.

Development partnerships emphasize long-term solutions over short-term fixes. They focus on strategies such as skill development, infrastructure investment, and holistic societal improvements, and craft innovative and context-sensitive solutions to complex developmental challenges.

To enhance development endeavors, it is crucial to underscore that development cooperation is conducted purely on business terms. This approach is based on mutual interest rather than charity, fostering a sense of shared responsibility and accountability among the partners. By aligning investment decisions with business logic, development cooperation creates a sustainable framework that enhances project viability.

A key aspect of this cooperation is the emphasis on foreign direct investments (FDI). By encouraging FDI, development initiatives stimulate economic activity and job creation in the recipient countries. FDI not only injects capital into local economies but also facilitates the transfer of technology, expertise, and market access, significantly boosting economic growth in the host country.

Development cooperation plays a vital role in promoting trade between developing and developed countries. By integrating developing countries into global supply chains and markets, increased trade fosters diverse economies, improves living standards, and strengthens global partnerships.

Development cooperation should transcend the traditional donor-recipient dynamic, fostering equality and mutual respect among stakeholders. This shift encourages collaborative problem-solving, with both parties working together towards shared goals rather than one side relying on the other.

The metaphor of treating both parties as travel companions aptly illustrates this partnership. Development cooperation involves collaboration, cultivating trust, and fostering long-term relationships essential for sustained growth and innovation.

Moreover, development cooperation aims to level the playing field by creating a more equitable framework for global partnerships. In this environment, every voice is valued, enabling smaller nations to compete fairly and contributing to a more balanced and equitable global economy.

Promoting local investment ownership is another critical solution. When local communities take ownership of development projects, the initiatives can be better aligned with their needs and aspirations. This ownership enhances commitment, sustainability, and the likelihood of successful results. It requires the formulation of appropriate macroeconomic policies, including sound fiscal and monetary policies, that promote entrepreneurship, encourage savings and investment, enhance exports, understand the need for strong trade relationships with neighbors and the outside world in general, and promote regional cooperation.

Finally, optimizing local resources is a fundamental aspect of effective development cooperation. By leveraging local capacities and resources, investments can achieve maximum impact while empowering communities to take charge of their development journeys. This not only leads to more sustainable outcomes but also fosters a deeper sense of ownership and agency among the local population. Overall, these strategies provide a robust foundation for developing more effective and meaningful initiatives.

Lessons for developing countries

For developing countries, the recent reduction in foreign aid should serve as a crucial wake-up call. These nations must understand that while foreign assistance can support local initiatives, it cannot be the primary driver of change.

As they navigate relationships with regional and international economic powers, developing countries should engage with international partners based on the principles of partnership. This approach requires mutual respect and collaboration to achieve the shared goals.

Furthermore, developing countries must develop and implement homegrown policies that effectively address the needs of their populations. Eliminating corruption is crucial, as it poses a fundamental barrier to progress in the country. Central to this effort is fostering good governance, characterized by the separation of powers, accountability, transparency, rule of law, establishment of robust institutions, and a commitment to combating corruption to enhance their ability to manage resources effectively. This means that African elites should have a renewed incentive to become more responsive to their citizens' needs.

Countries that are heavily reliant on foreign aid can become vulnerable to shifts in international policies. Developing nations should diversify their partnerships and seek broader collaborations with various stakeholders, including regional organizations, the private sector, and civil society. This will also require enhancing local skills, education systems, and human capital to empower citizens and create a skilled workforce that can drive development.

The development of these nations also depends on the strength and resilience of their private sectors. Developing countries can transition from being aid recipients to global players through mutually beneficial commercial partnerships. This also involves nurturing public-private partnerships and supporting investments in strategic sectors. Such efforts can facilitate sustainable economic growth and promote prosperity and improved livelihoods in developing countries. This synergistic approach aligns the interests of various stakeholders and unlocks the immense potential for transformative development outcomes.

Developing countries can achieve rapid progress by harnessing digital technology and artificial intelligence (AI) to leapfrog outdated systems. To fully capitalize on these advantages, investing in digital infrastructure, education, and consumer protection policies is essential. Collaboration with global technology companies and governments can provide the necessary resources and expertise. Key investment areas include enhancing mobile connectivity and developing educational capabilities. Additionally, digital e-commerce platforms enable local businesses to access broader markets, fostering entrepreneurship and economic diversification. Mobile payment systems and microfinance platforms also empower individuals without access to traditional financial systems to engage in the financial ecosystem, thereby supporting entrepreneurship and family risk management.

Developing countries must recognize that in today's interconnected world, isolation is not an option for survival, let alone for prosperity. Engaging with others to find mutually beneficial solutions is crucial. This approach promotes cooperation and negotiation rather than zero-sum games and underscores the importance of working together to address the complex challenges of a globalized society. Regional economic cooperation can enhance market access and improve the investment climate, as investors often seek stable and integrated markets with fewer barriers and reduced tariffs.

Economic diversification typically prevents nations from relying solely on a single revenue source, thus avoiding a mono-economy status and preparing them to absorb economic shocks. For instance, Mauritius has evolved from an economy based on sugar production to a more diversified and export-oriented economy.

It is also vital for the continent to prioritize growth and transformation by integrating markets and moving beyond the extraction and export of raw materials to processed commodities.

For example, countries such as Nigeria, which can produce 1.8 million barrels of oil per day, should not accept that approximately 40.1% of their population lives below the poverty line. Similarly, despite its natural resource wealth and a high GDP per capita of $8,017 in 2021, Gabon faces significant social challenges, with poverty and unemployment rates of 33.4% and 28.8%, respectively, in the same year. This stark contrast highlights the necessity of accountability and effective governance to ensure the equitable distribution of resources for the benefit of all citizens. By embracing these lessons, developing nations can pave the way for sustainable development and improve their people's living conditions, as demonstrated by the Southeast Asian economies. Adopting these principles will enable developing nations to forge a path toward sustainable development and enhance their citizens' quality of life.

In conclusion, developing countries should focus on creating sustainable economies that are less reliant on external assistance. This can be achieved by investing in local industries, promoting entrepreneurship, and fostering innovation.

Chapter 12

Diagnosing our Political Culture

Eritrea is characterized by political repression, strict control of thought, and a monopoly on truth, all of which are deeply embedded in its political culture. While numerous political actors, including individuals, groups, parties, and civic societies, engage in these practices, the primary architect of this situation is the PFDJ-led government. This entity's doctrine is to maintain power at all costs, employing terror, deception, and intimidation as its main tools to achieve its objectives.

The country's leadership is made up of a small group of top government officials, senior members of the ruling party, military commanders, and the state's security forces. Their primary goal is to safeguard their specific political interests. Clearly, as long as the pursuit of power continues, the political and financial benefits that come with it will remain unavoidable. However, the startling reality is that various distant pretexts and methods—such as propaganda, monopolizing the truth, repression, and creating artificial enemies—will continue to be employed.

To understand this, I find it necessary to refer to an analysis I wrote on January 29, 2009, under the pen name Tedros Tesfay. This analysis was an observation made at the time to illuminate the nature of the group. I would like to elaborate on this as follows:

> Let me be very explicit at this juncture as to what I mean when I refer to the party. I am referring to a person, Isaias, and a few of his cronies. It is about the machine created by him and for him, whose main task is to drain the Eritrean People's Liberation Front (EPLF) of its substance and deny the country its soul. I am referring to the tool created by him to legitimize the "Privatization" of all the structures and thus of the Eritrean society. All the rest, that is, the elimination of historical figures, is a reflection of this vacuum-cleaning act: snatching away decades of collective effort for the glory of one; the ultimate ripping-off of the gallant people of Eritrea. (Tesfai, 2001)

Furthermore, under the pen name Zeineb Ali, I wrote a detailed analysis on this issue in 2002, which roughly stated the following. This analysis was based on the understanding that the PFDJ has no ideology. I quote:

> The pretext: I am purposely avoiding concepts such as philosophy and ideology. I have carefully chosen the word "pretext" because I believe that the PFDJ has neither philosophy nor ideology. It started with a seemingly leftist/nationalist line of thought and ended with none. Please allow me to explain why it continues to maintain these characteristics:

> Everything originates from an inferiority complex, which stems from ignorance of global realities and is rooted in rigidity, dishonesty, and hatred. This hatred is directed towards people, anything new and un-PFDJ, organized institutions, democracy, and pluralism. Suspicion, mistrust, and contempt are at the core of this mindset, which emerges from disdain for alternative solutions. This attitude results from the government's highly protective and insular nature. When faced with

challenges and unable to defend itself rationally, it resorts to its notorious pretext of 'uniqueness.' Everything is deemed to be unique to Eritrea. The National Assembly does not convene regularly because Eritrea's situation is considered unique. Political parties are deemed unnecessary as they are perceived to conflict with Eritrea's unique circumstances. The prevailing notion of uniqueness in Eritrea today does not allow for independent press, democracy, or pluralism. Eritrea's multiethnic and multilingual society, with its diverse religious beliefs, further justifies this uniqueness. Do not be surprised if one day, the PFDJ uses the country's population size, varied topography, and climate as a pretext for ulterior motives. "Everything is unique, so the PFDJ has the right to choose unique solutions to problems." These solutions have never been applied in the history of modern human society.

Moreover, Eritrea's "uniqueness" is starkly highlighted by the fact that its fate rests in the hands of one man, the "Honorable" President, Isaias Afewerki. What an affront to the land of the Great Heroes!

A defining characteristic of the PFDJ is its adherence to absurdity. Lacking any vision, the PFDJ resorts to actions that are illogical, abnormal, oppressive, crude, deceitful, and vulgar. If it has any vision, it is one of destruction, aimed at dismantling the diversity of the Eritrean people, the deeply rooted social fabric, economy, and established culture. The PFDJ's objective is to obliterate anything that threatens its survival. When deemed necessary, it uses 'pretexts' to destroy any of these esteemed principles (Ali, 2002).

As previously mentioned, the PFDJ's existence is fundamentally rooted in creating and perpetuating uninterrupted terror. Any resistance or perceived threat to its power and existence is ruthlessly repressed. Beyond this, it fosters political polarization, establishes the groundwork for thought regimentation, and, most importantly, enforces the notion of a monopoly on truth. As a result of these practices, traits such as fear, conformity, hypocrisy, and mutual distrust have become widespread in Eritrean society. These characteristics have persisted within the country and have become prevalent among Eritreans in the diaspora. Eradicating this deeply ingrained political culture, which is exceedingly dangerous, demands a concerted effort and inevitably requires time.

This chapter is designed to illuminate the mechanisms the system uses to reinforce the previously mentioned characteristics. It aims to alert the Eritrean people from falling into the system's traps of deception. Furthermore, it is crucial to foster a healthy society in the long term and ensure that future generations remain untainted by these harmful traits.

Political polarization and its consequences

Political polarization is defined as the growing divide in political views and ideologies that appear irreconcilable, leading to starkly opposing positions on issues. This phenomenon often breeds hostility, resulting in either a deadlock (an inability to reach a consensus) or escalating into heightened conflict and strained communication. It manifests in various forms.

The first issue is the confusion and ambiguity arising from professing diverse ideologies. When significant ideological differences exist between two groups, the likelihood of reconciling their views diminishes, and the chance for constructive dialogue fades.

The second characteristic of this phenomenon is hostility rooted in partisanship, which fosters intense hatred and animosity among groups. At a higher level, political opponents are no longer seen as mere competitors but as mortal enemies. This culture promotes exaggerated competitiveness, wishing the worst for others, and employing every means to destroy one another. It can lead to extreme confrontations, such as the vicious or baseless threat, "I will dance on your grave." If anyone benefits from this situation, it is the political elite, who prioritize their narrow interests over those of the people.

Third, media outlets often begin to align with or show bias towards one side. In such scenarios, individuals tend to seek, believe, and share information that confirms and reinforces their existing beliefs. As a result, pre-existing divisions are renewed and deepened. Social media platforms such as Facebook and Twitter (now "X") create conditions that allow people to consume only information that aligns with their political beliefs, thereby shaping their opinions on various issues. When alternative views are ignored, it fosters an atmosphere conducive to polarization.

In Eritrea, the majority of the population residing within the country is deprived of alternative perspectives, creating an information vacuum where people are forced to rely solely on one-sided, non-interactive information.

Fourth, we can address what is firmly known as the politics of identity. This phenomenon occurs when political allegiance is strongly tied to a cultural, ethnic, or religious identity. When political groups engage in such practices, they create formidable barriers to achieving political compromise, thereby diminishing the potential for progress.

Mitigating political polarization for effective governance

Good governance flourishes through dialogue, whereas polarization erects barriers to achieving bipartisan or dualistic agreements. It impedes the development of a civilized political culture, and where such a culture exists, it leads to its decline. Consequently, public trust in institutions such as elections, courts, the media, and other organizations has gradually eroded in this flawed political environment. Each side perceives the other's statements as objectionable or portrays them as illegitimate, making this perception the norm. This inevitably cultivates an environment that fosters distrust.

Political polarization creates fertile ground for politicians eager to exploit divisions, contributing to the rise of populism and extremism, which presents itself as a defense of the people's interests. This polarization leads to social fragmentation and intensifies hostility among citizens, with the potential to incite violence. When politics devolves into a zero-sum game, it undermines democracy, mutual understanding, and dialogue, inevitably fostering apathy or events that lead to public frustration. Severe polarization cripples governance, causing instability and unrest and hindering efforts to achieve good governance.

To address these issues, a strong and free media, critical thinking, a culture of tolerance, and civic education that promotes these values are essential. Additionally, refining cross-party dialogue to build trust among leaders is crucial. Striking a balance between healthy political competition and constructive cooperation is indispensable for establishing a stable governance system.

The regimentation of thought

When religious institutions or organizations grounded in specific ideologies, especially political parties, deliberately employ sophisticated and systematic methods to control and standardize their followers' thinking, it leads to the regimentation of thought. In its extreme form, this phenomenon stifles and extinguishes freedom of thought and expression. Its goal is to shape and dominate individuals' thoughts, feelings, and characters, ultimately aiming to achieve narrow political objectives.

In today's world, populations face this phenomenon, where those in power exploit it to enforce conformity and suppress dissent, all while spreading dominant propaganda to maintain control or establish "ideological purity." This practice is prevalent across political, academic, religious, and cultural domains and can have both positive and negative effects on governance.

When the expression of alternative ideas is stifled, governance's ability to adaptively fulfill its responsibilities and address problems is increasingly compromised. For instance, the Marxist-Leninist ideology embraced by the Soviet Union prohibited economic and political reform, ultimately leading to the system's collapse. Numerous analysts contend that external pressure was the catalyst for change in the Soviet Union. However, I believe that the internal dynamics are the most crucial factor, fundamentally representing the internal decay of the system.

A rigid ideological framework can be effective in preventing political chaos, but it may also impede critical thinking. For instance, China's "socialist core values" promote patriotism and allegiance to the Communist Party, which might have played a role in maintaining the country's political stability. However, this stability comes at the expense of open dialogue. Only history and time will reveal how long this situation will endure.

Strict regimentation of thought can lead to censorship, propaganda, and persecution of dissenters. For example, North Korea's ideology, known as 'Juche,' is disseminated through intense, state-driven propaganda. Any deviation from this ideology is deemed a crime and results in severe punishment. The government exercises tight control over the media, which unconditionally praises the government and its leaders while attributing blame to external factors.

In the United States, narratives on issues such as immigration and climate change are often promoted by specific political parties. Some emphasize the dangers of climate change, while others deny its existence or interpret it as a political conspiracy. This significantly influences public opinions and policy decisions.

Moreover, strict regimentation of thought can lead to economic and policy inflexibility, hindering adaptability. Such rigidity can impede economic growth. For instance, the inflexible philosophy of Chavismo in Venezuela resulted in economic mismanagement, as it failed to account for evolving global conditions.

Additionally, regimentation can oversimplify or distort the decision-making process. For example, the military advantage of the Eritrean People's Liberation Front (EPLF) over the Eritrean Liberation Front (ELF) during the independence struggle was due to, among other factors, the regimented thinking fostered within the Front. This cohesion enabled the Front to endure and succeed within a military framework, albeit at the expense of political freedom.

Singapore serves as another example, where the governance model emphasizes pragmatism and strict discipline. While this approach has undeniably fueled rapid economic growth, it has also suppressed political dissent.

Furthermore, although regimentation can foster short-term stability and unity, prolonged control over thought ultimately undermines creativity, adaptability, and public trust. Ultimately, the most effective governance models are those that strike a balance between maintaining order and allowing freedom.

The tyranny of the single narrative: How one story shapes minds and societies.
The monopoly of truth as a mockery of alternatives
In our world, certain familiar entities belittle or ridicule alternative viewpoints while promoting the idea that only one truth exists, leaving no room for other interpretations of a situation or opinion. This is what we firmly refer to as a monopoly on truth. It manifests in various spheres of life, including politics, the media, religion, and academia. It often becomes entrenched when a political party consolidates its absolute hold on power by controlling information sources and leveraging social norms and organizational structures. When a dominant power insists that only its interpretation is valid, it hinders individuals from considering alternative perspectives or compels them to critically scrutinize their own beliefs.

This inevitably curtails the freedom and capacity to explore issues from multiple perspectives. Consequently, these issues are often poorly understood. By restricting access to diverse perspectives, truth-suppressing groups effectively turn individuals into adherents of a singular, distorted narrative.

The monopoly of truth as a tool of fear

In essence, the monopoly of truth creates an atmosphere of fear and anxiety, erecting barriers that prevent people from freely expressing their views. Moreover, censorship becomes an obstacle to the free flow of thought, hindering the flourishing of open dialogue. When a multitude of existing viewpoints are suppressed, it leads to political repression, forcing different political groups to adhere to and remain entrenched in their beliefs. This inevitably causes social fragmentation.

The monopoly of truth as a tool for dominant propaganda

In countries like Eritrea, where the notion of truth is stifled, those in power seize opportunities to manipulate narratives to serve their own narrow interests. By dictating what is presented as the sole "truth," they aim to shape the opinions and character of ordinary people. The pressure to conform to the dominant narrative fosters an atmosphere of anxiety and suspicion, especially towards those with differing views. This environment ultimately stifles critical thinking and intellectual freedom.

In the analysis I wrote on January 21, 2001, under the pseudonym Tedros Tesfai, I examined this issue and concluded that this framework remains relevant.

> The PFDJ's philosophical foundation is inherently anti-democratic and promotes totalitarian rule. It stems from the belief that "the PFDJ is

everything." The PFDJ encompasses politics, the economy, the nation, and its citizenry. It represents all that is good and sacred in Eritrea and claims an exclusive right to care for its people. The PFDJ genuinely believes that its monopoly over the nation's politics and economy is justified.

Isaias and his associates equate the PFDJ with national interest, asserting that it champions national development and reconstruction. They believe that the PFDJ is the sole possessor of the best ideas and consider themselves forward-thinking, unlike others. They maintain that the PFDJ is infallible, while others are inherently flawed. The PFDJ is seen as destined to lead, with others only fit to follow.

The PFDJ claims to have the wisdom and courage to interpret matters related to Eritrea's future. It asserts the exclusive right to speak for Eritrea's people and denies others this privilege. Only the PFDJ claims the authority to interpret information and events (Tesfai 2001).

The monopoly of truth as an antidote to misinformation

Encouraging diverse opinions is essential for building a society that can address complex challenges. Conversely, a lack of varied perspectives stifles creativity and hampers collaboration. Fundamentally, a political culture that suppresses the truth fosters an environment in which misinformation flourishes, gradually eroding people's ability to make decisions based on factual information.

The monopoly of truth as a mockery of academic freedom

Ideologies that undermine academic freedom by asserting a singular truth on various issues can adversely affect policy-making. Religions, grounded in their doctrines, have also been known to demand adherence to their beliefs as the absolute truth, branding those with differing opinions as heretics. This phenomenon persists to the present day.

The monopoly of truth detrimentally affects both individual and societal thinking, fostering a divisive culture that hinders genuine dialogue between people. Diverse viewpoints are vital for nurturing critical thinking and cultivating an open, resilient, and healthy society.

The triple pillars of control: How polarization, thought regimentation, and monopoly of truth sustain the Eritrean State

Similar to many liberation movements that emerged during the tumultuous 1960s and 70s, the Eritrean People's Liberation Front (EPLF) embraced Marxism-Leninism. Its fundamental principles encompassed the dictatorship of the proletariat, fostering solidarity between workers and peasants, constructing a fully egalitarian society, abolishing private property, and promoting unity, solidarity, and support for progressive movements worldwide. The EPLF adopted a highly centralized operational structure and mindset aimed at instilling its progressive ideology in every member of the organization. This approach reflects the military culture, mindset, and discipline.

However, there was no inherent culture of tolerance for political differences. This intolerance was evident in the manner in which political developments such as the "Menka'e"[xiii] of 1973 or "Yemin"[xiv] were suppressed. This was also reflected in the treatment of Front members who held differing opinions on various issues, including the group led by Osman Saleh Salih Sabbe.[xv]

At that time, it was deemed inconceivable to remain detached or uninfluenced by the globally impactful leftist ideology for obvious reasons. It is also challenging to assert that it played no role in supporting the national liberation movements. The liberation movement and progressive ideology have become so intertwined that they could no longer be viewed separately.

This issue persists today. Over the past fifty years, the world has undergone significant changes. Political and economic mechanisms have been tested to assess their effectiveness. The world is more interconnected than ever, and we have entered an era in which events in one part of the globe quickly impact others elsewhere. Persisting with ideologies that were effective in a different era, from this perspective, not only reveals a reluctance to acknowledge a lack of innovation but also fails to yield fruitful results. As the renowned physicist Albert Einstein famously stated, "Insanity is doing the same thing over and over again and expecting different results." Ineffective or outdated ideologies and perspectives that cannot be practically implemented have been discarded. However, the ruling group in Eritrea refuses to learn from a world that has changed dramatically, clinging to its own narrow interests and attempting to govern the 21st century with a 1960s ideology. Some of its stubborn characteristics are as follows.

Prevailing Realities
A grim, repression-heavy agenda

In Eritrea, a political culture characterized by strict regimentation forms the backbone of the system. The absence of dialogue, debate, and platforms for constructive conflict resolution is noteworthy. An entrenched "You are either with us or against us" mentality prevails. This may be a continuation of the repressive culture observed in the forties and fifties among various Eritrean political parties, which later, during the armed struggle, transformed into a rigid method of resolving internal conflicts. These conflicts, arising from power struggles between armed organizations, have led to tragic internal strife. However, this trajectory was neither inevitable nor linear. Thus, lessons from the past are invaluable. As people mature, their thinking evolves.

This phenomenon extends beyond the country's borders; media outlets aligned with the government or the diaspora, particularly YouTube channels, are known to amplify this culture of trolling. Some do not hesitate to employ divisive and provocative tactics that foster politics of hatred and violence. Politics seems to be conducted in a manner that borders on madness rather than promoting a healthy society. The diversity of opinions has reached a point where citizens who deserve respect and attention are accused of heresy. Terms such as traitor, reactionary, mercenary, saboteur, agent of foreign interests, CIA, spy, collaborator, and mercenary agent of foreign forces are prevalent in the lexicon of Eritrean politics. The harm inflicted on the population is not easily remedied. The aspiration to create a political space for reconciliation and coexistence also seems distant.

Eritrea's political culture is marked by the suppression of opposition and the violent eradication of differences. The PFDJ's existence is rooted in paranoia about perceived enemies, fine-tuning hostility as a strategy for maintaining power. It employs hatred as a foundational creed for mobilization and justifying its existence.

Ideological control forged by slogans

Under the PFDJ system, ideological control is enforced through slogans, compelling every citizen to align with the party's singular line of thought. This is achieved by systematically propagating distorted narratives, with slogans encapsulating these ideas regularly chanted. Each year, listeners are inundated with new slogans, often recycled from previous campaigns. Some of these slogans include "We will witness miracles in development as we did for our independence," "A clear vision, a firm conviction," "There is no honor without a nation," "Ready for Warsai Yikealo campaign," "United under one flag," "Synergy for national honor," "A quarter-century of national defense and development," "Resilient as ever," "Independent choice-backbone of Our Pride," "Our cohesion our armor," "Peace anchored on resilience," and so on.

Under the PFDJ, youth are subjected to psychological control by the state. This segment of society is targeted by PFDJ's social engineering projects to be molded into a "new person." The aim is to reshape the youth in the image of a freedom fighter and, beyond that, to make them think in the way the PFDJ desires, instilling and perpetuating the traits the PFDJ wants to cultivate, or rather, conditioning them for obedience. Its ultimate goal is to bring the people's thoughts and freedom under the absolute control of the PFDJ's narrative and to use them for its various immediate objectives. One of these is to use them as cannon fodder in its quest to defend the nation from "external threats." In general, it has created an intergenerational ideological and cultural gap that replaces natural intergenerational succession and the transmission of educational values to the younger generation. If this is not corrected, the resulting social fragmentation may be irreparable.

The militarization of the entire society

In Eritrea, militarization has been subtly and systematically woven into the cultural fabric of society. Citizens are organized to mirror military norms, structures, and priorities, aligning their civilian lives, governance, and culture with these principles. Under the guise of "national security," the suppression of free thought has become deeply entrenched. The Ministry of Defense's budget has increased significantly, often at the expense of other social services. The glorification of war and wartime heroism has reached new heights, profoundly influencing the regimentation of the Eritrean psyche. While it is admirable to celebrate our proud history, it is essential to prevent the system from exploiting this for its narrow interests, just as it manipulates the legacy of the martyrs.

A generation nurtured on information control and fear

As discussed in previous chapters, the regime in Asmara enforces strict control over information, stifling alternative media and perspectives. It expends vast energy and resources to deprive people of opportunities to access diverse opinions and narratives, compelling them to accept the regime's narrative as the sole truth. The Voice of the Broad Masses of Eritrea, Haddas Eritrea (a daily newspaper), and Eri-TV serve as the regime's primary propaganda tools. The Sawa Center and the political education center in Nakfa carry out sophisticated brainwashing efforts on the youth. Public meetings are meticulously organized to support these initiatives. As a result, the populace is left with a mindset that fosters the belief to "do whatever you are told or leave the country." The devastating consequences of these actions have not yet been fully realized.

As previously mentioned, narratives wield a significant influence on cultivating a culture of conformity among citizens. The relentless stream of brazen falsehoods and subtle deceptions can lead individuals to question their intellectual and natural instincts. In their quest to verify the truth of the narratives presented to them, they may find themselves trapped in a cycle of perpetual self-doubt.

A key factor driving this conformity is the fear of punishment arising from potential punitive actions that could be imposed on citizens. People often align with the regime's narratives, whether out of concern or coercion, to ensure their own safety and that of their families. Some individuals adopt the regime's narratives as a means of self-preservation, recognizing that voicing grievances can have severe and damaging consequences.

Conclusion

When political polarization, regimentation of thought, and a monopoly on truth take root in a nation, the chances of ensuring good governance are significantly diminished.

Regimentation deepens existing societal divisions, making efforts to resolve political differences through dialogue or compromise increasingly futile and ineffective. Strict ideological control, or regimentation, significantly hinders the development of political pluralism by suppressing dissent. This regimentation of thought conflicts with the promotion of critical thinking, as it aims to establish a culture of conformity that stifles innovation. Political regimentation enforces conformity by silencing free voices and actively promoting an "us versus them" mentality.

Politics marked by polarization prioritize victories based on partisan interests rather than the welfare of the populace, thereby justifying disproportionate measures against political opponents.

The monopoly on truth stifles debates grounded in facts and information, leading to a decline in citizens' trust in institutions and eroding mutual understanding and cooperation. This distortion of political debate results in flawed or irrational policy-making and the demonization of dissenting opinions.

To address these challenges, it is crucial to raise awareness of their existence. A responsible and free press can play a vital role in eradicating these issues. Achieving this requires a governance system that provides legal guarantees to protect the press. Challenging totalitarianism is a strategic necessity rather than a choice. A society that fails to consistently implement corrective measures is destined to face ongoing crises, instability, and eventual collapse. For Eritreans living abroad, we have the opportunity to express our opinions freely, even with those with whom we disagree. However, our choices should be expressed with integrity, and it is beneficial to embody these principles in a mature way. We have a duty to cultivate traits such as respect, tolerance, and acceptance of diverse opinions.

We must strive to create responsible press and media, negotiate our differences in a civilized manner, refrain from defamation, avoid labeling, view each other as political competitors rather than enemies, and conduct debates based on evidence rather than defamation. We must move away from politics rooted in hatred, mutual destruction, and repression. The only way to persuade others is by presenting ideas with evidence and logic and winning hearts and minds through proof. Despite our differences, we are all citizens of the same country. Governments are temporary, but people remain on their lands. We must prepare a better future for generations to come by building our country through mutual understanding and cooperation.

Chapter 13

African Economic Horizons: A Framework for Eritrea

Introduction

More than 60 years have passed since decolonization began in Africa, leading to the emergence of numerous independent nations in the region. Yet, the continent continues to be unfairly labeled as the 'dark continent,' a term synonymous with underdevelopment, poverty, disease, authoritarian rule, corruption, civil strife, and genocide. Africa is often depicted as a place of unchecked population growth, rampant malaria and HIV/AIDS, and ethnic diversity, which is seen as a liability rather than a strength. Additionally, Africa struggles with inadequate infrastructure, including inefficient communication and transportation systems, and rapid urbanization driven by rural poverty further strains its development.

However, the continent is rich in natural resources, including fertile land, rivers, lakes, minerals, and fossil fuels. It also takes pride in its energetic and hard-working population.[xvi] Africa is home to a rich and diverse culture, with traditions dating back thousands of years. The continent cherishes a wealth of social values that are deeply meaningful and worth preserving. Its vast, untouched forests are major tourist attractions. Moreover, numerous renowned anthropologists have affirmed that Africa is the cradle of humankind.[xvii] Furthermore, Africa's tradition of higher education dates back to the twelfth century, as exemplified by the historic scholarly hub of Timbuktu in present-day Mali.[xviii] Africa is also home to one of the world's youngest populations.

This chapter examines the foundational drivers of economic growth in Africa, first conceptualizing growth in its broadest terms, and then evaluating the continent's current developmental stage using established economic indicators. The analysis then assesses Africa's economic potential by drawing comparative lessons from regions with analogous socio-economic contexts and historical trajectories. Central to the discussion is the argument that deficient governance represents a critical barrier—one that not only hinders Africa's development but also contributes to its periodic regressions. In conclusion, this study offers

What is economic growth?
In "Modern Economic Growth: Findings and Reflections," Kuznets defines a country's economic growth as a long-term increase in its ability to provide an increasingly diverse array of economic goods to its population. This expanding capacity relies on technological advancements and the institutional and ideological adjustments they necessitate to be successful (Kuznets, 1973).[xix] In their textbook, "Economic Development," Todaro and Smith emphasize that all three components of this definition are crucial to economic development. They further explain that economic growth is evidenced by a sustained rise in national output, that technological progress is essential for continued growth, and that institutional and attitudinal changes are necessary to fully harness technology's potential (Todaro, 2003).[xx] In the same book, Todaro and Smith identify several key factors associated with growth: physical and human resource endowments; per capita income and GNP levels relative to the global economy; climate; population size, distribution, and growth; the historical role of international

migration; gains from international trade; scientific and technological R&D capacity; and the stability and adaptability of political and social institutions (Todaro, 2003).[xxi]

Additional considerations include geography, access to maritime trade routes, and forms of government. According to classical economics, economic growth is primarily gauged by the increase in the Gross National Product (GNP), which represents the market value of all final goods and services consumed by households, the government, and foreign entities within a given year. Furthermore, it suggests that growth should be evaluated using a standardized economic index, typically expressed as the rate of growth in income per capita, as a key indicator of development (Todaro, 2003).[xxii]

However, these observations are not universally applicable, and caution is advised when applying them. For example, countries with similar climatic conditions may experience significantly different levels of economic growth than other countries. Similarly, nations with limited natural resources often achieve greater prosperity than those with abundant resources. Additionally, democracies, especially those transitioning from authoritarian rule, sometimes face challenges in fostering growth, as competing interest groups can impede economic progress. Nonetheless, it is well-documented that stable democracies tend to achieve stronger long-term growth compared to authoritarian regimes (Todaro, 2003).[xxiii]

Africa's economic growth

In The Bottom Billion, Paul Collier underscores a stark global divide: while 80% of the world's population resides in rapidly developing countries, the poorest billion remain trapped in stagnant or declining economies. Collier observes that most of these nations are concentrated in Africa and Central Asia, where they grapple with civil conflict, disease, and a lack of knowledge. He cautions that as these left-behind economies fall further behind—diverging from a globalized world driven by technology, rapid growth, and rising incomes—their reintegration will only become more challenging (Collier, 2027).[xxiv]

Africa's persistent underdevelopment is often attributed to a complex interplay of factors, including colonial legacies, adverse climatic conditions, challenging terrain, and geographical disadvantages, such as limited coastlines relative to landmass. Ethnic fragmentation, often extending to sub-ethnic divisions, along with political instability fueled by border disputes, civil conflicts, and frequent coups, further complicates these challenges. The impact of foreign aid on Africa's economic growth remains hotly debated, with critics pointing to an inequitable global economic system that is structurally skewed against the continent (Calderisi, 2006).[xxv] Many African leaders and scholars trace the roots of these issues to historical injustices such as the transatlantic slave trade, colonialism, Cold War geopolitics, crippling debt burdens, and the policies of international institutions (Calderisi, 2006).[xxvi] Others argue that globalization has exacerbated Africa's economic struggles.

Colonialism indeed contributed to the creation of weak states in Africa, a consequence of the fragmented political landscape that emerged after centuries of the slave trade. Essentially, the political boundaries and governance structures of most African states today stem from the institutional legacies of European colonial rule in the nineteenth and twentieth centuries (Leonard, 2003).[xxvii] In Africa's Stalled Development: International Causes and Cures, David K. Leonard and Scott Straus argue that colonial institutions were primarily designed to serve a small settler community and, as such, were economically oriented toward exports (Leonard, 2003).[xxviii] This model is inappropriate for most of the African population.

The transatlantic slave trade deprived Africa of a substantial portion of its workforce for centuries. Many scholars contend that this prolonged phenomenon not only caused profound social instability but also triggered enduring demographic shifts across the continent (Leonard, 2003).[xxix]

The Cold War significantly impeded Africa's overall development. During this era, global superpowers supported authoritarian regimes across the continent to protect their strategic interests, including shipping lanes, military bases, and access to critical minerals and energy supplies in Africa (Calderisi, 2006).[xxx] However, it is crucial to remember that the Cold War played a significant role in accelerating decolonization (Calderisi, 2006).[xxxi] The end of the Cold War did not usher in a new political era, suggesting that the Cold War itself had little significant impact on Africa's economic stagnation (Calderisi, 2006).[xxxii] This implies that the prevalence of Marxist planned economies in Africa during the Cold War might have been a key factor in its economic underperformance.

The impact of foreign aid on Africa's economic growth—or stagnation—remains a hotly debated topic. Critics argue that aid has fostered a dependency syndrome, thereby contributing to the continent's sluggish economic development. Scholars such as Dambisa Moyo reject the notion that aid can alleviate poverty, dismissing it as a misconception. In "Dead Aid: Why Aid Is Not Working and How There Is a Better Way for Africa," Moyo asserts that aid has left millions poorer, exacerbating misery and deprivation rather than reducing them. She goes further, condemning aid as an unmitigated disaster—politically, economically, and humanitarianly—for much of the developing world, both historically and in the foreseeable future (Moyo, 2007).[xxxiii] In 1981, economist P. T. Bauer summarized the case against aid in three powerful sentences:

The argument that aid is indispensable for development runs into an inescapable dilemma: If the conditions for development other than capital are present, the capital required will either be generated locally or be available commercially from abroad to governments or businesses. If the required conditions are not present, then aid will be ineffective and wasted (Bauer, 1981).[xxxiv]

It can be argued that, despite its limitations, foreign assistance played a crucial role. Certain aspects of social progress, such as rural roads, primary schools, vaccination programs, family planning services, sanitation, and access to clean water, might not have been achievable without it.[xxxv] Some argue that foreign aid also has an economic rationale, exemplified by the creation of the World Bank in 1946 to foster global trade growth and rebuild the war-ravaged economies of Germany and Japan.[xxxvi] This, of course, targeted countries that already possessed the institutional capacity to absorb such assistance. Proponents of aid also argue that its benefits were more evident thirty years ago, when economic progress—and by extension, foreign aid—yielded clearer results. For instance, between 1950 and 1975, life expectancy in poor countries rose by 15 years (from 35 to 50), while adult literacy rates more than doubled, increasing from 30% to over 50%. Many countries also saw significant improvements in access to healthcare, education, and clean water during this period.[xxxvii]

In 'The Trouble with Africa: Why Foreign Aid is not Working,' Calderisi acknowledges that historical and structural factors, such as slavery, colonialism, the Cold War, international institutions, high debt, geography, Africa's numerous small states, and population pressures, have all shaped the continent's development. However, he argues that none of these fully explain why Africa has regressed economically over the past three decades, especially given its post-independence growth. Calderisi notes that after a prolonged period of contraction, African economies are now recovering, but only at a sluggish pace (Calderisi, 2006).[xxxviii] Such arguments suggest that the fundamental causes of Africa's economic stagnation must be sought elsewhere.

Prospects for Africa's economic growth

Addressing poverty requires sustained economic growth underpinned by sound policies and significant investments in education and health.

Without growth, large populations are trapped in poverty.[xxxix] True development is realized when growth leads to tangible improvements in people's lives through equitable wealth distribution. Ultimately, meaningful progress necessitates narrowing the gap between the wealthy few and the impoverished majority to enhance the overall quality of life.

Africa does not need to reinvent the wheel to achieve economic growth. While the continent has unique characteristics—including its history, culture, geography, natural resources, human capital, and climate—it can adapt proven growth strategies from countries with similar socioeconomic conditions.

In "Economic Development," Todaro and Smith emphasize that sustainable progress requires more than just efficient resource allocation (typically market-driven) and steady output growth. Nations must also establish the economic, social, and institutional frameworks necessary to deliver rapid and large-scale improvements in living standards. Crucially, this involves addressing fundamental questions about power and equity: who controls economic decision-making, and whose interests do these decisions serve? The authors further stress that international factors must be integral to any growth strategy (Todaro, 2003).[xl] These include the behavior of the international market, interest rates, and global economic health.

Another important factor to consider when examining Africa's economic growth is that the continent is far from homogeneous. Comprising more than fifty countries, each has its own distinct history, relationships with the West, intra-African dynamics, natural resource endowments, and governance structures. A striking comparison can be drawn between two landlocked diamond-rich nations: Botswana and the Central African Republic. Botswana has successfully transformed into a middle-income economy through sound governance, while the Central African Republic's economic progress has stagnated—primarily due to poor governance.[xli]

In Africa, strategies for economic growth often involve market-driven capital accumulation by local entrepreneurs, targeted investment policies (both domestic and foreign) in high-potential sectors (primary, secondary, or tertiary), sound macroeconomic management (fiscal and monetary policy), human capital development (education and health), and increased regional cooperation. The people themselves are central to this growth. African nations must empower the poor by expanding access to education, skills training, employment, entrepreneurship, and investment opportunities to alleviate poverty. As Paul Collier argues in his TED lecture, cultivating a critical mass of informed citizens is also crucial for sustainable development (Collier, 2008).[xlii]

To boost economic growth, Africa must establish a robust regulatory framework aligned with international standards, implement effective poverty reduction strategies, and foster an inclusive financial sector that serves marginalized populations. Strong institutions, the rule of law, fiscal discipline, and transparent governance, including checks and balances, anti-corruption measures, and efficient resource allocation, are vital for stability and sustained growth. Beyond institutional reforms, social foundations such as family structures, cultural values, and education also contribute to political stability, creating an environment where economies can thrive.[xliii]

Infrastructure forms the foundation of economic growth, whereas a skilled workforce serves as its backbone. Women are pivotal drivers of development, empowering households and lifting families out of poverty through economic contributions. In agrarian Africa, agriculture remains the dominant sector, fueling employment, ensuring food security, and holding untapped potential through technological innovation. However, progress must not come at an environmental cost; sustainable practices are essential to safeguard Africa's long-term economic stability.

Consequently, effective policies, legislation, and regulatory frameworks must be implemented to ensure the sustainable management of environmental resources and prevent ecological crises.[xliv] Responsible ecosystem management should be integrated into the ethical and religious values underpinning development. Renowned African economist and former Nigerian Finance Minister Ngozi Okonjo-Iweala emphasized this in her lecture, 'Want to Help Africa? Do Business Here!' She highlighted how privatization, market liberalization, improved financial management, economic diversification, market predictability, and banking system consolidation contributed to Nigeria's stronger economic performance in the early 2000s (Okonjo, 2008).[xlv] However, the key to all of the above is good governance. Without this, progress can be delayed.

In 2023, foreign aid to African economies totaled $73.6 billion, which was less than 10% of the continent's total revenue when compared to remittances at $90.8 billion, foreign direct investment at $97.1 billion, and tax revenues at $479.7 billion.[xlvi]

Good governance: the way out to Africa's economic growth

As discussed in Chapter 5, strong governance is crucial for Africa's economic growth, safeguarding against downturns and policy errors. Governance refers to how power is exercised in managing a country's resources for development. It was defined as the traditions and institutions through which authority is exercised, including government selection processes, policy implementation, and citizen-state relationships. The WB evaluates governance across six dimensions: voice and accountability, political stability, government effectiveness, regulatory quality, rule of law, and corruption control.

In Introduction to Sustainable Development, Rogers et al. emphasized that poor governance hinders development, distorts its processes, and disproportionately harms the poor. They argue that good governance relies on accountability, participation, decentralization, predictability, and transparency (Rogers, 2009).[xlvii] Accountability ensures that officials are answerable for their actions. Decentralization enhances participation by involving all stakeholders in decision-making, whereas predictability depends on the consistent enforcement of sound policies, laws, and regulations. Finally, transparency requires that citizens are fully informed about government actions and policies (Rogers, 2009).[xlviii]

Several African countries are notorious for their governance structures, often characterized by one-man rule, nepotism, corruption, lack of transparency and accountability, financial mismanagement, abuse of human rights, and ineffective approaches to combating corruption.

An article published in 2023 by the Council on Foreign Relations (CFR), a US-based research institute, titled "The Age of Exact Leaders," indicates that many African countries faced challenges in transferring power in the first fifty years after independence. The report notes that leaders who gained prominence during national independence movements tended to remain in power indefinitely once they assumed office. Furthermore, it states that in 2023, five leaders had been in power for over thirty years, namely: Teodoro Obiang Nguema Mbasogo in Equatorial Guinea, Paul Biya in Cameroon, Denis Sassou Nguesso in the Republic of Congo, Yoweri Museveni in Uganda, and Isaias Afwerki in Eritrea. In addition, the report confirms that more than sixteen leaders had stayed in power for at least ten years, and in two countries (Gabon and Togo), family dynasties had been established, lasting over fifty years.[xlix]

The institute also pointed out that some leaders appear to be transferring power to their family members, citing Zimbabwe's former president, Emerson Mnangagwa, as an example. For instance, President Mnangagwa appointed his son, nephew, and wife to the cabinet he formed. The institute, in its published article, explains that in recent years, leaders who had been in power for a long time were removed from their positions, and provides the following examples: in 2017, Angola's President José Eduardo dos Santos was forced out of office after thirty-eight years in power. Similarly, Zimbabwe's former President Robert Mugabe was removed from power by a military coup after thirty-seven years in office. Two years later, Sudan's Omar al-Bashir was forcibly removed from power after thirty years. In addition, Chad's leader, who had ruled for thirty years, was killed on the battlefield in 2021. The most striking reality is the ten military coup attempts carried out since 2020. These include Burkina Faso, Mali, and Niger. Recently (as of August 2023), Gabon's President, Ali Bongo Ondimba, was removed from power by the military after nearly fourteen years in office.[l]

This aligns with Paul Collier's characterization of African leaders in The Bottom Billion—individuals who attained power through extralegal means (Collier, 2007).[li]

According to Calderisi, economic growth is achievable, and foreign assistance proves most effective in countries where governments are already committed to sound governance—setting clear priorities, implementing coherent policies, and strengthening key institutions based on domestic needs rather than external expectations (Calderisi, 2006).[lii] Collier and Gunning, in an article titled 'Explaining African Economic Performance,' highlight an inverse relationship between economic growth and overseas development aid (ODA) in most African countries, attributing this trend to weak policy environments (Collier, 1999).[liii]

Paul Collier further expands on this theme in his seminal State Department lecture, 'New Rules for Rebuilding a Broken Nation,' emphasizing the critical role of clean government in fostering youth employment and equitable social services. Such reforms, he argues, can catalyze a shift from exploitative 'politics of plunder' to transformative 'politics of hope' (Collier, 2009).[liv]

Evidence suggests that without meaningful governance reforms, Africa's economic growth will remain stunted. African governments must move beyond protecting narrow interests and adopt inclusive, homegrown strategies tailored to their unique challenges rather than conforming to external political or economic agendas.

To achieve this, they must first address systemic inefficiencies by building robust and transparent institutions and implementing clear standards for policy execution. Corruption must be eradicated through stringent checks and balances, and meritocratic systems should cultivate a new generation of skilled professionals to drive transformative changes. Fostering inclusive governance is equally critical. Civil society organizations, NGOs, and other stakeholders must actively participate in both development discourse and decision-making processes to ensure equitable progress.

African nations must strengthen regional cooperation by establishing mechanisms that hold their governments mutually accountable to their citizens. The tolerance for lawlessness must end, with peer pressure ensuring adherence to governance standards that prioritize public welfare.

For the West, supporting Africa's economic growth is not merely altruistic; it is a strategic imperative. Such cooperation fosters global stability, strengthens economic ties, and advances shared prosperity. However, this requires fundamental rethinking and engagement. OECD economies must transition from a donor-recipient dynamic to a genuine partnership, recognizing Africa as an equal stakeholder. True collaboration demands jointly defined objectives and implementation strategies, relationships grounded in shared values and long-term vision, mutual respect for each party's contributions and capabilities, and institutionalized trust and solidarity in principle and practice.

This empowerment framework moves beyond transactional aid and creates sustainable pathways for collective progress.

Chapter 14

The Next Chapter: Integrating Transitional Justice into Eritrea's National Project

In Eritrea, the absence of justice and the rule of law has resulted in numerous cases of arbitrary detention, killings, torture, and disappearances, causing real suffering for the victims and their families. Additionally, divisive political cultures that thrive on polarization present significant challenges. This political culture suppresses free expression, encourages conformity, and fosters an "us versus them" mentality. While many political actors seem to accommodate this phenomenon, the ruling PFDJ system in Eritrea is its primary architect. This institution's doctrine focuses on consolidating power at all costs, using terror and repression as its primary tools.

To dismantle such a vicious culture and create conditions where victims of the oppressive system can seek justice in a post-change Eritrea, a credible, institutionalized process of accountability and implementation with a clear procedure is essential. This approach must provide victims with opportunities to seek justice. For effective implementation and realization, a transitional government based on good governance, a mechanism for transitional justice, economic reform, and trust cultivation within society are necessary. These strategies must be informed by Eritrea's unique history, multicultural fabric, and the nature of the authoritarian regime that subjugated the people.

A key expectation of a transitional government founded on the principles of good governance is to initiate a national healing process and implement peace and reconciliation programs. Achieving this requires a sound strategy and profound vision. The success of such efforts often depends on the inclusive participation and goodwill of all people, along with the support of the international community. Therefore, a transitional government in Eritrea should establish frameworks that facilitate the implementation of transitional justice, paving the way for a just and reconciliatory system. This will help address past crimes and foster national unity.

Transitional Justice
Transitional justice is crucial in addressing the injustices of societies transitioning from conflict, repression, and authoritarian rule to peace and democracy. This framework includes the principles, processes, and mechanisms used by transitioning societies to tackle widespread human rights violations and injustice. Its implementation demands meticulous planning and extensive public engagement to balance justice, reconciliation, and national stability. Despite its comprehensive nature, transitional justice serves as a tool to promote accountability, justice, reconciliation, and institutional reform following widespread abuse or human rights violations in a country while preventing their recurrence. This approach encompasses both judicial and nonjudicial measures.

Transitional justice becomes more effective and sustainable when tailored to local specificities while aligning with international norms and standards. Rather than relying solely on abstract concepts, transitional justice should ideally be developed and function by drawing on the experiences and norms cultivated and nurtured by society as a whole.

Consequently, favorable and accepted experiences and formulas that can bolster transitional justice in a country or society must be continuously developed and used. Leveraging these tools has the potential to make the learning process more inclusive and effective.

Transitional justice involves several key elements: truth-seeking and reconciliation; holding perpetrators accountable and prosecuting them; conducting official investigations to uncover crimes; creating conditions for victims to receive compensation; reforming or restructuring corrupt or abusive institutions; documenting crimes in historical records; constructing monuments; and establishing museums.

The transitional justice process must operate within a legal framework or institution that requires government support. Additionally, timely assessment of specific situations is crucial. A transitional justice process is more effective when it is inclusive and participatory, rather than exclusive. Moreover, it should be viewed as part of a broader framework and not as an isolated effort. Therefore, adopting a holistic approach is essential for addressing these issues.

Another important consideration is that the process should be designed and managed by dignified professionals and people with experience.

Transitional justice: When and how?

In societies with a history of widespread abuse, concerted efforts during the transition period are crucial for promoting accountability, delivering justice, and initiating reconciliation processes. Transitional justice encompasses various mechanisms and approaches to achieve these goals, including judicial and non-judicial mechanisms, individual prosecutions, reparations, truth-seeking, and institutional reforms. These approaches can involve a combination of elements, regardless of the level of international involvement.

Recent experiences underscore the importance of creating conditions that allow independent and sovereign institutions and commissions to operate within the national justice plan. The support or input of international bodies should also be considered, including:

a. Ensuring that such mechanisms and bodies are established at a sufficiently high level of authority;
b. Guaranteeing their independent operation and adherence to international standards; and
c. Ensuring that the mechanisms are owned and operated by sovereign nations.

When capacity-building initiatives are undertaken to support sovereign bodies in implementing these processes, there is an expectation that they will contribute to the sustainable improvement or reform of the justice system.

When transitional justice is necessary as a tool, the strategies pursued must be holistic. This means addressing individual prosecutions, issues of reparations, truth-seeking, institutional cleansing, and the dismissal of perpetrators from their positions. The goals and expectations of transitional justice should be legally mandated and implemented in a manner that is widely understood by the public. Hence, continuous public engagement is essential.

Truth commission

The establishment of a Truth Commission serves as a crucial mechanism for investigating and addressing human rights abuses. These commissions are official, temporary, and non-judicial bodies tasked with uncovering the truth. They are responsible for investigating human rights abuses committed over a specific period, following a victim-centered process. Their objectives culminate in a final report containing the findings and recommendations. To date, more than thirty countries, including Argentina, Chile, South Africa, Peru, Ghana, Morocco, El Salvador, Guatemala, Timor-Leste, and Sierra Leone, have established and operated Truth Commissions.

Truth Commissions assist societies emerging from conflict in officially acknowledging and establishing the facts concerning human rights violations. They promote accountability, preserve evidence, and identify perpetrators, while providing recommendations for reparations and institutional reform. By holding public hearings, victims of crimes and abuse can share their personal stories and gain public recognition, which helps a country reconcile with its history.

However, challenges are associated with the use of Truth Commissions. These may include weak civil societies, political instability, fear among victims and witnesses, a weak or corrupt justice system, insufficient time for investigations, and lack of public support and funding. If Truth Commissions are established hastily, without adequate preparation, or if they become politicized, their credibility is undermined. Nevertheless, when the selection process is inclusive, aligns with public opinion, and is merit-based, there is significant potential for positive outcomes.

Truth Commissions also require a robust outreach strategy to publicize their work. A transparency-centered outreach strategy creates a platform that meets the expectations of the people and victims. Furthermore, they must consider gender issues and highlight the abuse suffered by victims of sexual and gender-based violence (SGBV). Such commissions may require international support, and it is advisable for them to seek it.

The importance and benefits of transitional justice
Promoting accountability

Transitional justice is vital for ensuring accountability and prosecuting those who might otherwise evade punishment for their actions. During political conflicts, crimes such as murder, torture, disappearances, and sexual violence often occur with impunity. By implementing prosecutions and mechanisms such as Truth Commissions to identify and bring perpetrators to justice, transitional justice not only helps prevent the recurrence of such acts but also reinforces the legal culpability of these actions in the minds of those involved. It serves as a deterrent to potential rulers and future human rights violators by highlighting the consequences of their actions.

Acknowledging the suffering of victims

Transitional justice acknowledges victims' suffering and provides a platform for redress and restoration of human dignity. Victims, often silenced and marginalized after enduring abuse, frequently face stigma. Both the state and perpetrators may deny the abuse. Truth Commissions pave the way for healing by officially acknowledging victims' suffering. This formal process of public recognition affirms victims' experiences and validates their status as rights-bearing citizens. It is instrumental in facilitating the psychological healing and social reintegration of victims.

Uncovering and establishing the truth

Transitional justice plays a crucial role in uncovering and establishing the truth. Conflicts are often cloaked in propaganda, denial, and secrecy, leaving families without information about the fate of their loved ones. Societies become divided and cling to competing and conflicting narratives that serve their interests. Truth Commissions officially present declassified documents and reports detailing the events that occurred—where, how, who was responsible, and why they occurred. This process counters denial, thwarts attempts to manipulate history, and helps bring closure to cases of disappearances.

Creating a platform for reconciliation and social cohesion

Transitional justice fosters reconciliation and strengthens social cohesion. Societies emerging from political conflict are often deeply polarized, with widespread distrust, resentment, and trauma. By acknowledging the crimes committed and facilitating dialogue, transitional justice cultivates a shared historical understanding. It also creates opportunities to rebuild broken community ties, jointly plan for a shared future, and live together in peace.

Creating a platform for democratic transition and institutional reform

Transitional justice facilitates democratic transition and institutional reform. Conflicts often arise from unjust, abusive, and dysfunctional state institutions. By establishing vetting processes, transitional justice helps remove perpetrators from positions of power and influence. Institutional reform addresses the root causes of abuse and builds institutions that respect human rights and the rule of law, making the government more legitimate, credible, and acceptable to the public.

Preventing the recurrence of abuse

Transitional justice is pivotal in preventing the recurrence of abuse. When grievances are left unaddressed and institutions remain unreformed, they become fertile ground for future cycles of violence. By engaging all stakeholders in the transition process, transitional justice helps to prevent the emergence of new cycles of violence. Accountability serves as a deterrent for those considering future crimes, while institutional reform addresses and eradicates the root causes of abuse. By tackling grievances and offering solutions, it diminishes the likelihood of revenge-seeking behavior.

Providing legitimacy to the succeeding political system
A government established after political turmoil requires legitimacy, public trust, and popular support. Transitional justice legitimizes the political system that is formed after a conflict. A government built on justice, truth, and institutional reform has the potential to break from the past and gain popular acceptance.

Providing an opportunity for perpetrators to reform
Even for perpetrators condemned and ostracized for their crimes, transitional justice offers opportunities and platforms for reintegration through community-focused programs. These initiatives enable them to reconcile with the society they have wronged and to rebuild their lives with renewed purpose.

In conclusion, transitional justice offers immense benefits not only in addressing past grievances but also in shaping the future. Although its implementation requires strong will, it is the only process capable of guiding a society traumatized by political conflict toward lasting peace, democracy, and the restoration of human dignity. Ignoring the past is akin to ignoring a wound, which cannot lead to lasting peace. Transitional justice provides a healthy and constructive path for healing.

Some Examples Related to Transitional Justice
South Africa
In response to the forty-six-year apartheid regime rooted in racial discrimination (1948–1994), South Africa established the Truth and Reconciliation Commission (TRC) to prevent large-scale acts of revenge. This initiative involved several key mechanisms: prioritizing truth-seeking, allowing perpetrators to testify and undergo full rehabilitation, offering substantial reparations to victims of abuse, and avoiding widespread prosecution.

While the TRC played a significant role in promoting national healing, some victims felt that it lacked balance and accountability.

Argentina

The military junta that ruled Argentina from 1976 to 1983 was responsible for the disappearance and killing of many Argentine citizens. Following the regime's collapse, Argentina actively pursued justice. The country prosecuted senior military leaders, ensuring their sentencing, although these individuals were pardoned around 2000 and later retried. The National Commission on the Disappearance of Persons (CONADEP), established in 1983, documented these crimes in a report titled "Nunca Más" ("Never Again"). Additionally, a former torture center, known as ESMA, was transformed into a museum of remembrance and is now on the UNESCO World Heritage List. Through this historical process, Argentina has been recognized as a model for holding human rights violators accountable.

Post-Genocide Rwanda - Gacaca Courts

In the aftermath of the genocide that claimed the lives of over eight hundred thousand Rwandans, the country faced the challenge of delivering justice to the victims. The International Criminal Tribunal for Rwanda (ICTR) played a crucial role in ensuring that senior architects of genocide were held accountable. Meanwhile, the establishment of community-based judicial systems, known as Gacaca Courts, allowed alternative punishments, such as community service for lower-level perpetrators. Additionally, the government initiated reconciliation efforts as a strategy to address the issue. Although these community-based courts have resolved numerous cases, they have also faced criticism regarding their implementation.

The United Nations Security Council established the International Criminal Tribunal for Rwanda (ICTR) with the mandate to prosecute individuals responsible for genocide and other serious breaches of international humanitarian law committed in Rwanda and neighboring states between January 1, 1994, and December 31, 1994. The Tribunal was headquartered in Arusha, Tanzania, with an office in Kigali, Rwanda, and The Hague, Netherlands, serving as an additional location. Established in 1995, the Tribunal tried 93 individuals accused of serious violations of international law, including senior military and government officials, politicians, businessmen, religious leaders, and numerous militia and mass media leaders.

Post-Communist Eastern Europe

Following the collapse of communism between 1989 and 1991, nations such as the Czech Republic and Poland took steps to bar state officials, particularly those from the secret police, from occupying public office. In Poland, the Institute of National Remembrance was established to document these crimes.

Post-Conflict Colombia - The Peace Agreement

Established in 2016, the Special Jurisdiction for Peace (SJP) is a pivotal component of Colombia's transitional justice system. Its mission is to investigate crimes committed during the conflict between the Colombian government and the FARC guerrilla movement, aiming to hold perpetrators accountable while balancing justice, reconciliation, and lasting peace. In 2018, it was ratified and integrated into the country's legal framework, establishing mechanisms for truth-seeking, justice, reparations, and ensuring that such events are not repeated in the future. This process involved all FARC members responsible for crimes, state officials, and other entities implicated in these offenses. Thousands of former guerrillas and state agents faced justice, and investigations were initiated into the actions of several senior military leaders. Consequently, previously concealed truths about the conflict have emerged. The Special Jurisdiction for Peace (SJP) is the cornerstone of Colombia's peace process.

Beyond its primary objectives, the SJP employed both retributive and restorative approaches. This includes adjudicating large-scale criminality and human rights violations and determining the appropriate sanctions. Additionally, through forgiveness, reconciliation, healing, and fostering conditions for reconciliation between victims and perpetrators, it crafted a roadmap that contributed to mending the country's social fabric.

Colombia's situation was distinctive because its justice sector comprises top academic institutions, intellectuals, lawyers, and civil society members. These individuals had the capacity to consult and conduct training sessions with international experts, significantly enhancing the potential for successful results.

Chapter 15

The Fate of the Fragmented Landscape of Eritrean Opposition

Introduction

In a single-party authoritarian regime or a government established through force, legitimate or peaceful opposition is not permitted. Typically, the ruling party wields absolute power in the country, portraying any opposition as illegal or a conspiracy with national adversaries. Disagreement with government policy or opposition to the government is swiftly suppressed by the security forces. In such systems, the existence of opposition is neither acknowledged nor allowed to function as a viable entity in the political arena. The only options are to operate clandestinely, act from exile, or express opposition through methods shrouded in silence. Resistance within the country does not function as a political force that can operate freely, but as a "dissident." Even if opposition exists, it ultimately has no choice but to operate outside the country.

Currently, the Eritrean opposition appears to be fragmented, disorganized, and lacking cohesion. Despite the earnest efforts of responsible members to unite under a common umbrella with a basic program, tangible results have yet to be achieved. This is a matter of concern for the future.

There are more opposition movements than normal, with operations primarily concentrated in the Middle East, Africa (notably Ethiopia), Europe, Australia, and North America. Despite their differing worldviews, these movements share similar objectives. They aim to instigate change within Eritrea and establish a constitutional government through a transitional administration. Questions that are raised by the opposition include: the organization of post-change Eritrea, the challenges it will encounter, the utilization of its resources, and its role in the region and the world. Undoubtedly, these and similar issues will be addressed by the transitional government in a democratic and inclusive manner, following the change in government.

Among these varied forms of opposition, some have historical ties to the Eritrean Liberation Front (ELF), while others are former members of the Eritrean People's Liberation Front (EPLF). Additionally, some have emerged independently of these two main organizations.

These opposition entities express their platforms in different ways: some as political organizations, others as movements, and others categorize themselves as civic society. They all utilize social media to advance their political agendas, organize dialogue events, and raise awareness within Eritrean communities, positively influencing their audiences. However, their discourse often includes language rife with personal attacks and insults. Consequently, these social media platforms have also become tools for spreading discord and deepening divisions among various opposition groups and organizations, which is regrettable and should be addressed.

Historical redress

In the early phases of the armed struggle, dissent was not tolerated; differing opinions were often suppressed or met with hostility. The eradication of the renowned Eritrean Liberation Movement (also known as Haraka) in the Sahel region, the senseless civil war that dragged on for nearly a decade between the Eritrean Liberation Front and the Eritrean People's Liberation Forces (later the Eritrean People's Liberation Front) until the Eritrean Liberation Front was compelled to exit Eritrea, and the military clashes between the Eritrean People's Liberation Front and various splinter groups of the Eritrean Liberation Struggle from 1981 to 1991 are notable examples of this. These internal conflicts among the fronts fostered divisive sentiments among Eritreans, both within and outside the country, sowing discord between supporters and sympathizers of the different organizations. This was the result of a political culture that opted to resolve differences of opinion through violent confrontation and elimination rather than through dialogue. In subsequent years, it set a negative precedent for the future. The ELF's dissolution had unprecedented consequences, culminating in the marginalization of a huge segment of society (mainly Muslims and lowlanders) in Eritrea's political arena. This was the last nail in the coffin for the opposition.

In his unpublished manuscript on the history of the armed struggle, Ibrahim Totil[iv] notes that the serious dispute and subsequent military conflict in 1965 between the ELF and the Eritrean Liberation Movement (Haraka) over establishing a military wing unit in the Sahel, which led to the ELF's liquidation of Haraka, indicates that the long-standing political dispute between the two organizations, existing since the establishment of the ELF in 1960, had reached its peak.

Within the Eritrean Liberation Front, difficulties and shortcomings were frequently addressed through violence. The movements that led reform initiatives are known by different names. Ibrahim Totil describes the "Islah" (Reform) movement as follows:

> The founders of the "Islah" (Reform) movement were young individuals who served in the Revolutionary Command units and participated in

the Kassala Conference, while others came from military cadres, particularly the First Division. Most of these individuals, who had been part of the Revolutionary Command units since their inception, were recruited in 1966 and 1967. They possessed the most comprehensive knowledge of the internal dynamics of the Revolutionary Command and were closely connected to the realities on the ground. Consequently, they were not only aware of the abuses committed against the army and its various bodies, but they were also capable of devising remedial measures due to their deep understanding of the leadership's deficiencies. (Ibrahim Totil: Date not available).

Continuing this movement, the Aradayeb meeting and the Adobha conference, held between 1968-69 E.C., should also be recognized. These gatherings, led by veteran and senior ELF fighters, aimed to highlight the ELF's shortcomings, strategically reposition the Eritrean army, and address the needs of both the people and the fighters.[lvi]

In the early 1970s, motivated by the belief that "the Eritrean field cannot accommodate more than one organization," efforts were made by the ELF to eliminate factions that had split from it for various reasons—specifically, the People's Forces (Group One), the People's Forces (Group Two), and the Eritrean Liberation Forces (Obel)—in the most extreme manner. This not only squandered the liberation army's resources, which were crucial for confronting the primary enemy, but also left decades of unhealed wounds.

Within the Eritrean People's Liberation Forces, which later evolved into the Eritrean People's Liberation Front, the response to the 1973 Reform Movement and other similar movements, whether they emerged as groups or individuals, was predominantly violent. This approach mirrored the measures taken within the ELF, underscoring that intolerance of political differences had become a deeply ingrained aspect of the Eritrean political culture.

As the Eritrean People's Liberation Front demonstrated its resilience through confrontation, a deadlock persisted between the two opposing fronts, namely the ELF and the EPLF. The internal fratricidal conflict continued until the Eritrean Liberation Front, overwhelmed by external conflicts with the EPLF and the Tigray People's Liberation Front (TPLF) and plagued by internal divisions, was forced to withdraw from the Eritrean arena in 1981.

In the complex and demanding political and military landscape, the Eritrean People's Liberation Front (EPLF) emerged as Eritrea's dominant political and military force. As it began to assert its influence over Eritrean politics, it started to display a similar political culture of intolerance towards other organizations. This stance was confirmed by the President of the current Government of Eritrea, who declared on Eritrea's Martyrs' Day, "We will not allow Eritrea to be the playground of organizations outside the People's Front in Eritrea," marking the highest official endorsement of this belief.

Consequently, numerous political organizations, movements, groups, and individuals abroad, who were prepared and capable of engaging in nation-building and were waiting outside Eritrea, were marginalized or ignored. Consequently, the capacity intended for nation-building was diminished, resulting in a loss for Eritrea.

In the years following independence, no force within Eritrea posed a challenge to the Eritrean People's Liberation Front (EPLF), later renamed the People's Front for Democracy and Justice (PFDJ). It faced no internal or external competition, and potential threats from within were minimal.

Despite the immense and irreparable losses stemming from the political differences between the EPLF and ELF, it was crucial for the EPLF to establish principles and strategies to ease political tensions and pursue reconciliation and recovery after independence. When a political organization emerges as dominant, one will expect it to exhibit qualities such as humility, patience, tolerance, and inclusiveness. This environment had the potential to materialize in post-independence Eritrea. The PFDJ had the historical opportunity to demonstrate wisdom, caution, foresight, inclusiveness, and tolerance to initiate national dialogue and reconciliation more effectively. Surprisingly, steps were taken to prevent key members of the ELF and other organizations, who could have significantly contributed to nation-building, from returning to their homeland and being utilized. And that's not all.

The centralization and culture of political regimentation fostered inside the EPLF during the armed struggle persisted after independence. For instance, the measures taken during the 1993 veterans' protest, which demanded basic living standards, exemplified this. Similarly, the violence in 1994 concerning disabled former freedom fighters, the political marginalization of the group known as G-13,[lvii], and the raids and arrests of the group known as G-15 further illustrate this trend. Additionally, actions against places of worship, the arrests of figures like Hajji Musa, accused of leading the Akriya School movement, and individuals such as Biteweded Abraha, as well as measures against senior and mid-level members of the civil service, military, and the PFDJ involved in the Forto movement of January 2013, which called for government reform, underscore the ongoing repression. Furthermore, thousands of citizens accused of having links to 'Islamic extremism' have been removed from their positions and remain imprisoned to this day.

Eritrea is a nation without a free press, where the government maintains absolute control over all domestic media outlets, using them as tools and mouthpieces for propaganda. The current regime has significantly stifled the country's burgeoning free-press culture. In 2001, citing national security, the government banned the free press, resulting in the closure of all privately owned newspapers and the imprisonment of eleven journalists. According to reports from the Committee to Protect Journalists, Eritrea is the most censored country globally and has the highest number of imprisoned journalists in Sub-Saharan Africa.[lviii]

The current state of the opposition

Given the nature of the ruling party, opposition forces in the diaspora should have created conditions favorable for uniting under a single, inclusive political platform or minimum program, thereby emerging as an alternative political force. To achieve this, they must develop strategies, consolidate their capacities, and commit to collaboration. When comparing the opposition camp to the ruling party, the former faces notable disadvantages. These include a lack of resources, increasing detachment from the country's realities over time, intelligence infiltration by the ruling party into their structures, geographical dispersion, and a lack of transparency and accountability in their operations. In light of this, the opposition forces need to cultivate qualities such as adaptability to changing circumstances, resilience to understand the struggle's fluctuations, and perseverance to maximize their limited resources. It is also appropriate for the opposition camp to assess itself using the aforementioned indicators. These include the following: What is the level of organizational capacity within the opposition? How clear are its goals, and how realistic and viable is its ideology? To what extent is the formulated strategy popular? What is its capacity to foster democratic discourse? What is the level of mobilization capability? etc. We now examine these factors one by one.

Organization

Efforts to unite opposition organizations in the diaspora under a single umbrella have been significant. There have been moments when hope seems to be within reach, although it ultimately remains unfulfilled. While these opposition groups share the common goal of opposing the regime in Asmara, they often expend more energy on internal conflicts than on building a robust political and diplomatic front against the ruling party. This is evident in the mutual accusations they level at each other. The absence of a unified platform to confront the Asmara regime, combined with the narrow interests of these groups, results in some, perhaps unintentionally, prioritizing harm to the opposition over the broader goal of change. Additionally, many entities within the opposition camp are hesitant to step out of their comfort zones, which can hinder the development of a platform that adapts to the changes occurring around it. Movements driven by personal positioning, ambition, and individual egos are also common. Historical legacy remains a significant obstacle, too.

In response to this situation, several social media platforms, aware of the harmful effects of such discord, are working to promote more constructive interactions and create communication channels among opposing movements. This is a promising development.

In an article published on Awate.com on August 31, 2025, Semere Habtemariam explored the challenges faced by the opposition. He notes that attempts to form alliances, such as the Eritrean Democratic Alliance in 2011 and the Eritrean National Council for Democratic Change in 2014, failed to unite all organizations under a single platform or to gain widespread support. He comments, "Instead of directing our resources to challenge the government, we find ourselves wasting our potential on trivial pursuits. The pursuit of unity has remained elusive." Semere elaborates that, as a former member of the now-defunct "Medrek" platform, he personally encountered significant difficulties in uniting diverse groups and acknowledges their failure in this endeavor. Through this account, he suggests that their efforts were characterized by a transactional approach, lacking the long-term commitment and essential qualities such as maturity, integrity, honesty, and structural soundness needed for a successful platform. Additionally, he criticized that while this experience provided a valuable lesson, it amounted to little more than that. In conclusion, he asserts, "Without structure, form, trust, and a shared vision, even the most earnest efforts will remain fragmented."

Semere observes that what is ultimately lost is trust, the opportunities we fail to seize, and the increasing suffering of the people we claim to represent. He also lists several established and attempted alliance initiatives: "UL-ELF-O (1989), EDLF (1991), ENPA (1992), DUE (1996), AENF (1999), ENA (2002), Four+One, ENDF (2004), ENSF (2004), EDF (2005), and others." Finally, Semere notes that even if some of these alliances are technically still in existence, their effectiveness falls short of expectations.

The infiltration of the PFDJ into the opposition

It is public knowledge that the PFDJ's intelligence network seeks to infiltrate opposition groups and sow discord among them by exploiting ethnic, regional, and religious differences, even going so far as creating divisions along regional lines. It is important to recognize the potential for such infiltration to severely undermine the unity of the opposition. The opposition lacks awareness of the regime's operational modalities and has not demonstrated the willingness or capability to address this issue with the necessary seriousness. Some even fail to acknowledge its existence.

The generational gap

Another source of division is the gap within the opposition camp between older citizens and the youth. This generational gap has led to differences in prioritizing issues and changing strategies. However, some serious veteran freedom fighters are creating opportunities to facilitate the transfer of experience between these generations. Because the transfer of experience is an important asset for the struggle.

The political positions of the diaspora

The relationship that the Eritrean opposition had with different administrations in Ethiopia was not encouraging. These relationships have not helped their growth as independent political entities. The Ethiopian regimes have not created an environment conducive to operating independently to challenge the Eritrean regime. Instead, they have repeatedly attempted to bring the opposition under their control and influence, using it as a tool for their political ambitions. This situation, coupled with the weakness of the alliances active on those platforms, has not helped the struggle against the Eritrean government. Moreover, it is crucial to note that the turmoil within Ethiopia over the past seven years has generated significant suspicion among opposition organizations.

Numerous members of the opposition camp, whether organizations, groups, or individuals, have been observed attempting to take a stand in the intricate military and political developments of neighboring Ethiopia, often at the cost of their reputations, and sometimes even overlooking the broader context of their actions.

Some have aligned themselves with either Prime Minister Abiy or his rival faction, the TPLF. Others argue that the war is a consequence of internal conflicts arising from political differences between competing forces in Ethiopia and should have been addressed through peaceful means and dialogue. The latter group advocates diplomacy as the sole solution, emphasizing the necessity of negotiation and perseverance.

Furthermore, there is contention regarding Eritrea's involvement in the conflict between the two Ethiopian factions. Some assert that such involvement not only complicates the situation but also represents an irresponsible act by the PFDJ, framing it as a military and political gamble.

Under the pretense of "eradicating the TPLF," some individuals aligned themselves with the military forces of Eritrea or the regime during the ensuing war. These differing viewpoints further weakened the opposition's ability to develop a clear and popular strategy for addressing the Ethiopian conflict.

The resolution of Ethiopia's internal affairs, marked by political disagreements and conflicts, should rest solely in the hands of Ethiopians. If Eritrea or any other neighboring country were to become involved, their role should be limited to facilitating dialogue between the parties, acting as a mediator to promote resolution. The involvement of Eritrean military forces in the conflict is unwarranted and should be condemned.

Young Eritreans abroad - Blue Wave or Briged Nhamedu

The deteriorating political situation in Eritrea has become a driving force pushing hundreds of thousands of young people into exile (to seek a better political, economic, and social life). Unlimited national service, the absence of the rule of law and justice, the suppression of political rights, worsening economic conditions, mass detention, etc., are some of the key drivers of exile. The regrettable thing is that, as a result of this misguided government policy, Eritrea's stability is in a worrying state of decline.

Youth frustration and anger have been fueled by this phenomenon, leading to the emergence of movements such as the Blue Wave or Briged Nhamedu, which call for governmental change and justice. Initiated in 2021 and predominantly led by young people, this movement included many former members of the national service. Their grievances and dissatisfaction with the regime arise from the severe repression they have endured and the future taken from them.

Young individuals are fleeing their beloved country to escape the interminable "national service," which they equate to forced labor and modern slavery, as well as to avoid relentless persecution by security forces and the military. Most cited the ongoing, indefinite national service as the primary reason for their decision to leave.

Many of them have been shot while crossing the Eritrea-Sudan and Eritrea-Ethiopia borders to flee the indefinite national service; they have endured various abuses while traversing the Sahara Desert in pursuit of hope, and some have even perished while crossing the Mediterranean Sea. These young men and women harbor profound hatred for the system that has destroyed their youth. They are also deeply resentful of this system.

Politically conscious and committed to their cause, they are leading a movement that has shaken the fear instilled by the Eritrean government in the Eritrean diaspora.

This Eritrean youth movement, symbolized by the Blue Wave, is not an isolated occurrence. Instead, it is part of an unstoppable global youth movement characterized by discontent and anger, which is spreading and will continue to do so. Recent youth movements in the Arab World, Nepal, Kenya, Madagascar, Morocco, and Georgia, as well as the Qeerroo movement in Ethiopia, have been instrumental in shaking the foundations or toppling corrupt and authoritarian regimes in these countries. The spirit of youth resistance holds a significant place in Eritrean history, too.

In the forties and fifties, and during the armed struggle, Eritrean youth were the leaders and backbone of the fight for independence. Their heavy sacrifices secured Eritrea's sovereignty. Today's youth inherit this legacy, but their struggles occur under different circumstances. They are not fighting colonial powers, but an oppressive system entrenched in the country, plundering its resources and leading it to ruin. This system has betrayed the goals for which their parents paid a lot of sacrifice.

Frustration, anger, rage, and discontent among the youth have given rise to this movement, which demands change and justice from the government. This movement represents a state of dissatisfaction. It is organized around local groups or chapters, has a global reach, and routinely experiences friction among its various chapters. It operates in many parts of the world, including Germany, Israel, the Netherlands, Sweden, Denmark, the USA, Canada, Switzerland, Ethiopia, and Uganda.

The confrontational methods employed to express the movement during its inception leave much to be desired. Other shortcomings were also evident. As a result, the movement has paid a significant price. However, contrary to the claims of the PFDJ regime, the movement has been driven by its internal dynamics rather than being manipulated by external forces. Movements like these, led and sustained by youth, naturally arise from unjust and oppressive systems. The phenomenon that unfolded in Eritrea is not an exception.

At this juncture, the internal differences within the Blue Wave appear to pose a greater threat than the inevitable pressure from the regime itself. Interestingly, these differences do not stem from the fundamental goals of the struggle itself. Instead, they center on the manner in which their struggle is conducted, the organization of the movement's chapters across different continents, and the nature and maturity of the political alliances or coalitions being formed.

Even if the current discord is fueled by personal or group interests and ambitions, a significant challenge lies in the potential for it to cause irreparable harm to the youth movement itself. The primary concern is how to overcome these challenges and elevate the movement to a higher level of effectiveness. Ultimately, what are the choices? Should the internal conflict persist, be managed, or be resolved? Should it be escalated or stabilized?

Escalating this will not yield any results. Eritrea cannot afford to look back and dwell on a struggle for which such a heavy price has been paid to achieve. The efforts of these youth are an invaluable national asset that must not be squandered. There is no alternative to resolving differences through dialogue. Such crises are inevitable in movements of this nature. The key is to manage and resolve disputes in the spirit of goodwill.

For the Blue Wave movement to be effective, it must engage in self-reflection, maintain its dynamic essence, clarify its direction, and evolve organically. Supporters of this movement need to view the pressing questions before them as a wake-up call in their pursuit of reconciliation, understanding, and integrity. The Blue Wave movement should prioritize and address the following issues:

- Centering the struggle around fundamental goals that align with the aspirations of all Eritrean youth seeking justice;

- Establishing strong connections with pro-change forces operating in Eritrea;
- Ensuring that, through their voices and actions, they become genuine partners with citizens striving for change in Eritrea;
- Moving beyond a reactive strategy of merely responding to the regime's provocations and adopting proactive and savvy measures;
- Actively confronting the regime's system of extorting the 2% tax, which it coercively imposes on citizens living abroad;
- Making the world aware of the regime's crimes and its unparalleled cunning in destabilizing the region in a clear and intelligent manner; and
- Engaging in alliances based on partnerships with democratic forces worldwide.

This strategic thinking and maturity are not indicators of the movement's weakness but rather evidence of its wisdom and strength. These are the primary tools used to dismantle a deeply entrenched dictatorship.

This path of struggle demands patience, focus, profound political wisdom, and commitment. It requires rising above personal egos, grudges, and resentments. The movement is responsible for choosing a trusted and effective approach, but this cannot be accomplished without guidance.

Elderly citizens in the diaspora, who have experience in the struggle, have a duty to intervene as mediators to resolve the temporary crisis within the movement. However, this must be performed without exerting pressure. Ultimately, the goal is to establish a common, all-inclusive, and broad political umbrella that serves as a center for hosting dialogues and reconciling political differences. This common political umbrella should pursue the following three fundamental objectives:

- Changing the regime without compromising Eritrea's sovereignty;
- Establishing a broad-based transitional government; and
- Building a constitutional Eritrea.

All members of the Blue Wave movement should set aside personal, group, or individual interests to prioritize the needs of the people and the cause. The Eritrean youth are intelligent and capable of achieving remarkable things. Their awareness of the detrimental effects of division within the struggle is greater than that of others. Their determination to resist the fear that the regime seeks to instill is commendable and should be supported. At this juncture, they must exhibit wisdom to maintain their unity, as their strength lies in this trait. It is the only tool that can facilitate such changes. We must ensure that the Blue Wave remains a unifying force, rather than one that divides.

Consequences of a weak opposition

A weak opposition breeds frustration and confusion among its members and supporters, while offering relief to its adversaries. Ultimately, the people suffering under dictatorial rule bear the brunt of this weakness. The fragmentation within the opposition has shattered, or at least shaken, the hopes of those seeking justice, eroding their faith in the opposition's role in the struggle for change in the country. This disarray has also led to an increase in the number of people choosing silence. Many citizens who were once vocal now find themselves participating in festivals and events organized by the PFDJ/Eritrean embassies, with some even reaching despair. Fear-induced self-censorship has become the norm. For those abroad who dare to speak out, it is common to hear, "Why don't they lead a peaceful life rather than confront a cruel regime?" or "They are getting nowhere." Expressing one's opinion is seen as foolishness, while silence is regarded as a virtue.

This internal division within the opposition fuels silent anger, frustration, and sometimes hopelessness among Eritreans living in the country. The tendency to side with the regime or avoid confrontation can partly be attributed to the crisis and internal fragmentation within the opposition.

In the absence of convincing opposition, alternatives have gradually disappeared, hindering the formation of a common platform of resistance with those fighting against the regime.

The Eritrean diaspora community, mired in divisive politics, has failed to function cohesively. The hope that Eritrean citizens residing in Eritrea once placed in the opposition camp has diminished. Speaking without verifying facts only highlights the opposition's weaknesses.

Countries and organizations that support the Eritrean people also perceive the opposition camp not as a viable option with potential but as a group prone to internal conflicts, leading them to dismiss it as a solution. In essence, international civil society does not regard the opposition as a credible political alternative or institution. The sporadic diplomacy occasionally undertaken, even if it achieves some results, fails to persuade as it should. Resources are squandered, appearing unconvincing and duplicative.

The opposition's weaknesses have allowed the PFDJ to freely maneuver abroad. The Regret Form[lix] for the individuals who wish to express regret (for opposing the regime) acts as a pretext for citizens wishing to return to their homeland. The 2% tax sent from abroad serves as a financial source for the PFDJ. Additionally, festivals sponsored by the Asmara regime are expanding in type and scale, justified for various occasions.

Eritreans abroad are deprived of the services they should receive as citizens. Notably, deceased individuals are not repatriated for burial in their homeland. Furthermore, violent clashes between regime supporters and opponents sometimes result in fatalities. The tragic incident in Israel between government supporters and opponents exemplifies this phenomenon. The opposition camp has also failed to halt this trend.

Currently, Eritreans in the diaspora are divided into two major groups: regime supporters and opponents of the Eritrean government. There is also a group known as the "silent majority." The PFDJ, which holds power in Eritrea, exploits and fuels the division among Eritreans living abroad.

This situation appears to be politically polarized. The Eritrean government exercises strict control over the diaspora community, and citizens who criticize the system are faced with intimidation. This phenomenon can be described as transnational aggression.

The form of opposition in a post-change scenario

While it is anticipated that the form of opposition will become more institutionalized during the transitional government period in a post-change scenario, and even legally justified, it is not too early to explore some useful preliminary ideas. This primarily concerns the question of what kind of political system will best represent the interests and welfare of Eritrea's people. As detailed in Chapter 2, the transitional government must determine the type of constitutional government to be established in Eritrea. It, representing all Eritrean people and citizens abroad, will be tasked with establishing a governance structure rooted in democratic principles, reflecting Eritrea's socio-economic formation, and prioritizing the interests and welfare of the Eritrean people. However, opposition must be understood within the context of this comprehensive framework. Opposition is the lifeblood of a democracy. It should not be regarded as an enemy or threat; rather, it is an integral and legal component of the political system itself.

The primary function of the opposition is to scrutinize the actions, policies, and laws of the ruling party or government. It represents citizens who do not support the current system, voice their concerns and interests, and hold the system accountable in the public arena. A credible opposition party develops and presents alternative policies and visions to citizens, offering voters a clear choice in future elections. By employing parliamentary and popular oversight, the government is compelled to be accountable for its revenue, expenditures, and shortcomings. However, the opposition underscores a fundamental truth: its mission is to strive for a share of power and not to be perceived as an adversary.

For the opposition to achieve its goals through popular means and for the spirit of democracy to take root and thrive on both sides, it is essential that fundamental principles exist that both the government and the opposition should uphold. Both sides must have faith in the Constitution and the government. The opposition challenges the political party in power at the time but does not oppose the government, the constitution, or the democratic laws of the system. Its aim is to come to power and replace the government, not through confrontation but through constitutional means and persuasion.

The opposition holds the right to critique and scrutinize the government; however, this criticism should be constructive and prioritize national interests. Beyond merely highlighting the government's errors, it is also tasked with suggesting better solutions. Indiscriminate obstruction can harm political systems and erode public trust. Moreover, the opposition must graciously accept its electoral defeat and allow the victorious party to form a government. Both sides must also demonstrate their commitment to democratic principles, including parliamentary procedures, freedom of expression, and institutions such as the judiciary and media.

The ways in which opposition is expressed in the political arena differ across systems. These methods may include participating in parliamentary debates to express views, posing questions to various ministries about their performance, serving on parliamentary committees that oversee government policies and their implementation, and amending or improving bills presented by the government to the parliament. While these roles are carried out within the parliament, the opposition also has roles outside it. These may involve publishing research-based policy proposals, organizing forums to gauge and gather public opinion, meeting with the media to communicate proposals to the public, and using the media to inform the public about the government's shortcomings and present new ideas.

Additionally, the opposition can challenge or oppose government actions deemed unconstitutional through the judicial system.

The vitality of democracy is reflected in the strength of its opposition. A dynamic, courageous, and widely supported opposition indicates a confident and democratic system. Conversely, when opposition is restricted, silenced by governmental pressure, or suppressed through unlawful means, it signals a decline in democracy. A balanced governance system is crucial, where one side upholds the core principles of governance and the other side ensures government accountability. This balance is achieved when both sides exhibit mutual commitment to fundamental democratic principles and rules.

Conclusion

Envisioning a New Eritrea

As you delve into "Renewing the Promise: A New Vision for Eritrea," the content unfolds page by page, offering both diagnostic insights and prescriptive solutions. This book seeks to thoroughly explore the entrenched challenges confronting Eritrea as a nation and proposes foundational ideas for constructing a new Eritrea. These ideas are not presented as the musings of an outsider but rather from the perspective of someone deeply committed to the vision of a sovereign and prosperous Eritrea. The goal of this concluding chapter, however, is not to reiterate the arguments presented in the earlier sections. Instead, it weaves interconnected themes into a cohesive narrative. It presents a vision that embodies the actionable practices and aspirations of the people, envisioning a post-transformation or a new Eritrea.

From the detailed text emerges a central, compassionate thesis: prioritizing human welfare is a fundamental pillar of national growth. This is not merely a slogan; it is the foundation upon which Eritrea must be built. As repeatedly emphasized throughout the book's chapters in various forms, sovereignty and improving the standard of living for all citizens are inseparable. If treated separately, they become empty and meaningless phrases. If economic progress cannot be measured by the level of health, education, and the dignity of each citizen, it cannot be considered meaningful or complete. Furthermore, if national security is not based on the active participation of the people and does not align with the governmental priorities trusted by the people, its chance of success is doubtful.

Synthesizing the core argument

Our analysis begins with an examination of the current situation in the country. This comprehensive assessment elucidates the scope and magnitude of the challenges encountered (Chapter 1) in Eritrea. Building on this foundation, the book delves into pivotal moments or prospective political transitions, analyzing and discussing the tasks and essential steps for a transitional government (Chapters 2 and 13). The mission of this entity, the transitional government, is to promote sustainable growth and stability by fostering political dialogue that embraces Eritreans with diverse perspectives (Chapter 14).

The detailed roadmap for economic development, outlined in Chapters 3 and 4, is based on a human welfare-based development approach. This approach prioritizes advancements in education, health, and food security, presenting them not as secondary objectives but as the primary foundations for long-term economic growth. This people-centered development model is intricately linked to the symbiotic relationship between economic development and good governance, as extensively discussed in Chapter 5. Development cannot be realized without institutions characterized by transparency and accountability, free from corruption, that prioritize the rule of law and provide a framework of predictability for both citizens and investors. Good governance can be described as the conduit through which economic policies are translated into the well-being of the people.

When a government serves its people, it forms the foundation of national sovereignty (Chapter 6). A nation composed of capable and healthy citizens who actively engage in shaping their collective future strengthens its sovereignty and can better withstand unforeseen challenges. This internal resilience is further bolstered when Eritrea's rich cultural heritage (Chapter 7) and the Eritrean diaspora—a vast reservoir of untapped potential—are integrated into the development process (Chapter 8). When effectively harnessed, culture can act as an ethical catalyst for economic growth while fostering social cohesion and national unity. Meanwhile, the Eritrean diaspora provides a wide network of skilled human capital, expertise, and global connections that are essential for national reconstruction.

A country prioritizing domestic development requires a strategic, cost-effective, and credible defense posture. The doctrine of deterrence outlined in Chapter 9 is not about militarizing society or glorifying military actions; rather, it envisions creating a conducive environment for unhindered development. As discussed in Chapter 10, this defensive stance is complemented by a sophisticated foreign policy that includes strategic patience, non-alignment, and economic diplomacy. This approach can transition Eritrea from isolation to confident partnerships, aiming to establish reciprocal frameworks that promote incremental mutual benefits rather than zero-sum outcomes.

Ultimately, the foreign policy direction proposed in the book sets the stage for the detailed policy shift outlined in Chapter 11: transitioning from an aid-dependent model to a development partnership grounded in national sovereignty. To achieve this, Eritrea must prioritize its interests when engaging with international partners. At a broader level, the envisioned partnership should align with and support the national development roadmap. Success in this endeavor hinges on absorbing the lessons—both positive and negative—that Africa has learned during this period (Chapter 13). By learning from the experiences of other nations, Eritrea can protect itself from potential pitfalls on its development path and emulate the best practices. In doing so, it will position itself as an integral member of the African community, capable of making unique contributions.

The unified vision: A cohesive framework for action

Integrating all the elements mentioned above can potentially establish a robust and resilient framework for the development journey. Good governance promotes economic growth that prioritizes human welfare, which inevitably bolsters national sovereignty. A sovereign and prosperous nation with credible and acceptable defensive capabilities is well equipped to pursue a confident foreign policy and secure peace, which is crucial for its development. This virtuous cycle is driven by skilled Eritrean human capital, both within the country and in the diaspora, and unified by a shared cultural identity.

The discussion on conventional political opposition in a New Eritrea (Chapter 15) does not involve dismantling the government from its core. Instead, it aims to infuse the government with a new spirit of governance. A system focused on good governance views the opposition not as a threat but as an essential tool for accountability, innovation, and policy enhancement. It represents a patriotic effort that showcases the government's ability to achieve the ambitious goals it has set to enhance the Eritrean people's well-being.

A call for conscience and action

The roadmap outlined in this book is undeniably ambitious, necessitating a fundamental reassessment of the relationship between the state and its citizens. This, in turn, calls for contributions, sacrifices, and a deep sense of shared responsibility from all sectors of society. From the leaders of the transitional government to the youth who will follow them, from ordinary citizens to skilled professionals in the diaspora, from religious to traditional leaders, and from the youngest to the oldest, everyone is involved.

The challenges are vast, but so are the opportunities they bring forth. Eritrea is a nation of strong and resilient people, strategically located with untapped potential. Most importantly, it boasts an indomitable history of struggle and proven capacity for collective action. The spirit of struggle that achieved liberation must now be directed towards the national reconstruction project.

This conclusion should not be seen as an end but rather as a beginning—a call to action for the decisive struggle being waged today. It is a struggle to build a peaceful, just, stable, and prosperous Eritrea. An Eritrea that has paid a heavy price should not merely survive by chance but must become a nation that transforms the lives of both present and future generations. The narrative is complete, and the vision is now clear to the reader. The next chapter will not be written with ink but with the resolve, hard work, and collective action of the Eritrean people. The responsibility lies with us. The time is now.

ENDNOTES

i   On September 18, 2001, senior Eritrean politicians were arrested. They have been detained for over 20 years after advocating for the National Assembly to convene as planned and for a constitution to be enacted, as well as criticizing Eritrea's President, Mr. Isaias Afwerki. Most of these individuals were senior veterans known as the "Group of 15" (G-15), who were part of the Central Committee and the Political Bureau of the Eritrean People's Liberation Front (EPLF). Among those who raised concerns, 11 members of the 'Group of 15' were imprisoned on September 18, 2001, while the remaining four were forced into exile. One of them, Ambassador Adhanom Ghebremariam, died in February 2021. The three who remain in exile are: Mr. Mesfin Hagos, former Minister of Defense and Governor of the Southern Region; Mr. Mahmoud Burhan Blata, former administrator of Dekemhare city and veteran of the Eritrean struggle; and Mr. Haile Menkerios, who was Eritrea's Ambassador to the United Nations and later served as a senior UN official.

ii   Phone conversation with Kebreab Yimesghen, November 30, 2025

iii   UN Human Rights Council (2025) UN Rights Council Rejects Bad-Faith Bid to End Eritrea Scrutiny | Human Rights Watch)

iv   UNDP Eritrea – 2024 Annual Report UNDP Eritrea Annual Report 2024

v   What is the Red Sea crisis, and what does it mean for global trade? The Guardian, January 03, 2024 https://www.theguardian.com/world/2024/jan/03/what-is-the-red-sea-crisis-and-what-does-it-mean-for-global-trade

vi   Al Majala, Why do so many foreign powers have military bases in Djibouti? London, March 21, 2023 https://en.majalla.com/node/288091/politics/why-do-so-many-foreign-powers-have-military-bases-djibouti

vii   Addis-Djibouti Corridor to Get Major Upgrade That is Key to Unlocking Connectivity and Trade for Ethiopia and the Horn of Africa, The World Bank, July 20, 2023 https://www.worldbank.org/en/news/press-release/2023/07/20/addis-djibouti-corridor-to-get-major-upgrade-that-is-key-to-unlocking-connectivity-and-trade-for-ethiopia-afe-hoa viii "Thus as far as authoritarian leadership dynamics in concerned, an overwhelming majority of dictators lose power to those inside the gates of the presidential palace rather than the masses outside. The predominant political conflict in dictatorships appears to be not between the ruling elite and the masses but rather among regime insiders." (Svolik, Milan, (2012) The Politics of Authoritarian Rule, Milan W. Svolik, Cambridge, London.

ix The philosophy or intent behind political marginalization can vary, often serving as an instrument employed by those in power to maintain control. By suppressing specific groups or individuals, authorities can sustain their influence unopposed. Factors such as the political convictions of individuals or the absence of loyalty to the government may be utilized to perpetuate this practice. "Mdskal" or to be frozen out or sidelined, represents one form of political marginalization.

The impact of "Mdskal" can be profound on individuals and their mindsets. The state of mind of those who experience "Mdskal" can vary widely based on the context and the individual's resilience. It is crucial to note that individuals respond to "Mdskal" in diverse ways, and resilience can play a significant role in shaping their mental and emotional well-being. Additionally, societal and systemic factors contribute to the overall state of mind, with common outcomes being feelings of not being valued or respected. Moreover, "Mdskal" negatively affects trust between colleagues and with the broader society in general. This practice can lead to emotions of exclusion, isolation, and powerlessness, creating a sense of alienation and frustration that impacts psychological well-being. This can contribute to a feeling of being trapped in a quagmire or conundrum, resulting in diminished self-esteem, affecting confidence and self-worth, and even leading to apathy and a lack of interest in politics. This experience can be compounded when members of your community believe that the government may have had a reason to sideline you or put you in that situation.

x   Dr. Natasha Ezrow is a senior lecturer at the University of Essex. Recently, she has published a new book titled "Failed States and Institutional Decay," and in 2011, she also published two books on dictatorships. "The Politics of Dictatorship" serves as an introduction to the topic and is an academic text concerning dictatorial systems.

xi   National Charter: The following elements may be included:·
- Preamble: This concise statement will emphasize the significance of the charter, outline the vision of a transitional government, and may also incorporate fundamental national principles, values, and the country's historical context.
- Objectives and Principles: These may encompass guiding principles such as democracy, justice, human rights, social justice, and economic development.·
- Administrative Structure: This may involve the separation of the three branches of government (legislative, judicial, and executive) and the electoral systems.
- Rights and Freedoms: This section may address the civil, political, economic, social, and cultural rights of citizens, as well as equality before or under the law.·
- Duties of Citizens: This section outlines the civic responsibilities of citizens towards their country, including respecting the law and contributing to society.
- Accountability Mechanisms: This covers the accountability of the government and public officials, checks and balances, transparency, and public participation in the decision-making process.
- Conflict Resolution and Management of Differences: Recognizing the importance of political differences, this stipulates methods for resolving disputes, such as dialogue, mediation, and other conflict-resolution mechanisms.
- Amendment Procedures: This section outlines the procedures for amending the charter as circumstances evolve.

- Implementation Procedures: This section specifies the rules and procedures for implementing the principles and objectives of the National Charter, including the ultimate judicial procedures.
- National Unity and Reconciliation: This involves developing a strategy to promote coexistence and prevent conflict among different groups.·
- International Commitments: This stipulates the country's respect for and adherence to international laws, treaties, agreements, etc., in alignment with the charter.

xii Normalcy involves reestablishing a peaceful and functional society where the rule of law is upheld, essential services are provided, and citizens can live their daily lives without the threat of political persecution. Restoring normalcy requires reviving economic stability and ensuring citizens have access to basic necessities. It envisions a scenario where children can enjoy their childhood without being overwhelmed by political rhetoric, and where the youth can aspire to a promising future, complete their education, find employment, establish families, own homes, and raise children in safety. This means farmers can tend to their land without disruption, workers can earn a sustainable livelihood to support their families, and parents and grandparents can enjoy a peaceful retirement. It also involves respecting churches and allowing them to offer unhindered spiritual services to their communities, as well as honoring local traditions. This transformation embodies the aspiration for a society where peace, stability, and prosperity are not just ideals but the lived reality of every citizen.

xiii The members of the 1973 movement were primarily intellectuals and students. Their core demands focused on protecting the democratic rights of front members, implementing checks and balances, ensuring accountability, upholding freedom of expression, and ending the misuse of power by some veterans against new members. The movement was ultimately suppressed, with its main leaders arrested, degraded, and humiliated. It was labeled as "opportunistic," "sectarian," "destructive," "divisive," and so forth, leading to its dissolution. Among the prominent leaders sentenced to death were Mussie Tesfamichaael, Yohannes Sebhatu, Tareke Yehdego, Habteselassie Gebremedhin, Afeworki Teklu, Debessay Gebreselassie, Doctor Rissom, Ghebreamlak Issac, Doctor Michael, Germay Berhe, Tewelde Iyob, Dahab Tesfatsion, Aberash Melke, Messih Rissom, Michael Bereketab, Samuel Gebredengl, Alem Berhe, Tekle Gebrekristos, Goitom Berhe, and Haile Yohannes.

xiv In his book, Mesfin Hagos notes that within the Eritrean People's Liberation Front, a faction labeled "Yemin" or "Yemanawyan" (meaning "rightists") was disparaged by Isaias and his associates. Subsequently, Isaias, acting on his own, ordered their execution without informing the other Polit-bureau members (Hagos M., 2023). For instance, Iyob Ghebrelul, a scholar who studied geography in the Soviet Union, was arrested for asserting that there was no ideological difference between the Eritrean Liberation Front and the Eritrean People's Liberation Front. Before his execution, a comprehensive campaign was launched to purge and eliminate the group. Among those targeted were Mehari Ghirmatsion, Ghebremichael Meharezgi, Iyob Ghebrelul, Haile Jebha, Solomon Weldemariam, Araia Semere, and Kidane Abeto, to name a few.

xv The late Osman Saleh Sabbe was a dedicated fighter for Eritrea's independence from the mid-1950s until his death, presenting the struggle on an international stage. Alongside Idris Mohamed Adem and Osman Galawdewos, he served for many years on the Supreme Council of the Eritrean Liberation Front (ELF). He also contributed to the establishment of the Eritrean People's Liberation Forces (the First Group). In the mid-1970s, due to disagreements with the leadership of the Eritrean People's Liberation Forces (later known as the Eritrean People's Liberation Front, EPLF), he continued his struggle through other means.

xvi Africa Environment Outlook: Past, present and future perspectives, GRID-Arendal and UNEP,
http://www.grida.no/publications/other/aeo/

xvii	http://www.bbc.co.uk/worldservice/specials/1624_story_of_africa/page92.shtml
xviii	Shamil Jeppie and Souleymane Bachir Diagne (eds). The Meanings of Timbuktu, CODESRIA/HSRC, 2008, 416 p., http://www.codesria.org/spip.php?article643&lang=en
xix	Simon Kuznets, Modern Economic Growth: Findings and Reflections, American Economic Review 63, 1973, 247-258.
xx	Michael P. Todaro and Stephen C. Smith, Economic Development-8th ed. (Boston: Addison Wesley, 2003), 85.
xxi	Ibid. 91-99
xxii	Michael P. Todaro and Stephen C. Smith, Economic Development-8th ed. (Boston: Addison Wesley, 2003), 15
xxiii	Ibid. 98
xxiv	Paul Collier, The Bottom Billion (New York: Oxford University Press, 2007), 3-4.
xxv	Robert Calderisi, The Trouble with Africa, Why Foreign Aid is not Working (New York: Palgrave Macmillan, 2006), 14.
xxvi	Ibid. 7
xxvii	David K. Leonard and Scott Straus, Africa's Stalled Development: International Causes and Cures (Colorado: Lynne Reinner Publishers, 2003), 8.
xxviii	Ibid. 10
xxix	Ibid. 8
xxx	Robert Calderisi, The Trouble with Africa, Why Foreign Aid is not Working, (New York: Palgrave Macmillan, 2006), 26.
xxxi	Ibid. 27
xxxii	Ibid. 27
xxxiii	Dambisa Moyo, Dead Aid: Why Aid is not Working and How There is a Better Way for Africa, (New York: Farrar, Straus and Girous, 2007), xix.
xxxiv	P. T. Bauer, Equality, the Third World, and Economic Delusion, (Cambridge: Harvard University Press, 1981), 100.

xxxv   Robert Calderisi, The Trouble with Africa, Why Foreign Aid is not Working (New York: Palgrave Macmillan, 2006), 160.
xxxvi   Ibid. 156
xxxvii   World Bank, World Development Report, pp. 33-35
xxxviii   Robert Calderisi, The Trouble with Africa, Why Foreign Aid is not Working (New York: Palgrave Macmillan, 2006), 14.
xxxix   http://www.yara.com/sustainability/global_trends/growth/index.aspx
xl   Michael P. Todaro and Stephen C. Smith, Economic Development-8th ed. (Boston: Addison Wesley, 2003), 23.
xli   Paul Collier, The Bottom Billion (New York: Oxford University Press, 2007), 53-58.
xlii   Paul Collier, On the Bottom Billion, TEDGlobal, May 2008 http://www.ted.com/speakers/paul_collier.html
xliii   CIDA, Stimulating Sustainable Economic Growth, http://acdi-cida.gc.ca/INET/IMAGES.NSF/vLUImages/EconomicGrowth/$file/Sustainable-Economic-Growth-e.pdf
xliv   Ibid.
xlv   Ngozi Okonjo-Iweale, Want to Help Africa, Do Business Here, TEDGlobal, 2008 http://www.ted.com/talks/ngozi_okonjo_iweala_on_doing_business_in_africa.html
xlvi   The Africa Report. Mo Ibrahim and the multipolar world order. January 03, 2026. https://www.theafricareport.com/403243/mo-ibrahim-and-the-multipolar-world-order/?utm_source=Facebook&utm_campaign=Facebook&utm_medium=Social%20media#=
xlvii   Peter P Rogers, Kazi F Jalal, and John A Boyd, An Introduction to Sustainable Development (London: Earthscan, 2009), 62.
xlviii   Ibid. 63
xlix   Council on Foreign Relations Africa's 'Leaders for Life' | Council on Foreign Relations September 2023
l   Ibid.

li	Paul Collier, The Bottom Billion, (New York: Oxford University Press, 2007), 4.
lii	Robert Calderisi, The Trouble with Africa, Why Foreign Aid is not Working (New York: Palgrave Macmillan, 2006), 160.
liii	Paul Collier and Jan Willem Gunning, "Explaining African Economic Performance." Journal of Economic Literature 37, no. 1 (1999): 64-111.
liv	Paul Collier, New Rules for Rebuilding a Broken Nation, TEDGlobal, 2009, http://www.ted.com/talks/paul_collier_s_new_rules_for_rebuilding_a_broken_nation.html
lv	Ibrahim Totil Ibrahim Totil was a senior veteran of the Eritrean independence struggle. In 1987, during the "Unity" congress of the Eritrean People's Liberation Front, he joined the movement and continued fighting for independence. Although he was appointed head of the Northern Red Sea Zone after independence, the regime disregarded his experience and knowledge for many years. On February 8, 2013, he was arrested under the pretext of having participated in the Forto movement. He remains imprisoned in the regime's jail.
lvi	ዝክሪ መስከረም ካብ ካይሮ ክሳብ አዶብሓ፡ ጋዜጣ ሓዳስ ኤርትራ፡ መስከረም 23, 2025 (September Memorial, From Cairo to Adobha, Haddas Eritrea, September 23, 2025)
lvii	The movement, known as Group 13 (G-13), consisted of 13 prominent Eritrean intellectuals living in the diaspora. In October 2000, they sent a letter to the President of Eritrea, Mr. Isaias Afwerki. This letter addressed various issues, including a call for an end to one-man rule and matters of political reform.
lviii	https://www.hrw.org/world-report/2020/country-chapters/eritrea
lix	The Regret/Remorese Form is a document used in Eritrea's taxation of its diaspora, who left without permission. This document expresses remorse for an unauthorized departure and/or non-payment of the 2% diaspora tax while abroad. By completing the form and paying owed taxes,

individuals legitimize their status with the Eritrean government, access consular services such as passports and identity documents, and ensure they can visit Eritrea without the risk of detention for avoiding national service or taxes.

BIBLIOGRAPHY

Chapter 1

African Development Bank. Eritrea Economic Outlook | African Development Bank Group

Council on Foreign Relations, Al Shabaab, December 6, 2022

The Economist Intelligence. Eritrea Economy, Politics and GDP Growth Summary - The Economist Intelligence Unit

The Economist Magazine. Somalia's state-building project is in tatters The Economist Magazine, July 24th 2025

Human Rights Concern Eritrea, Eritrea: Hajji Ibrahim Younus Dies in Custody, February 6, 2019, https://hrc-eritrea.org/eritrea-hajji-ibrahim-younus-dies-in-custody/

UN Human Rights Council (2025) UN Rights Council Rejects Bad-Faith Bid to End Eritrea Scrutiny | Human Rights Watch)

UNDP Eritrea – 2024 Annual Report UNDP Eritrea Annual Report 2024

UNHCR (2023) – Eritrea Country https://www.unhcr.org/countries/eritrea

Chapter 2

Ezrow, Natasha M., and Erica Frantz, Dictators and Dictatorships— Understanding Authoritarian Regimes and their Leaders, Bloomsbury, London, 2011

Authoritarian breakdown -- how dictators fall | Dr. Natasha Ezrow | TEDxUniversityofEssex, https:// www.youtube.com/watch?v=6ECTcaSXeI1 Accessed on October 7, 2023

Brownlee, J. (2012). Democracy Prevention: The Politics of the U.S.-Egyptian Alliance. Cambridge University Press.

Doyle, M. W., & Sambanis, N. (2006). Making War and Building Peace: United Nations Peace Operations. Princeton University Press.

Geddes, B., Frantz, E., & Wright, J. (2018). How Dictatorships Work: Power, Personalization, and Collapse. Cambridge University Press.

Huntington, S. P. (1991). The Third Wave: Democratization in the Late Twentieth Century. University of Oklahoma Press.

International Crisis Group (ICG). (2021). Mali's Transition: A Fragile Path to Democracy. CrisisGroup.org (https://www.crisisgroup.org)

Kotkin, Stephen, Modern Authoritarianism and Geopolitics: Thoughts on a Policy Framework, Stanford CDDRL, April 11, 2022

Linz, J. J., & Stepan, A. (1996). Problems of Democratic Transition and Consolidation: Southern Europe, South America, and Post-Communist Europe. Johns Hopkins University Press.

Nordlinger, E. A. (1977). Soldiers in Politics: Military Coups and Governments. Prentice-Hall.

O'Donnell, G., & Schmitter, P. C. (1986). Transitions from Authoritarian Rule: Tentative Conclusions about Uncertain Democracies. Johns Hopkins University Press.

Paris, R. (2004). At War's End: Building Peace After Civil Conflict. Cambridge University Press.

Slovik, Milan W., The Politics of Authoritarian Rule (Cambridge Studies in Comparative Politics) Cambridge University Press, September 17, 2012

Solomon, Semere, ረዚን ዋጋ ዝተኸፍሎ ናጽነት ኤርትራ ንዘተጠልመ መብጽዓን፥ ብአረአአያ ሓደ ገዳም ተጋዳላይ፥ IngramSpark Publishers, La Vergne, TN, 2024

Syria's Transitional Government: Challenges, Policies, and Prospects Syria's Transitional Government: Challenges, Policies, and Prospects - Arab Center Washington, DC May 22, 2025 Arab Center Washington, DC

United Nations Development Programme (UNDP). (2012). Tunisia's Transition: One Year After the Revolution. UNDP Reports https://www.undp.org

U.S. Institute of Peace (USIP). (2004). Establishing the Rule of Law in Afghanistan. USIP.org https://www.usip.org

Chapter 3

African Development Bank, https://www.afdb.org/en/countries/central-africa/gabon/gabon-economic-outlook Accessed on March 5, 2025

Agence des Participations de l'État (APE). (2022). Annual Report. Retrieved from [https://www.economie.gouv.fr/agence-participations-etat/rapports-annuels]

Amsden, A. H. (1992). Asia's Next Giant: South Korea and Late Industrialization. Oxford University Press.

Beacon, C. (2018). "Mobile Money and Financial Inclusion in East Africa." Yale Global Online. Retrieved from [Yale Global](https://yalebooks.yale.edu/yale-global-online/mobile-money-and-financial-inclusion-in-east-africa)

Burnside, C., & Dollar, D. (2000). "Aid, Policies, and Growth." American Economic Review, 90(4), 847-868.

Calderisi, Robert. (2006) The Trouble with Africa, Why Foreign Aid is not Working, New York, Palgrave Macmillan

Chen, S., & Yang, R. (2020). "Digital Economy Empowering Rural E-commerce Development in China." Computers in Human Behavior, 108, 105147. doi:10.1016/j.chb.2020.105147

Defense Advanced Research Projects Agency (DARPA). (2024). FY 2025 President's Budget Request. https://www.darpa.mil/sites/default/files/attachment/2024-11/darpa-2024-afr-final.pdf

Easterly, W. (2006). The White Man's Burden: Why the West's Efforts to Aid the Rest Have Done So Much Ill and So Little Good. New York: Penguin Press.

Financial Times (2025). "Development is how we compete, grow and stay secure Private investment flows only where the right conditions exist and where there's a clear probability of return" by Ajay Banga https://www.ft.com/content/3e5d55bb-0c0d-40e6-a15c-5187c8a021b2

Gouvernement.fr. (n.d.). France 2030: A 10-year plan to innovate, invest and industrialise. Retrieved from [https://www.gouvernement.fr/en/france-2030]

Hudson, A. (2000). "Foreign Aid: A Key to Development?" International Development Review, 42-43.

International Monetary Fund. (2023). World Economic Outlook Database. Retrieve data on government finances, including tax revenues. Available at: [IMF World Economic Outlook] (https://www.imf.org/en/Publications/WEO)

Kharas, H. (2011). "Trends and Issues in Development Aid." Global Economy & Development Working Paper 1. Brookings Institution.

Kharas, H. (2008). "Measuring the Effectiveness of Development Assistance." World Bank Policy Research Working Paper 4664. Washington, DC: World Bank.

Mercy Corps. (2020). "The Importance of Foreign Aid and Development Assistance in Responding to Humanitarian Crises". Available at: https://www.mercycorps.org/research/global-aid

Morris, M., & E. J. W. V. D. (2016). "The Role of International Trade in Sustainable Development: A Review of the Literature." Journal of International Trade and Economic Development.

Moyo, D. (2009). "Dead Aid: Why Aid Is Not Working and How There Is a Better Way for Africa." New York: Farrar, Straus and Giroux.

Nigeria Bureau of Statistics, Nigeria launches its most extensive national measure of multidimensional poverty, Press Release, 17 November 2022 – Abuja

Norges Bank Investment Management (NBIM). (2023). Government Pension Fund Global Annual Report 2022. Retrieved from [https://www.nbim.no/en/publications/reports/2023/annual-report-2022/]

OECD (2018). Development Cooperation Report 2018: Joining Forces to Leave No One Behind. Paris: OECD Publishing.

OECD (2011). The Busan Partnership for Effective Development Cooperation. Paris: OECD Publishing.

OECD Development Assistance Committee (DAC). (2020). "Beyond the Tipping Point: The future of development assistance". Available at: https://www.oecd.org/development/dac/

OECD. (2023). Revenue Statistics 2023. This publication provides comprehensive data on tax revenues among OECD countries. Available at: [OECD Revenue Statistics](https://www.oecd.org/tax/revenue-statistics-26121331.htm)

OECD. (2011). Corporate Governance of State-Owned Enterprises in Asia: An Overview. Chapter on Singapore. Retrieved from [https://www.oecd.org/corporate/ca/corporategovernanceof-state-ownedenterprises/48444832.pdf]

OECD Guidelines on Corporate Governance of SOEs: This is a key international standard advocating for the very principles in your text: clear mandates, professional management, transparency, and equitable treatment with the private sector.

OECD. (2015). OECD Guidelines on Corporate Governance of State-Owned Enterprises, 2015 Edition. OECD Publishing, Paris. https://doi.org/10.1787/9789264244160-en

Riddell, R. (2007). Does Foreign Aid Really Work? Oxford: Oxford University Press.

Riddle, L. (2014). "The End of Aid? How Development Cooperation Is Changing the Game." Global Policy, 5 (4), 477-486.

Rogers, Peter P, Kazi F Jalal, and John A Boy. (2009) An Introduction to Sustainable Development, London, Earthscan.

Runde, Daniel, (2023) The American Imperative, Reclaiming Global Leadership through Soft Power, New York · Nashville, Post Hill Press

Solomon, Semere (2024). "Eritrea's Hard-won Independence and Unmet Expectations". USA, KDP

Solomon, Semere (2003) "Being Responsive to Locally Led Development: Beyond Channeling Funds to Local Organizations". Creative Associates International. USA.

Solomon, Semere (2022) "U.S.-Africa Leaders Summit: How Can the US Contribute to Africa's Development?". Creative Associates International. USA.

Temasek. (2023). Temasek Review 2023: The Resilient Dawn. Retrieved from [https://www.temasek.com.sg/en/our-financials/temasek-review-2023]

The Economist (2025). "The Demise of Foreign Aid Offers an Opportunity - Donors Should Focus on What Works. Much aid currently does not." The Economist.

The Economist (2025). "Aid Cannot Make Poor Countries Rich." The Economist.

The Economist (2025). "Why Some Africans See Opportunity in Foreign-aid Cuts." The Economist.

Todaro, Michael P. and Stephen C. Smith (2003). Economic Development-8th ed. Boston: Addison Wesley,

UNCTAD. (2023). Investment Policy Reviews and other related publications. Offers insights into tax policies in developing countries.

Available at: [UNCTAD Publications](https://unctad.org/webflyer/world-investment-report)

UNESCO. (2020). Education and the Digital Revolution: How technology can support learning. Retrieved from [UNESCO](https://en.unesco.org/themes/education-and-digital-transformation)

UNDP (2011), "Human Development Report 2011, Sustainability and Equity: A better Future for All"

United Nations Development Programme (UNDP). (2019). UNDP Strategic Plan 2018-2021: Priorities and Programmatic Approaches for Development Cooperation.

United Nations Office for the Coordination of Humanitarian Affairs (OCHA). (2021). "Global Humanitarian Overview". Available at: https://www.unocha.org/global-humanitarian-overview

World Bank. (2012). World Development Report 2012: Gender Equality and Development. Washington, DC: World Bank Group.

World Bank. (2021). "The Role of Foreign Aid in Global Development". Available at: https://www.worldbank.org/en/topic/aid

World Bank. (2016). Digital Dividends: World Development Report 2016". Retrieved from [World Bank] (https://www.worldbank.org/en/publication/wdr2016)

World Bank. (2023). World Development Indicators. Data on tax revenue as a percentage of GDP. Available at: [World Bank Data] (https://data.worldbank.org/indicator/GC.TAX.TOTL.GD.ZS)

World Bank. (2022). Tax Revenue (% of GDP). Access and view tax revenue statistics by country. Available at: [World Bank Tax Revenue] (https://data.worldbank.org/indicator/GC.TAX.TOTL.GD.ZS)

World Bank. (2020). China - Deepening Reform of State-Owned Enterprises for Sustainable Growth. Retrieved from [https://www.worldbank.org/en/country/china/publication/china-deepening-reform-of-state-owned-enterprises-for-sustainable-growth]

World Bank. (1993). The East Asian Miracle: Economic Growth and Public Policy. Oxford University Press. (Chapter 6 specifically discusses Korea's coordinated industrialization).

Chapter 4

Cypher, James M. and James L. Dietz, (2004). The Process of Economic Development, New York, Routledge.

Daly, Herman E. (1996). Beyond Growth, Bacon Press.

Daly, Herman E. and Joshua Farley. (2009). Ecological Economics: Principles and Applications, Island Press.

Easterlin, R. (1974). Does Economic Growth Improve the Human Lot? NBER Chapters. https://mpra.ub.uni-muenchen.de/111773/1/MPRA_paper_111773.pdf

Milanovic, B. (2019). Capitalism, Alone: The Future of the System That Rules the World. Harvard University Press.

Nussbaum, M. (2013). Creating Capabilities: The Human Development Approach. Harvard University Press.

OECD. (2020). How's Life? 2020: Measuring Well-being. https://www.oecd.org/statistics/better-life-initiative.htm

Solomon, S (2024). Eritrea's Hard-won Independence and Unmet Expectations: From the Perspective of a Veteran Freedom Fighter, Ingramspark.

Stiglitz, J., et al. (2018). Beyond GDP: Measuring What Counts for Economic and Social Performance. OECD.

Todaro, Michael P. and Stephen C. Smith. (2003). Economic Development-8th ed. Boston: Addison Wesley.

UN. (2015). Transforming Our World: The 2030 Agenda for Sustainable Development. https://docs.un.org/en/A/RES/70/1

United Nations, "What is the Rule of Law?" (UN.org) UNDP (2020). Human Development Report 2020: The Next Frontier – Human

Development and the Anthropocene. http://hdr.undp.org/en/content/human-development-report-2020
UNDP. (2022). Human Development Report. https://hdr.undp.org/
World Bank (2020). World Development Report: Trading for Development in the Age of Global Value Chains. https://www.worldbank.org/en/publication/wdr2020

Chapter 5

African Development Bank, https://www.afdb.org/en/countries/east-africa/eritrea/eritrea-economic-outlook Accessed on June 21, 2024

Calderisi, Robert. The Trouble with Africa, Why Foreign Aid is not Working, New York, Palgrave Macmillan, 2006, p. 160

Central Intelligence Agency, https://www.cia.gov/the-world-factbook/field/real-gdp-per-capita/countrycomparison/ Accessed on June 21, 2024

Collier, Paul and Jan Willem Gunning. "Explaining African Economic Performance, Journal of Economic Literature 37, no. 1, 1999, p. 64, 111

Collier, Paul Collier. New Rules for Rebuilding a Broken Nation, TED Global, 2009

Guled, Ahmde. Djibouti needs a Plan B for the post-Guelleh era, Middle East Institute, July 20, 2021, https://mei.edu/publications/djibouti-needs-plan-b-post-guelleh-era Accessed on May 24, 2025

Rogers, Peter P, Kazi F Jalal, and John A Boyd. An Introduction to Sustainable Development, London, Earthscan, 2009, p. 62

Solomon, Semere. ረዚን ዋጋ ዝተኸፍሎ ናጽነት ኤርትራን ዝተጠልመ መብጽዓን, Jan. 2025, USA

Tazebew, Tezera, Ethiopia's Quest for Utilizing the Port of Berbera, Somaliland, since 2010: Drivers, Processes, and Challenges, JES Vol LVI, No. 1 (June 2023)

The Economist, Vietnam's diaspora is shaping the country their parents fled – As well as sending remittances, many are returning to their homeland, May 22, 2025|

TradeEconomics, https://tradingeconomics.com/country-list/gdp-per-capita-pppp?continent=africa Accessed on June 21, 2024

United Nations Economic and Social Commission for Asia and the Pacific, https://www.unescap.org/ttdw/ppp/ppp_primer/51_functions_of_a_regulator.html Accessed on September 25, 2023

Webster's II New Riverside University Dictionary, Boston, The Riverside Publishing Company, 1984

World Bank, https://data.worldbank.org/indicator/NY.GDP.PCAP.CD Accessed on June 21, 2024

World Bank, Worldwide Governance Indicators, A global compilation of data capturing household, business, and citizen perceptions of the quality of governance in more than 200 countries and territories, http://info.worldbank.org/governance/wgi/index.asp Accessed on October 11, 2023

Chapter 6

Acemoglu, D., & Robinson, J. A. (2013). Why Nations Fail: The Origins of Power, Prosperity, and Poverty. Crown Business.

Anderson, B. (2026). Imagined Communities: Reflections on the Origin and Spread of Nationalism, Verso.

Chang, H.-J. (2002). Kicking Away the Ladder: Development Strategy in Historical Perspective. Anthem Press.

Fukuyama, F. (2014). Political Order and Political Decay: From the Industrial Revolution to the Globalization of Democracy. Farrar, Straus and Giroux.

International Court of Justice (ICJ) – Cases on State Sovereignty. https://www.icj-cij.org/

Gellner, E. (1983). Nations and Nationalism, Cornell University Press.

Krasner, S. D. (1999). Sovereignty: Organized Hypocrisy. Princeton University Press.

Milanovic, B. (2019). Capitalism, Alone: The Future of the System That Rules the World. Harvard University Press.

Philpott, D. (2001). Revolutions in Sovereignty: How Ideas Shaped Modern International Relations. Princeton University Press.

Rodrik, D. (2011). The Globalization Paradox: Democracy and the Future of the World Economy. W.W. Norton & Company.

Sen, A. (1999). Development as Freedom. Oxford University Press.

Smith, A. D. (1993). National Identity, University of Nevada Press.

Solomon, S (2024). Eritrea's Hard-won Independence and Unmet Expectations: From the Perspective of a Veteran Freedom Fighter. Ingramspark.

Stiglitz, J. E. (2007). Making Globalization Work. W.W. Norton & Company. United Nations Charter (1945). Article 2(1) – Sovereign Equality of States. https://www.un.org/en/about-us/un-charter

United Nations, "What is the Rule of Law?" (UN.org) UNDP (2020). Human Development Report 2020: The Next Frontier – Human Development and the Anthropocene. http://hdr.undp.org/en/content/human-development-report-2020

Waltz, K. N. (1979). Theory of International Politics. Addison-Wesley.

WHO. (1948). Constitution of the World Health Organization. https://www.who.int/about/governance/constitution

World Bank. (2021). Poverty and Shared Prosperity Report. https://www.worldbank.org/en/topic/poverty

Chapter 7
Pollera, Aleberto, (1935) La Popolazione Indgine Dell'Eritrea, E. Cappelli, Editore, Bologna,

Negash, Ghirmai. (2017), መገዲ ዓድና (Megedi Adinaa: The Road to the Land). SP.

Chapter 8
Cohen, R. (2008). Global Diasporas: An Introduction (2nd ed.). Routledge.

International Organization for Migration (IOM) (2021). Diaspora Engagement in Development: Policy Perspectives

Kapur, D. (2010). Diaspora, Development, and Democracy: The Domestic Impact of International Migration from India. Princeton University Press.

Levitt, P. (2001). The Transnational Villagers. University of California Press.

Migration Policy Institute (MPI) (2022). "Beyond Remittances: The Role of Diaspora in Poverty Reduction." https://www.migrationpolicy.org/sites/default/files/publications/Beyond_Remittances_0704.pdf

Solomon, Semere (2024). ረዚን ዋጋ ዝተኸፍሎ ናጽነት ኤርትራን ዝተጠለሙ መብጽዓን (Eritrea's Hard-won Independence and Unmet Expectations). Ingramspark.

The Economist, Vietnam's diaspora is shaping the country their parents fled – As well as sending remittances, many are returning to their homeland, May 22, 2025 https://www.economist.com/ https://www.economist.com/asia/2025/05/22/vietnams-diaspora-is-shaping-the-country-their-parents-fled

UNHCR (2023) – Eritrea Country https://www.unhcr.org/countries/eritrea

World Bank Group/KNOMAD Remittances Slowed in 2023, Expected to Grow Faster in 2024 Migration and Development Brief 40 June 2024 World Bank Document https://documents1.worldbank.org/curated/en/099714008132436612/pdf/IDU-a9cf73b5-fcad-425a-a0dd-cc8f2f3331ce.pdf

Chapter 9

Aldrich, R. J. (2010). GCHQ: The Uncensored Story of Britain's Most Secret Intelligence Agency. HarperCollins.

Betts, R. K. (2009). Enemies of Intelligence: Knowledge and Power in American National Security. Columbia University Press.

Biddle, S. (2006). Military Power: Explaining Victory and Defeat in Modern Battle. Princeton University Press.

Byman, D. (2011). A High Price: The Triumphs and Failures of Israeli Counterterrorism. Oxford University Press.

Freedman, L. (2004). Deterrence. Polity Press.

Freedman, L. (2017). The Future of War: A History. PublicAffairs.

Freilich, C. D. (2018). Israeli National Security: A New Strategy for an Era of Change. Oxford University Press.

Gabriel, R. A. (1990). The Culture of War: Invention and Early Development. Greenwood Press.

George, A. L., & Smoke, R. (1974). Deterrence in American Foreign Policy: Theory and Practice. Columbia University Press.

Gray, C. S. (1999). Modern Strategy. Oxford University Press.

Gray, C. S. (2011). The Strategy Bridge: Theory for Practice. Oxford University Press.

Horowitz, M. C. (2010). The Diffusion of Military Power: Causes and Consequences for International Politics. Princeton University Press.

Ikenberry, G. J. (2000). After Victory: Institutions, Strategic Restraint, and the Rebuilding of Order After Major Wars. Princeton University Press.

Jervis, R. (1976). Perception and Misperception in International Politics. Princeton University Press.

Kroenig, M. (2020). The Logic of American Nuclear Strategy. Oxford University Press.

Lieber, K. A., & Press, D. G. (2020). The Myth of the Nuclear Revolution: Power Politics in the Atomic Age. Cornell University Press.

Luttwak, E. N. (1987). Strategy: The Logic of War and Peace. Harvard University Press.

Mazu TV "ንሓጕስ ክሻ ተኸታቲልናዮ" | "ኮምፒዩተር ኢሳያስ ነቢል ይቄጻጸራ" | ምስጢራት ሳይበር ህግደፍ የቃልዕ… | ምስ ኮሎኔል ቢኒያም ተወልደ | Muza Tv March 30, 2025

Mearsheimer, J. J. (2001). The Tragedy of Great Power Politics. W.W. Norton. https://samuelbhfaure.com/wp-content/uploads/2015/10/s2-mearsheimer-2001.pdf

Morgan, P. M. (2003). Deterrence Now. Cambridge University Press.

Nye, J. S. (2017). The Future of Power. PublicAffairs.

Pomerantsev, P. (2019). This Is Not Propaganda: Adventures in the War Against Reality. PublicAffairs.

Schelling, T. C. (1960). The Strategy of Conflict. Harvard University Press.

Snyder, G. H. (1997). Alliance Politics. Cornell University Press.

Solomon, S. (2024) ረዚን ዋጋ ዝተኸፍሎ ናጽነት ኤርትራን ዝተጠልመ መብጽዓን (Eritrea's Hard-won Independence and Unmet Expectations). Ingramspark.

Solomon, S. (2025) ልኡላውነት፡ ድሕንነት ደቅሰብ (human welfare) ዘግእከለ ክኸውን ይግባእ፡ ዳህሳሳዊ ሓተታ ብዛዕባ ኤርትራ www.semeresolomon.com

Tan, A. T. H. (2007). Singapore's Defence: Capabilities, Trends, and Implications. Marshall Cavendish.

Walt, S. M. (1987). The Origins of Alliances. Cornell University Press.

Chapter 10

Acharya, A. (2018). Constructing Global Order: Agency and Change in World Politics. Cambridge UP.

Allison, Graham (2017). Destined for War: Can America and China Escape Thucydides's Trap? Boston: Houghton Mifflin Harcourt.

Barston, R. P. Modern Diplomacy. 3rd Edition, Pearson Education Limited, 3rd Edition, Harlow. 2006.

Charap, Samuel, and Timothy J. Colton (2017). Everyone Loses: The Ukraine Crisis and the Ruinous Contest for Post-Soviet Eurasia. London: Routledge (for the International Institute for Strategic Studies).

Cooper, A. F., & Shaw, T. M. (Eds.). (2009). The Diplomacies of Small States: Between Vulnerability and Resilience. Palgrave Macmillan.

Hey, J. A. K. (Ed.). (2003). Small States in World Politics: Explaining Foreign Policy Behavior. Lynne Rienner.

Ikenberry, G. John, Michael Mastanduno, and William C. Wohlforth, eds. (2009). International Relations Theory and the Consequences of Unipolarity. Cambridge: Cambridge University Press.

Kissinger, Henry, Diplomacy. Simon and Schuster. New York. 1994.

Muldoon P. James, Joann Fagot Aviel, Richard Reitano, and Earl Sullivan. Multilateral Diplomacy and the United Nations Today. Westview Press. Cambridge, MA, USA. 2005.

O'Neill, Jim (2001). "Building Better Global Economic BRICs." Global Economics Paper No: 66, Goldman Sachs.

Panke, D. (2010). Small States in the European Union: Coping with Structural Disadvantages. Routledge.

Porter, Patrick (2018). "Why America's Grand Strategy Has Not Changed: Power, Habit, and the U.S. Foreign Policy Establishment." International Security

Solomon, Semere (2024), ረዚን ዋጋ ዝተኸፍሎ ናጽነት ኤርትራን ዝተጠልመ መብጽዓን, Ingramspark.

Solomon, Semere (2024). Eritrea's Hard-won Independence and Unmet Expectations: From the Perspective of a Veteran Freedom Fighter. KDP.

Stent, Angela E. (2019). Putin's World: Russia Against the West and with the Rest. New York: Twelve.

Teschke, Benno (2003). The Myth of 1648: Class, Geopolitics, and the Making of Modern International Relations. Verso Books.

The U.S. Department of Defense. (Annual). Military and Security Developments Involving the People's Republic of China (Report to Congress).

Thorhallsson, B. (2018). "Small States in the UN Security Council: Means of Influence?". Hague Journal of Diplomacy. Small States in the UN Security Council: Austria's Quest to Maintain Status in: The Hague Journal of Diplomacy Volume 16 Issue 1 (2021)

Watson, Adam. Diplomacy: The Dialogue between States. Routledge. New York. 1991. Questia, Web, 9 June 2011.

http://unfccc.int/files/press/news_room/unfccc_in_the_press/application/pdf/int-01sep02.pdf (accessed June 11, 2009)

http://assembly.coe.int/Documents/AdoptedText/TA03/ERES1318.htm (accessed June 09, 2011).

Zakaria, Fareed (2008). The Post-American World. New York: W.W. Norton & Company.

Chapter 11

African Development Bank, https://www.afdb.org/en/countries/central-africa/gabon/gabon-economic-outlook Accessed on March 5, 2025

Beacon, C. (2018). "Mobile Money and Financial Inclusion in East Africa." Yale Global Online. Retrieved from [Yale Global https://yale-books.yale.edu/yale-global-online/mobile-money-and-financial-inclusion-in-east-africa)

Burnside, C., & Dollar, D. (2000). "Aid, Policies, and Growth." American Economic Review, 90(4), 847-868.

Calderisi, Robert.(2006) "The Trouble with Africa, Why Foreign Aid is not Working." New York, Palgrave Macmillan

Easterly, W. (2006). "The White Man's Burden: Why the West's Efforts to Aid the Rest Have Done So Much Ill and So Little Good." New York: Penguin Press.

Mercy Corps. (2020). "The Importance of Foreign Aid and Development Assistance in Responding to Humanitarian Crises". Available at: https://www.mercycorps.org/research/global-aid

Morris, M., & E. J. W. V. D. (2016). "The Role of International Trade in Sustainable Development: A Review of the Literature." Journal of International Trade and Economic Development.

Moyo, D. (2009). "Dead Aid: Why Aid Is Not Working and How There Is a Better Way for Africa." New York: Farrar, Straus and Giroux.

Nigeria Bureau of Statistics, Nigeria launches its most extensive national measure of multidimensional poverty, Press Release, 17 November 2022 – Abuja https://www.mppn.org/nigeria-launches-its-most-extensive-national-measure-of-multidimensional-poverty/

OECD (2018). Development Cooperation Report 2018: Joining Forces to Leave No One Behind. Paris: OECD Publishing. https://www.oecd.org/content/dam/oecd/en/publications/reports/2018/12/

development-co-operation-report-2018_g1g92803/dcr-2018-en.pdf
OECD (2011). The Busan Partnership for Effective Development Cooperation. Paris: OECD Publishing. https://www.oecd.org/content/dam/oecd/en/publications/reports/2011/12/busan-partnership-for-effective-development-co-operation_29eb4a17/54de7baa-en.pdf
Riddell, R. (2007). Does Foreign Aid Really Work? Oxford: Oxford University Press.
Riddle, L. (2014). "The End of Aid? How Development Cooperation Is Changing the Game." Global Policy, 5 (4), 477-486.
Solomon, Semere (2024). "Eritrea's Hard-won Independence and Unmet Expectations". KDP.
Solomon, Semere (2024). "ረዚን ዋጋ ዝተኸፍሎ ናጽነት ኤርትራን ዝተጠልሙ መብጽዓን". Ingramspark
Solomon, Semere (2003) "Being Responsive to Locally Led Development: Beyond Channeling Funds to Local Organizations". Creative Associates International. USA. Being responsive to locally led development: Beyond channeling funds to local organizations | Creative Associates International
Solomon, Semere (2022) "U.S.-Africa Leaders Summit: How Can the US Contribute to Africa's Development?". Creative Associates International. USA. U.S.-Africa Leaders Summit: How can the U.S. contribute to Africa's development?
The Economist (2025). "The Demise of Foreign Aid Offers an Opportunity - Donors Should Focus on What Works. Much aid currently does not." The Economist. https://www.economist.com/leaders/2025/03/06/the-demise-of-foreign-aid-offers-an-opportunity
The Economist (2025). "Aid Cannot Make Poor Countries Rich." The Economist. https://www.

economist.com/finance-and-economics/2025/03/06/aid-cannot-make-poor-countries-rich

The Economist (2025). "Why Some Africans See Opportunity in Foreign-aid Cuts." The Economist. https://www.economist.com/middle-east-and-africa/2025/03/06/why-some-africans-see-opportunity-in-foreign-aid-cuts

UNESCO. (2020). "Education and the Digital Revolution: How technology can support learning." Retrieved from UNESCO https://en.unesco.org/themes/education-and-digital-transformation

United Nations Development Programme (UNDP). (2019). UNDP Strategic Plan 2018-2021: Priorities and Programmatic Approaches for Development Cooperation. file:///C:/Users/Semere%20Solomon/Downloads/UNDP--EN--Strategic-Plan-2018-2021-N1733496-20171128.pdf

United Nations Office for the Coordination of Humanitarian Affairs (OCHA). (2021). "Global Humanitarian Overview". Available at: https://www.unocha.org/global-humanitarian-overview

World Bank. (2012). World Development Report 2012: Gender Equality and Development. Washington, DC: World Bank Group. https://openknowledge.worldbank.org/bitstreams/ff4bacaa-5fca-5875-b704-ef8418c40b72/download

World Bank. (2021). "The Role of Foreign Aid in Global Development". Available at: https://www.worldbank.org/en/topic/aid

World Bank. (2016). "Digital Dividends: World Development Report 2016." Retrieved from [World Bank](https://www.worldbank.org/en/publication/wdr2016)

Chapter 12

Ali, Zeineb (2002). A decade since 1991: Life under PFDJ, Asmarino.com.

Arendt, H. (1973). The Origins of Totalitarianism.

Barr, M. D. (2013). The Ruling Elite of Singapore: Networks of Power and Influence.

Bernays, Edward (2004). Propaganda. Ig Publishing

Byman, D., & Lind, J. (2010). Pyongyang's Survival Strategy: Tools of Authoritarian Control in North Korea. International Security, 35(1), 44-74.

Corrales, J., & Penfold, M. (2015). Dragon in the Tropics: Venezuela and the Legacy of Hugo Chávez.

Dahl, R. A. (1991). Democracy and Its Critics. Yale University Press

Dikötter, F. (2011). Mao's Great Famine: The History of China's Most Devastating Catastrophe, 1958-1962.

Foucault, M. (1995). Discipline and Punish: The Birth of the Prison.

Fukuyama, F. (2014). Political Order and Political Decay: From the Industrial Revolution to the Globalization of Democracy. Farrar, Straus and Giroux.

Gentzkow, M. (2016). Polarization in 2016. Stanford University Working Paper. https://web.stanford.edu/~gentzkow/research/PolarizationIn2016.pdf

Herman, Edwards and Naom Chomsky (2002). Manufacturing Consent: The Political Economy of the Mass Media. Knopf Doubleday Publishing Group

Kornai, J. (1992). The Socialist System: The Political Economy of Communism.

Iyengar, S., Lelkes, Y., Levendusky, M., Malhotra, N., & Westwood, S. (2019). The Origins and Consequences of Affective Polarization in the United States. Annual Review of Political Science, 22, 129-146. https://www.annualreviews.org/content/journals/10.1146/annurev-polisci-051117-073034

Lewandowsky, S., Ecker, U. K. H., & Cook, J. (2017). Beyond Misinformation: Understanding and Coping with the "Post-Truth" Era. Journal of Applied Research in

Memory and Cognition, 6(4), 353-369. https://research-information.bris.ac.uk/ws/portalfiles/portal/152516154/Pages_from_JARMAC_2017_59_Revision_1_V1.pdf

Levitsky, S., & Ziblatt, D. (2018). "How Democracies Die." Crown.

McCoy, J., Rahman, T., & Somer, M. (2018). Polarization and the Global Crisis of Democracy: Common Patterns, Dynamics, and Pernicious Consequences for Democratic Polities. American Behavioral Scientist, 62(1), 16-42.

Mounk, Y. (2018). The People vs. Democracy: Why Our Freedom Is in Danger and How to Save It. Harvard University Press.

Nathan, A. J. (2003). Authoritarian Resilience. Journal of Democracy, 14(1), 6-17.

OECD (2020). Governance in the 21st Century: Overcoming Polarisation and Gridlock. https://www.oecd.org/gov/governance-in-the-21st-century-3d1a6f3e-en.htm

Oreskes, N., & Conway, E. M. (2010). Merchants of Doubt: How a Handful of Scientists Obscured the Truth on Issues from Tobacco Smoke to Global Warming. Bloomsbury Press.

Pew Research Center (2022). Political Polarization in the American Public. https://www.pewresearch.org/politics/2022/03/10/political-polarization-in-the-american-public/

Scott, J. C. (1999). Seeing Like a State: How Certain Schemes to Improve the Human Condition Have Failed.

Sen, A. (2000). Development as Freedom. Anchor.

Solomon, Semere (2024). ረዚን ዋጋ ዝተኸፍሎ ናጽነት ኤርትራን ዝተጠለመ ሙብጽዓን. Ingramspark

Sunstein, C. R. (2017). Republic: Divided Democracy in the Age of Social Media. Princeton University Press.

Svolik, M. (2019). Polarization Versus Democracy. Journal of Democracy, 30(3), 20-32.

Tesfai, Tedros. (2001). Where did things go wrong for the "party of the people? Asmarino.com.
Trouillot, Michel-Rolph (2015). Silencing the Past: Power and the Production of History. Beacon Press.
V-Dem Institute (2023). Democracy Report: Defiance in the Face of Autocratization. https://www.v-dem.net/documents/29/v-dem_dr2023_lowres.pdf
Zuboff, Shoshana (2019). The Age of Surveillance Capitalism: The Fight for a Human Future at the New Frontier of Power. PublicAffairs.
Zubok, V. (2007). A Failed Empire: The Soviet Union in the Cold War from Stalin to Gorbachev. The University of North Carolina Press.

Chapter 13

Africa Environment Outlook: Past, present and future perspectives, GRID-Arendal and UNEP, http://www.grida.no/publications/other/aeo/
Bauer, P. T. Equality, the Third World, and Economic Delusion. Cambridge: Harvard University Press, 1981.
BBC, http://www.bbc.co.uk/worldservice/specials/1624_story_of_africa/page92.shtml
Calderisi, Robert. The Trouble with Africa: Why Foreign Aid is not Working. New York: Palgrave Macmillan, 2006.
CIDA, "Stimulating Sustainable Economic Growth," http://acdiida.gc.ca/INET/IMAGES.NSF/vLUImages/EconomicGrowth/$file/Sustainable-Economic-Growth-e.pdf
Collier, Paul. The Bottom Billion, New York: Oxford University Press, 2007.
Collier, Paul and Jan Willem Gunning. "Explaining African Economic Performance". Journal of Economic Literature 37, no. 1. 1999. 64-111

Collier, Paul. "On the Bottom Billion," TEDGlobal, May 2008 http://www.ted.com/speakers/paul_collier.html

Collier, Paul. "New Rules for Rebuilding a Broken Nation," TEDGlobal, 2009 at http://www.ted.com/talks/paul_collier_s_new_rules_for_rebuilding_a_broken_nation.html

Council on Foreign Relations Africa's 'Leaders for Life' | Council on Foreign Relations September 2023

Daly, Herman E. and Joshua Farley. Ecological Economics: Principles and Applications. Washington: Island Press, 2009.

Jeppie, Shamil and Souleymane Bachir Diagne (eds). The Meanings of Timbuktu, CODESRIA/HSRC, 2008, 416 p., http://www.codesria.org/spip.php?article643&lang=en

Kuznets, Simon. Modern Economic Growth: Findings and Reflections. American Economic Review 63, 1973.

Leonard, David K. and Scott Straus. Africa's Stalled Development: International Causes and Cures. Colorado: Lynne Reinner Publishers, 2003.

Mayo, Dambisa. Dead Aid: Why Aid is not Working and How There is a Better Way for Africa. New York: Farrar, Straus and Giroux, 2007.

Okonjo-Iwaele, Ngozi. "Want to Help Africa, Do Business Here," TEDGlobal. 2008. http://www.ted.com/talks/ngozi_okonjo_iweala_on_doing_business_in_africa.html

Polity IV Project, "Political Regime Characteristics and Transition, 1800-2006," at http://www.systemicpeace.org/polity/polity4.htm

Rogers, Peter P, Kazi F Jalal, and John A Boyd. An Introduction to Sustainable Development. London: Earthscan, 2009.

Todaro, Michael P. and Stephen C. Smith, Economic Development 8th ed. Boston: Addison Wesley, 2003.

Webster's II New Riverside University Dictionary. Boston: The Riverside Publishing Company, 1984.

World Bank, World Development Report, pp. 33-35)
World Bank, http://info.worldbank.org/governance/wgi/index.asp
Yara, http://www.yara.com/sustainability/global_trends/growth/index.aspx

Chapter 14

Akhavan, P. (2001). "Beyond Impunity: Can International Criminal Justice Prevent Future Atrocities?" American Journal of International Law, 95(1), 7–31.

Colombia | International Center for Transitional Justice

de Greiff, P. (Ed.). (2006). The Handbook of Reparations. Oxford University Press.

ESMA Museum and Site of Memory

Former Clandestine Detention, Torture and Extermination Center ESMA Museum and Site of Memory | Argentina.gob.ar

Gibson, J. L. (2004). Overcoming Apartheid: Can Truth Reconcile a Divided Nation? Russell Sage Foundation.

Hayner, P. B. (2011). Unspeakable Truths: Transitional Justice and the Challenge of Truth Commissions (2nd ed.). Routledge.

International Center for Transitional Justice (ICTJ). (2023). "What is Transitional Justice?" ICTJ Official Website

Killean, Rachel & Elizabeth Newton (Published online: 13 May 2025) THE INTERNATIONAL JOURNAL OF HUMAN RIGHTS. University of Sydney Law School, Sydney, Australia. https://doi.org/10.1080/13642987.2025.2502561

Méndez, J. E. (1997). "Accountability for Past Abuses." Human Rights Quarterly, 19(2), 255–282.

Orentlicher, D. F. (1991). "Settling Accounts: The Duty to Prosecute Human Rights Violations of a Prior Regime." Yale Law Journal,

100(8), 2537–2615. https://digitalcommons.wcl.american.edu/cgi/viewcontent.cgi?article=2717&context=facsch_lawrev

Robinson, N. (2022). Conceptualising historical legacies for transitional justice history education in postcolonial societies. History Education Research Journal, 19(1), 10. https://doi.org/10.14324/HERJ.19.1.10

Seth, Shivangi. (2025). Global South States and Transitional Justice: Beyond Politicization. The International Journal Of Transitional Justice, Vol. 00, 2025, 1–18 doi: https://doi.org/10.1093/ijtj/ijaf015

Sikkink, K. (2011). The Justice Cascade: How Human Rights Prosecutions Are Changing World Politics. W.W. Norton & Co.

Sriram, C. L. (2007). "Justice as Peace? Liberal Peacebuilding and Strategies of Transitional Justice." Global Society, 21(4), 579–591.

Solomon, Semere (2024. ረዚን ዋጋ ዝተከፍሎ ናጽነት ኤርትራን ዝተጠልሙ መብጽዓን, Ingramspark

Solomon, Semere (2024). Eritrea's Hard-won Independence and Unmet Expectations: From the Perspective of a Veteran Freedom Fighter. KDP.

Teitel, R. G. (2000). Transitional Justice. Oxford University Press.

The ICTR in Brief | United Nations International Criminal Tribunal for Rwanda The ICTR in Brief

United Nations. (2010). Guidance Note of the Secretary-General: United Nations Approach to Transitional Justice. UN Report https://www.un.org/ruleoflaw/files/TJ_Guidance_Note_March_2010FINAL.pdf

UN Security Council, The rule of law and transitional justice in conflict and post-conflict societies Report of the Secretary-General https://docs.un.org/en/S/2004/616

Chapter 15

Cabinet Office. (2011). The Cabinet Manual. (1st ed.). https://assets.publishing.service.gov.uk/media/5a79d5d7e5274a18ba50f2b6/cabinet-manual.pdf

Dahl, R. A. (1971). Polyarchy: Participation and Opposition. Yale University Press.

Inter-Parliamentary Union (IPU). (2019). Parliamentary Oversight: Parliament's Power to Hold Government to Account.

Levitsky, S., & Ziblatt, D. (2018). How Democracies Die. Crown.

Linz, J. J. (1990). The Perils of Presidentialism." Journal of Democracy, 1(1), 51–69. https://muse.jhu.edu/article/225694/pdf

Norton, P. (2005). Parliament in British Politics. Palgrave Macmillan.

Schattschneider, E. E. (1942). Party Government. Holt, Rinehart and Winston.

Scheppele, K. L. (2018). "Autocratic Legalism." The University of Chicago Law Review, 85(2), 545–583.

Solomon, Semere. (2025. The Blue Wave at a Crossroads: Preserving a Movement for Eritrea's Future The Blue Wave at a Crossroads: Preserving a Movement for Eritrea's Future

The Concept of "Her Majesty's Loyal Opposition"

The Venice Commission (European Commission for Democracy through Law).

www.ingramcontent.com/pod-product-compliance
Lightning Source LLC
Chambersburg PA
CBHW051623010526
44119CB00040B/484/J